T0298516

China's Rise in the World ICT Industry

One of the most striking phenomena of China's remarkable economic growth is that its huge volume of exports are becoming high-tech. China is now the world's largest information and communication technology (ICT) exporter, having overtaken Japan and the European Union in 2003 and the United States in 2004. China's ICT industry is also the largest manufacturing sector within the Chinese economy. This book examines how China has attained this leading position and presents one of the first accounts of China's ICT development model, with specific reference to the experiences of East Asian 'tigers'. It shows how the development of the industry was military-driven before 1978, and how subsequently Chinese policymakers, struggling with domestic market reform and challenged by trade liberalization and globalization, managed to push through ICT development strategies. Overall, it discusses the debates between policymakers as to the most appropriate economic development strategy for 'catching-up' and demonstrates how China moved away from the across-the-board protectionist and interventionist industrial policies pursued by many developing countries, but has not wholeheartedly followed the neo-liberal free trade and market polices favoured by the World Bank, World Trade Organization and International Monetary Fund. By doing so, it sheds light on the limitations of China's strategies for moving forward, and identifies policy lessons for other developing countries.

Lutao Ning is a political economist at the Department of East Asian Studies, Cambridge University. He was a visiting scholar at the Chinese Academy of Social Sciences and Peking University. His research interests include globalization and industrial and trade policies in developing countries.

China policy series
Edited by Zheng Yongnian
China Policy Institute, University of Nottingham, UK

China's Rise in the World ICT Industry

Industrial strategies and the catch-up development model

Lutao Ning

Routledge
Taylor & Francis Group

LONDON AND NEW YORK

First published 2009
by Routledge
2 Park Square, Milton Park, Abingdon, Oxon OX14 4RN

Simultaneously published in the USA and Canada
by Routledge
270 Madison Ave, New York, NY 10016

Routledge is an imprint of the Taylor and Francis Group, an Informa business

© 2009 Lutao Ning

Typeset in by Times New Roman by GreenGate Publishing, Tonbridge, Kent

British Library Cataloguing in Publication Data
A catalogue record for this book is available from the British Library

Library of Congress Cataloging in Publication Data
Ning, Lutao.

China's rise in the world ICT industry : industrial strategies and the catch-up
development model / Lutao Ning.
p. cm. -- (China policy series ; 10)
Includes bibliographical references and index.
1. High technology industries--Government policy--China. 2. High technology
industries--China. I. Title.
HC430.H53N55 2009
338.4'760951--dc22
2008049957

ISBN10: 0-415-48224-0 (hbk)
ISBN10: 0-203-87742-X (ebk)

ISBN13: 978-0-415-48224-0 (hbk)
ISBN13: 978-0-203-87742-5 (ebk)

Contents

Figures

Tables

Preface

After three decades of reform, China has re-emerged as one of the most dynamic countries in the world economy, as it was a few centuries ago. Its steady growth continues to amaze the world. China is now the largest exporter in the world information and communication technology (ICT) industry, having overtaken Japan and the European Union in 2003 and the United States in 2004, and China's ICT industry is the largest sector within the Chinese economy. How has China achieved this leading position in one of the world's most capital- and technology-intensive industries? Is China's rise in the ICT sector really as impressive as it appears? Is China another economic 'miracle', following in the footsteps of the East Asian 'tigers'? Is China's 'catching up' strategy still relevant, given the dynamic changes in global competition? What can other developing countries learn from this 'catching up' experience?

With these questions in mind, this book investigates how China has managed its ICT industry and risen in the world market. It aims to interpret the role of the state and presents one of the first accounts of China's ICT industry's development with specific reference to the East Asian development model. The rationales of China's leaders' policies concerning the priority development of the high-tech industries, such as the ICT industry, have not so far been well understood by the outside world, and are often ignored or overlooked by existing literature. This book features rare archival data and thoughts on industrial development expressed by Chinese policymakers. It shows how the development of the industry was military-driven in the period 1949–1978, and how subsequently Chinese policymakers, struggling with domestic market reform and challenged by trade liberalization and globalization, managed to push through ICT development strategies over time. More specifically, this book looks at the rapid growth of China's ICT industry against the background of China's overall economic reform and the big picture of the shifting architecture of global competition. It intends to show readers China's development scenario from the inside, so that they can experience and feel the striking economic miracle China achieved from the perspective of the leaders whose decisions made it possible, and to understand the logic behind their policies.

The central theme of this book falls within the broad debate over the role of the state in economic development. Through exploring the development of the

Chinese ICT industry, the book discusses the debates between policymakers as to the most appropriate economic development strategy for 'catching up', demonstrating how China has moved beyond the across-the-board protectionist and interventionist industrial policies pursued by many developing countries, and also beyond the neo-liberal free trade and market polices favoured by the World Bank and International Monetary Fund (IMF). The book also explores the key issues of China's intention to emulate the industrial policies of the East Asian 'tigers' since the 1990s, to promote its ICT industry as a top priority in response to increasing degrees of economic liberalization and globalization. Debates over the unorthodox industrial policies of South Korea and Japan are extended to the case of China.

The book argues that the availability of a cheap labour force has been essential for China to enter the industry, but has hardly been sufficient. The emergence of a set of more selective policies towards foreign trade and investment, heavy R&D spending, and defence procurement has been important. However, most of China's successes are in the low-value-added end of global ICT production networks. China's strategies have not made China the real leader of the industry. This is mainly because China now faces a very different global and domestic economic and political environment, and a different set of opportunities and challenges from those experienced by the East Asian tigers. Its nationalistic industrial strategy, originally designed to create a highly independent ICT industry, has become irrelevant and difficult to pursue today. The international political environment, influenced by Cold War thinking, has constrained the possibilities for China to acquire technologies in the same way as did the East Asian latecomers. World Trade Organization (WTO) rules now restrict China's ability to support the industry. Challenges for China also come from the global business revolution in the Western models of capitalist organization and governance, which has changed the focus of international competition from manufacturing to services, innovation, and activities controlling sales and global production networks.

There is no denying the fact that China's strategies have successfully overcome unfavourable transitional economic and political conditions to initiate the industry. They have enabled domestic firms to improve their capabilities by taking advantage of the emerging opportunities that result from transformations in the world ICT industry. China's rise in the world ICT industry in fact demonstrates that governmental involvement in industrial development, such as guided liberalization and selective state intervention, can be beneficial if these actions can help the domestic industry and firms overcome historical, economic and political barriers to improve their competitiveness in accordance with the dynamic development of the world economy. China's experience shows that a successful policy that draws upon the experiences of other countries should still be development-centred, learning-focused and selective, and take into account the economic and historical differences embedded in industrial strategies adopted from other countries.

This book builds upon my doctoral research at Cambridge and 12 months' fieldwork in China. I spent the first year of my research working on Part I of the book, which is the introductory section. Chapter 1 is devoted to some general issues concerning China's policy priority towards the development of the ICT industry. Chapter 2 serves as a theoretical foundation for understanding industrial and trade policies during the economic liberalization process. Thanks to my appointments as visiting scholar at both the China Academy of Social Science and Peking University during my fieldwork, I had opportunities to access some rare records, out-of-print books, academic and internal journals, public speeches, and reports written by former ministers and high-ranking officials. This archival research, presented in Part II (Chapters 3 and 4), provides the proper context for the argument of this book and demonstrates the evolution of China's industrial planning and policies in the process of economic and political transition, the changing thoughts of policymakers as well as historical and international influences on their policy designs.

Part III (Chapters 5–8) looks at three main strategies of China's 'pillar' industrial development policy, the design of which was based on the East Asian model, to promote some strategic high-tech industries such as the ICT industry. The first strategy I look at is China's planning concerning big business and small- and medium-sized enterprises, which is intended to increase the scale of production and to build up the whole ICT supply and production chain in China. After spending time collecting and analysing research data, I travelled the east coast of China to experience the changes brought about by economic reform and to conduct research visits to some electronics plants, which resulted in long informal discussions with local leaders, and founders or chief executive officers/chief financial officers of companies. These visits provided me with some insights into how firms perceived the industrial policies of their own government, and strategies they formed or instructions they received from the state in response to deepening economic liberalization. Technological innovation and upgrading are still the central issues, but are not what worried firms most. Enterprises originating from former state-owned enterprises (SOEs) emphasized internal management problems left by the full state ownership, while private firms stressed the importance of network building with local governments in gaining preferential policies. These thoughts are discussed in Chapter 5.

During the time when I was visiting China, Chinese policymakers began to embark intensively on the 'walking out' export and outward foreign direct investment promotion strategy in addition to 'attracting in', the selective introduction of inward foreign direct investment (FDI), foreign technologies and an imports policy. The notable event of Lenovo's acquisition of IBM's personal computer business marked the beginning of China's response to ongoing global business restructuring. It seems that more attention should be paid to the ambition of Chinese policymakers to build 'national champions' that can catch up with leading multinational firms in both global coverage and technological capability, while the Chinese ICT industry as a whole is becoming integrated with the rest of the world economy. In Chapter 6, I consider whether China's 'walking out' and 'attracting in' strategies have been successful in achieving Chinese leaders' ambitious goals, and the effects of trade and market liberalization on the Chinese ICT industry. This is done through exploring China's position in global production chains, and its export, import and technological structures.

In 2004, China received its first ever WTO trade complaint from the United States over semiconductors, one of the strategic sectors of the ICT industry, just two years after it had joined the WTO. Chapter 7 considers the development challenges of China's 'breaking through' strategy. The government has used this East Asian tiger-style strategy to promote some 'strategic' ICT sectors such as semiconductors in order to improve the industry's overall global competitiveness. This chapter explores the core industrial and technological development strategies that Japan, Korea and Taiwan undertook, and compares them with the strategies China adopted in the development of semiconductor industries. It then examines the nature of semiconductor trade disputes with the United States, and thereby hopes to tackle the issues surrounding conflicts between Western economic orthodoxy and East Asian development policies, which were eventually revealed to be pitfalls for China in following the East Asian strategies.

In the final part of the book, Part IV, Chapter 8 sketches China's ICT development model and discusses its limitations and potential pitfalls. Chapter 9 concludes the book and examines implications for both economic development theories and popular debate concerning the causes of China's economic miracle. It also asks what other developing countries can learn from China's experience.

It should be emphasized that China's ICT development model has exhibited some pragmatic characteristics for industrialization in the process of trade liberalization and globalization, although the model and even the whole economic reform are still fraught with nationalism, contradictions, tensions and pitfalls in many respects. This book does not seek to underplay China's great potential and capabilities. China's strategies may not help domestic enterprises to be as innovative and powerful as leading flagships, but do allow them to leverage great cost advantages to surpass other developing countries. A time will come when Chinese firms find it expeditious to move towards the frontier of competition. However, in order to achieve such potential quickly, China needs to realize that its national objectives are ambitious and continuously reform its transitional economy.

Acknowledgements

I have incurred many debts of gratitude in finishing this book. I would like to thank Dr Wei Zhang, Jin Zhang and David Kou of Cambridge University, Dr Gregory Linden of the University of California at Berkeley, Professor Mike Hobday of the University of Sussex in the United Kingdom, Professor Yongnian Zheng and Dr Dylan Sunderland of the University of Nottingham, Professor Jinzhi Tong and Bin Yang of Xiamen University, Professor Tongshan Wang and Dr Tao Zhang, senior economists at the Chinese Academy of Social Sciences, Dr Jianbo Lou of Peking University and Peter Sowden, editor at Routledge, for their helpful comments and suggestions on this book and some of its chapters. I would also like to thank many anonymous Chinese officials and managers of ICT firms in China who generously took time out of their busy schedules to talk with me about my research and the development of China's ICT industry.

Benjamin Charlton, my friend and student at Cambridge, deserves special thanks for spending hours reading and improving this book.

I must acknowledge financial assistance from Dr Wei Zhang of Cambridge University, the Suzy Paine Fund, the Faculty of Economics and Politics, the University of Cambridge, Queens' College Cambridge Travel Fund, the Worts Travel Fund, the University of Cambridge, the Sino-British Fellowship Trust, the Great Britain-China Centre and the United Kingdom's Economic History Society for my fieldwork in China, and the Cambridge Trust in supporting my PhD study.

Finally, I would like to acknowledge the tremendous support of my family. I could never thank them enough for encouraging and supporting my studies and research.

The initial version of Chapter 5 was published as 'Economic Liberalization for High-Tech Industry Development? Lessons from China's Response in Developing the ICT Manufacturing Sector Compared with the Strategies of Korea and Taiwan' in the *Journal of Development Studies*, vol. 43, issue 3, pp. 562–587 (2007).

The initial version of Chapter 6 has been accepted for publication as 'China's leadership in the World ICT Industry: A Successful Story of its "Attracting-In" and "Walking-Out" Strategy?' in *Pacific Affairs*, vol. 82, no. 1, pp 67–91 (2009).

The original version of Chapter 7 was published as 'State-Led Catching Up Strategies and Inherited Conflicts in Developing the ICT Industry: Behind the US–East Asia Semiconductor Disputes', in *Global Economic Review*, vol. 37, issue 2, pp. 265–292 (2008).

Abbreviations

BTIB	Broadcasting and TV Industry Bureau
CA	comparative advantage
CAD	Computer-aided design
CAE	Computer-aided engineering
CAM	Computer-aided manufacturing
CCID	China Centre for Information Industry Development
CEO	chief executive officer
CFO	chief financial officer
CIB	Computer Industry Bureau
CCP	Chinese Communist Party
DOC	Department of Commerce (United States)
DRAM	dynamic random access memory
EC	European Commission
EOS	economies of scale
EPROM	erasable programmable read-only memory
EPZ	export processing zone
FDI	foreign direct investment
FIE	foreign-invested enterprise
FYP	Five-Year Plan
GATT	General Agreement on Tariffs and Trade
GDP	gross domestic product
GPN	global production network
HDTZ	High-Technology Development Zone
HO	Heckscher–Ohlin
IC	integrated circuit
ICT	information and communication technology
IMF	International Monetary Fund
IPR	intellectual property right
ISI	import substitution industrialization
ISIC	International Standard Industrial Classification
ITA	Information Technology Agreement
ITC	International Trade Commission (United States)

JSC	joint-stock companies
JV	joint venture
LCD	liquid crystal display
LLC	limited liability companies
M&A	mergers and acquisitions
MEI	Ministry of the Electronics Industry
MII	Ministry of the Information Industry
MITI	Ministry of International Trade and Industry (Japan)
MNEs	multinational enterprises
MOC	Ministry of Commerce
MOFTEC	Ministry of Foreign Trade and Economic Cooperation
NAICS	North American Industry Classification System
NBSC	National Bureau of Statistics of China
NIEs	newly industrialized East Asian countries
OBM	own brand manufacturing
ODM	original design manufacturing
OECD	Organisation for Economic Co-operation and Development
OEM	original equipment manufacturer/manufacturing
OLI	ownership, location and internalization
PC	personal computer
PRC	the People's Republic of China
RMB	renminbi (official currency of China)
S&T	science and technology
SAP	Structural Adjustment Programme
SCE	state-controlled enterprise
SEZ	Special Economic Zone
SIA	Semiconductor Industry Association
SMEs	small and medium-sized enterprises
SOE	state-owned enterprise
SP	Stabilization Programme
SRAM	static random access memory
STZ	Special Technology Zone
TNC	transnational corporation
TSMC	Taiwan Semiconductor Manufacturing Company
TVEs	township and village enterprises
UMC	United Microelectronics Corporation
UNCTAD	United Nations Conference on Trade and Development
USSR	Union of Soviet Socialist Republics, the former Soviet Union
USTR	US trade representative
VAT	value added tax
VCR	video cassette recorder
WFOE	wholly foreign-owned enterprise
WFOS	wholly foreign-owned subsidiary
WSC	World Semiconductor Council
WTO	World Trade Organization

Part I

The role of the state in industrial and trade development

1 Introduction

A European friend who is a scientist once asked me why we were undertaking this [high-tech] project when our economy was still underdeveloped. I answered that we had our eyes on long-term development, not just immediate needs... It has always been, and will always be, necessary for China to develop its own high technology so that it can take its place in this field. If it were not for the atomic bomb, the hydrogen bomb and the satellites we have launched since the 1960s, China would not have its present international standing as a great, influential country. These achievements demonstrate a nation's abilities and are a sign of its level of prosperity and development.

(Deng Xiaoping 1988)

The surest way to do more to help the poor is to continue to open markets . . . the developing countries that are catching up with rich ones are those that are open to trade; and the more open they are, the faster they are converging. That is particularly good news for China. The liberalization that joining the WTO requires will give another big boost to Chinese living standards.

(Mike Moore, former Director-General of the WTO, 16 June 2000)

When you open the door, some flies inevitably come in.

(attributed to Deng Xiaoping)

If China wants to join the WTO and to be integrated in the international community, it must play the rules of the game. China cannot do that without making concessions.

(Zhu Rongji, 1999)

The rise of the East Asian countries was one of the greatest economic miracles of the late twentieth century. By shifting from an inward- to an outward-oriented economic development approach, they became integrated into the global economy, expanding their exports, acquiring technology and accessing foreign investment. A wide array of selective industrial policies implemented by their governments contributed to their successful catching up experiences (Chang 2003b). Soon afterwards, in the past three decades, China has emerged as another economic miracle. Like its newly industrialized East Asian neighbours, China has demonstrated an extraordinary economic take-off after opening up to the outside world. From 1979 to 2004, it sustained an average annual growth rate of real GDP of 9.3 per cent and so far shows no sign of slowing down. China also successfully overtook the United Kingdom in 2002 to become the world's fifth largest trading economy and Japan in 2004 to become the third (after the United States and Germany). The Organization for Economic Co-operation and Development (OECD) even predicts that exports from China will surpass those from Germany in 2008 and rise to 10 per cent of the global market share by 2010 to overtake the position of the United States (OECD 2005).

One of the most striking phenomena in this picture of China's growth is that its huge volume of exports are becoming high-tech and a number of large domestic enterprises are approaching multinational stages, operating worldwide and acquiring firms in advanced economies. For example, in 2003 China successfully overtook Japan and the European Union and than in 2004 took the lead over the United States to become the biggest ICT exporter in the world (see Figure 1.3). China's global ICT production share rose from 2.3 per cent in 1993 to close to 15 per cent in 2004. By 2007, the Chinese ICT market was forecast to be worth US$215 billion, accounting for about 16 per cent of the global market. The average annual growth rate for the domestic market will reach 13 per cent per annum, whereas the US share has remained at 4 per cent in the same period, 2003–2007 (OECD 2006b; Yearbook of World Electronics Data 2004). The rise of Chinese multinational corporations was exemplified by Lenovo's acquisition of IBM's PC operation in 2005 (see Chapter 6).

Very little is known about how a less developed country like China can achieve a lead-taking position in some of the world's most capital- and technology-intensive industries, such as in the ICT industry. It seems that China is now making a leap from being a simple manufacturing centre to becoming an advanced technology 'superstate'. How has China altered its developmental rationales and put them into practice in achieving such tremendous growth? Is the growth really as impressive as it appears? Has China really become more competitive and taken a lead in some high-tech industries? How important has the state been in bringing this about? What role has the Chinese government played in fostering industrial growth? Is China another state-led economic 'miracle', following in the footsteps of the East Asian 'tigers'? Is China's 'catching up' strategy still relevant, given the dynamic change of global competition? Does the Chinese government have to move closer to more 'Western' neo-liberal models of capitalist organization and governance if it wants to achieve sustainable industrial growth?

This book explores China's experience in managing the growth of the sector, in the face of increasing economic liberalization and against the background of its own economic transition. More specifically, it investigates how the challenges of trade liberalization along with the trend towards globalization affect China's industrial reform intended to develop the competitiveness of high-tech industry in the

WTO era. It hopes to provide a more complete and solidly grounded understanding of how the industry evolved and the reasons behind its rapid growth, especially since 1979. The book is of a descriptive nature, as relatively little is known of China's strategies and reform process in this particular sector. It also aims to identify and analyse the problems and obstacles faced by the sector as it continues to grow, especially the constraints generated by the blueprint-style reform, administrative regulations and the international competition environment.

There are several reasons why a study of the Chinese ICT industry has important implications for both theory and policy, and is also well placed to enable us to understand the development issues surrounding China's industrial and technological upgrading during globalization. From a theoretical perspective, the theme addressed by this book at the broadest level is the role the Chinese government played in fostering industrial growth against a backdrop of increasing economic liberalization and globalization. This question is not only very complicated to answer, but also now needs to be discussed in a new context, as China became the 143rd member of the WTO in 2001. To comply with the WTO agreement, China has undertaken a considerable reform of its economic policies and regulatory landscape. By 2005, China committed itself to minimizing trade tariffs, barriers and related subsidies, as well as other state interventional policies for protecting the domestic market and restricting foreign investment.

Arguments soon arose over whether the further trade and industrial reform led by the WTO following the trend towards trade liberalization is propitious for industrial development in developing countries like China. On the one hand, there were some proponents of the view that Chinese growth will accelerate. Trade in accordance with comparative advantage can produce mutual welfare gains as a result of specialization, economies of scale, and efficient allocation of resources. It brings to a country a greater availability of inputs, knowledge and technologies, foreign investment and human capital. These in turn enable further knowledge creation and technological progress, which are regarded today as the major factors in boosting a country's economic growth rate (see Chapter 2). On the other hand, some scholars dispute this view and argue that lower- and middle-income countries will suffer from the controversial effects of free trade as the underdevelopment of infrastructure, institutions and human capital create difficulties in adapting and developing new technologies. Trade liberalization would lead to their specialization in primary goods and more labour-intensive lower-tech industries because they normally hold comparative advantages in these sectors. They also warn that openness would be detrimental to technological development and might either stop or slow developing countries' manufacturing sectors, which are capital- and technology-intensive and with higher export earning growth. These developing nations need at least temporary assistance in the form of protection for the newly emerging manufacturing sectors; otherwise, such countries would not be able to achieve industrialization and may consequently lose their potential ability to catch up. How should the governments of developing countries such as China struggle against the controversial trade liberalization and formulate their policies to promote industrial competitiveness?

The rapid emergence of China's ICT industry in the world market provides us with an unprecedented opportunity to explore some of the arguments of the large body of literature that attempts to explain the role of the state in industrial development and trade. Given the complexity of policy issues in the big picture of China's economic rise, however, the goal of this book is not to provide definitive answers to prove or disprove the deleterious effects of trade liberalization and globalization on China's technology-based industries and the effectiveness of the governmental promotion strategies in late industrialization, nor to predict their future trend. Rather, it brings readers into China's industrial development scenario linked with historical events, governmental policies, as well as the thoughts of Chinese leaders and economists. This book attempts to bring to light some new insights and materials overlooked by scholars of China's industrial development more fully to inform the debate on the state's role in trade and economic development.

By concentrating on investigating China's economic policies towards one of its targeted high-tech sectors, the ICT industry, over the course of its entire development trajectory, this book can also avoid intellectual pitfalls in generalizing the issues across all industries and the whole of the economy.[1] The ICT industry was referred to in China as the electronics industry prior to the late 1990s. As opposed to primary products, the information-related industries are large and intricate, as they are truly global and highly competitive, with rapidly changing technologies and declining costs. Their products are often referred to as the large number of electronic means that are used to display, capture, process, store and disseminate information (Duncombe and Heeks 1999; OECD 2002). These features imply that it is not so easy to define these industries. Their market segmentations are often complicated, with rapid change in demand patterns and unpredictable technical changes. For example, electronic devices can in most cases be distinguished on the basis of their functions and usage. However, some components are more difficult to separate from electrical and even mechanical types, and the definition may vary from country to country.

In 1998, an administrative reform took place. The Ministry of the Information Industry (MII) was created by merging the Ministry of Posts and Telecommunications and the Ministry of Electronics. It was hoped that this administrative restructuring would better reflect the nature and international development of the ICT industry as well as increase linkages between services, R&D and manufacturing activities within the sector (see Chapter 5 and Appendix 1). This book emphasizes the manufacturing side of the ICT industry, consistent with the focus of China's industrial strategy. Appendix 1 shows the coverage of the ICT industry that this book discusses.

From a policy perspective, the choice of the ICT industry for studying the role of the state in industrial development comes naturally. The industry has long been regarded as a key input into an economy. Much as the development of steam power and electricity did in earlier centuries, its growth creates profound linkage effects that alter cost structures, quality and productivity in most other industries and sectors, enabling them to expand, and therefore has the potential to stimulate economic progress (Gordon 2002; OECD 2003a). Also, the ICT sector with its technology-intensive nature both is integral to, and reflects the ongoing trend towards, a knowledge-based economy, in which ideas and innovation have become as important as tangible goods. Moreover, developing the ICT sector nowadays appears to be occupying an increasingly important place on the policy agenda of governments. Both advanced industrial countries and developing countries are attempting to promote indigenous capabilities in high-tech industries, especially the ICT sector, to improve either their positions in the world political economy or their current economic conditions. There are some countries, for example the United States, the United Kingdom and France, that have traditionally emphasized the development of the ICT sector for national defence. Conversely, most governments in developing countries have expressed particular interest in the labour-intensive commercial side of the industry, because it has the potential to generate employment and exports, attract foreign capital, and advance domestic technologies and human resources (Dahlman *et al.*, 1993; Mathews and Cho 2000). Together with the highly competitive and dynamic nature of the industry, the role of governments is very prominent and therefore lends itself to in-depth analysis.

The evolution of the ICT industry can be seen as exemplifying China's overall reform experimentation. It bears many of the aspirations of Chinese leaders for China to rise in the world, economically and politically. Deng Xiaoping's words of 24 October 1988 clearly state this:

> It has always been, and will always be, necessary for China to develop its own high technology so that it can take its place in this field. If it were not for the atomic bomb, the hydrogen bomb and the satellites we have launched since the 1960s, China would not have its present international standing as a great, influential country. These achievements demonstrate a nation's abilities and are a sign of its level of prosperity and development.
>
> (Deng 1988)

The Chinese communist government since its establishment in 1949 had emphasized military as opposed to civilian purposes for the strategic importance of the ICT/electronics industry. During the market-oriented economic reforms of the mid-1980s, the government began to promote the growth of commercial ICT goods for export and to consider it one of the 'pillar' industries for economic growth. In 1999, the Chinese National Congress made a decision on the priority development of the high-tech sectors. Two high-tech sectors, the ICT and biotechnology industries, were selected as China's crucial base for industrialization, national economic strength, international competitiveness and national defence in the twenty-first century. To promote the ICT industry further, in 2004 China highlighted the national goal of becoming a large, strong and competitive ICT nation in the world by 2020. The strategies regarding large firms, which originated in 1993, as well as supporting industrial policies, are emphasized as the main means by which to achieve this goal and assist China to move from its current low-end to high-end sectors of the global value chain.

Furthermore, several high-ranking Chinese officials who laid down the national economic restructuring principles, and were previously assigned to be in charge of the electronics/ICT industry throughout the early reform era. They include Jiang Zemin, who later, from 1993 to 2003, became the president of the People's Republic of China (PRC), and was the Minister of the Electronics Industry from 1983 to 1985. Another was Li Tieying, vice-chairman of the Standing Committee from 1993 to 1998, who succeeded Jiang and was in office from 1985 to 1987. Li in turn was succeeded by Hu Qili, a Standing Committee member of the Politburo as well as Secretariat member of the CCP's Central Committee from 1987 to 1989, who served as the minister from 1991 to 1993. The industry has been used to conduct reform experiments and is thus always a forerunner of broader trends in China's economic transformation. The industry's catalytic role has become even clearer now that Chinese leaders have placed the country's development priority on science- and technology-intensive industries (*keji xingguo*). Through exploring the development of the Chinese ICT industry, this book can address the broader question of how China's industrial policies evolved over time in response to economic liberalization while complying with the WTO agreement.

Moreover, the growth of the ICT sector is one of the features that contributed significantly to the East Asian economic miracle. It has similarly shown its significance in the Chinese economy. In terms of shares of export and sales of industrial output, the ICT sector has remained the largest of all China's manufacturing industries since the mid-1990s (see Figures 1.1 and 1.2). The ICT industry's contribution to the annual GDP growth rate also rose from 0.32 per cent to 1.32 per cent from 1998 to 2004 (see Table 1.1). China's policymakers have publicly expressed their ambitions to follow their East Asian neighbours and develop an internationally competitive ICT industry as a driver of China's rise (see Figure 1.3). The ICT industry is therefore very valuable in helping us understand the challenges that China

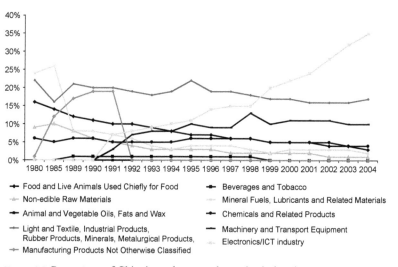

Figure 1.1 Percentage of China's total exports by major industries.

Source: *China Statistical Yearbook*; Information Technology Yearbook; *Yearbook of the Electronics Industry*; various years.

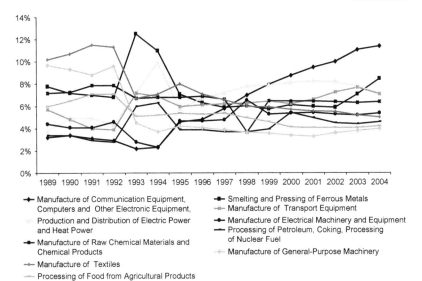

Figure 1.2 China's sales of industrial output by major industries.

Source: *China Statistical Yearbook*; Information Technology Yearbook; *Yearbook of the Electronics Industry*; various years.

faces in creating indigenous technological capabilities for late industrialization in the WTO era. Debates on the unorthodox industrial and trade policies of South Korea and Japan can be carried over to the case of China.

The entry of the East Asian economies into the high-tech ICT sectors in fact goes beyond the simple form of upgrading from labour-intensive to capital-intensive industrialization through the improvement of the general macroeconomic framework. The technological achievements of these countries have not relied heavily on domestic R&D activities, but rather on linkages with foreign companies in various forms such as OEM (original equipment manufacturing) and JV (joint venture) licensing. This allows the present study to show that differences in historical, economic and political conditions between countries determine the success of firms in obtaining and absorbing technologies and upgrading from imitation to innovation. No optimal policy regime could be constructed independent of time and circumstances.

Table 1.1 The ICT industry's contribution to the annual GDP growth rate

	1998	1999	2000	2001	2002	2003	2004
GDP growth rate	7.8%	7.1%	8.0%	7.3%	8.0%	9.1%	9.5%
ICT contribution	0.32%	0.34%	0.78%	0.4%	0.39%	0.64%	1.32%

Source: Information Technology Yearbook; *Yearbook of the Electronics Industry*; various years.

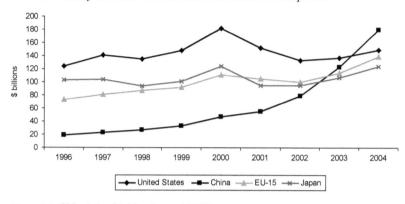

Figure 1.3 China's lead-taking in world ICT exports.

Source: OECD 2006.

Note: Data for the European Union exclude intra-EU trade.

Synopsis of the book

This book presents four general themes while following a modified chronological order in the setting of China's overall economic reform. Because of this arrangement, some continuous time series data are relevant to several different chapters. For easy reading and comprehension of China's strategy, Chapter 6 is organized to contain these data, which readers may occasionally want to refer to. The book proceeds as follows: Chapters 1 and 2 serve as the introductory part, Part I. They describe the broader theme this book addresses, and aim to make a link between the economic development of China and that of the rest of the world. Chapter 2 tends towards a more theoretical approach, examining the broader debate related to the competing paradigms of developmental and national competitive issues. It shows the international experiences of industrial, trade and economic progress. Relying on both historical facts and theoretical debate, Chapter 2 argues that there are deficiencies within the free trade and market system that the Bretton Woods institutions have pressed developing states to adopt. Neither intensive protectionist nor interventionist policies, widely supported in developing nations, were the right way to achieve industrialization and economic progress. Rather, guided liberalization, together with flexible state intervention that constantly responds to the dynamic development of the world economy, has been more effective.

Part II traces the development of the industry from the very beginning to the opening up period, showing China's distinctive development conditions. Chapter 3 describes the first four periods of the industry under the extreme statist command economy of the 1949–1978 period. Unlike in all the other latecomers, China's extreme level of state involvement was partly determined by the Stalinist-style centrally planned system and was seen as partially necessary to meet military needs in response to changes in the international political environment. Chapter 4 describes Deng's opening up period. As a specific development strategy for the ICT industry had not yet been formed, it emphasized four important reform processes within the overall development reorientation strategy applied to the sector: the shift towards civilian production, enterprises' autonomy and industrial restructuring, the management of trade and investment, and technology leverage.

Part III moves on to examine China's 'pillar' industrial strategy, which was based on the East Asian model and sought to promote some strategic high-tech industries such as the ICT industry. Part III's first chapter, Chapter 5, focuses on the big business and small business strategy, arguing that a successful strategy should be country-specific. Chapter 6 examines the 'attracting in' and walking out' strategies, which demonstrate the illusory nature of China's ICT catching up phenomena, and the inflexible role of the state in achieving dynamic growth. Chapter 7 discusses the challenges of the 'breaking through' strategy that the government used to improve China's overall ICT competitiveness by promoting some 'strategic' sectors, and focuses on the semiconductor sector.

Part IV, the concluding part of the book, summarizes and synthesizes China's ICT development model and its limitations. Chapter 9 attempts to draw some major theoretical and practical policy lessons from China's ICT development experience.

2 Economic liberalization and industrial policies

The state's role in economic development

Before probing into the specific issues of China's ICT industrial growth, this chapter serves to establish a theoretical foundation for China's industrial and trade policies during its economic liberalization process, and reviews them in their historical context. This review is essential to understanding China's industrialization and development strategy, not least because China's past and present industrial policy, along with its decision on WTO entry, are integral to the world's development. They reflect China's economic and political reaction to changes in the global political economy over time. An analysis of the implications of domestic economic policy needs to be considered in relation to international dimensions. In other words, the role of the Chinese government in developing the competitiveness of a particular industry should be examined from international, domestic and historical perspectives. It might be highly misleading to visualize China's three decades of industrial reform without taking into account the bigger picture of world development.

The main purpose of this chapter is to fit the case study of a specific Chinese industry, the ICT industry, into the context of the theoretical debate. As extensive literature exists in this field of study, this chapter cannot cover the entire spectrum of the debates but is limited to those aspects that can facilitate the analysis of the research question. This book hopes to show how China's industrial strategy was designed and has evolved in response to increasing economic liberalization. It will therefore follow the development of theories mainly related to the starting point of economic liberalization and globalization, which is international trade. It is also the area in which China's industrial policy ultimately aims to achieve success.

Industrial and trade policies will not be discussed separately in this book since they both affect industrial development in the process of economic liberalization, and their functions often overlap (Chang 2002, 2003a; Lall 2001, 2004; Lall and Urata 2003). The terms 'industrial policy' or 'industrialization strategy' do not have universally agreed definitions. Broadly defined, industrial policy covers:

> manpower policy, fiscal and financial incentives for investment, public investment programmes, public procurement policies, fiscal incentives for R&D, firm-level policies such as specific R&D support, anti-trust policy,

merger policies to create 'national champions', support for small firms, regional policies such as the development of physical and social infrastructure and the establishment of industrial complexes, generalized trade protection, sectoral policies such as the organization of recession cartels in depressed industries, product upgrading in labour-intensive industries.

(Pinder 1982, cited in Chang 2003a: 110)

In this book, industrial policy or industrial strategy refers to those state actions aimed at promoting the growth of a particular industry in order to achieve outcomes perceived by the state to be efficient for the whole economy.[1] Trade policies are integrally tied up with the overall industrial policy of a country and are those regulating the import or export of particular industrial goods and thus determining which specific industries will be open to the global market, and the degree to which international factors affect industry's growth. Nor will trade-related measures such as those affecting the flow of foreign capital and driving factors for globalization like multinational corporations be separately discussed, as this book mainly concerns the reform of China's broadly defined industrial and trade policies as a response to increasing economic liberalization and globalization.

The first part of this chapter reviews neo-liberal propositions to developing countries regarding trade and industrial reform. It traces the origin of the controversy on universal trade and market liberalization and shows the role played by the comparative advantage theory in the economic policy reform of developing countries. The second part reveals criticisms of the universal free market and trade, and support for selective state-led industrial and trade strategies. Historical and empirical evidence is presented alongside the theoretical discussion.

The neo-liberal 'catching-up' policy propositions to developing countries

Central to globalization and international competitiveness, the opening up to trade and foreign investment is often a key topic in any debate on policies designed to improve economic prospects for developing countries. Several centuries ago, scholars had already begun to ask what gives rise to a country's economic prosperity. Nowadays, theorists submit well-researched policy implications to governments on how some nations emerged with strong competitiveness by promoting production and engaging in trade, and what goals in trade and investment a country needs to secure for the purpose of sustainable development.

The first answer comes from mercantilism, which dominated economic thought and practices in Western Europe from the fifteenth to the late eighteenth century. Under the mercantilist view, the world economy is an arena of competition among states. The primary objectives of governments were to strengthen their power and to accumulate wealth (in the form of precious metals). States therefore needed to play an active role in building up industry and encouraging domestic production for all foreign import substitutes in order to maximize exports. A substantial surplus on a nation's balance of trade (exports exceeding imports) would ensure the influx of precious metals (e.g. gold and silver), which could be used to equip larger armies and navies. The enhanced military forces in turn could be utilized to defeat rivals, expand colonies, conquer new markets and control trade routes, which bring in wealth and power to the nation. Free trade, in the view of mercantilism, is a zero-sum game that leads to outflow of wealth for exchanging foreign goods. It would weaken a nation's political and military power (Vaggi and Groenewegen 2003).

In rejecting the mercantilist view, Adam Smith (1723–1790), in *An Inquiry into the Nature and Causes of the Wealth of Nations*, published in 1776, argued that the most important source of wealth creation is not the accumulation of precious metals, but the division of labour, with different people performing different tasks, obtaining what they need through exchange in the market. The benefit of the division of labour is that each individual worker becomes a specialist in his or her area of production, which increases that worker's efficiency. This will lead to an increase in overall productivity. Smith then posited that the division of labour could be limited by the extent of the market, which determines the variety of products that can be freely exchanged. For example, in Smith's observation a country carpenter had to perform most production tasks himself, whereas in a large market his job could be broken down into several trades (e.g. wood carver, wagon maker and cabinetmaker).

In general, Smithians believe that the more advanced a society, the greater the division of labour. The government should promote the division of labour by enlarging rather than disturbing the market. In doing so, a country needs to move from domestic to more extensive global markets to allow further division of labour and lead to productivity growth. As international trade takes place when two nations voluntarily exchange goods that they can produce with less labour than anywhere else in the world, both trading nations will be able to increase their output of goods in which they possess an *absolute advantage*. A part of the increase could be used to trade for more of those goods that each country cannot produce efficiently. The higher the level of international division of labour, the greater the potential gain from trade for both nations. Therefore, Smith (1776) advocated 'the system of natural liberty' in which free markets and trade should prevail against the mercantile and physiocratic systems.

The idea of Smith's absolute advantage is simple and intuitive. A question that arose, however, was whether countries will cease to trade when one nation holds an absolute advantage in all goods.[2] To adjust Smith's theory, David Ricardo (1772–1823) formalized the concept of *comparative advantage*, drawing references from Mill (1821) and Torrens (1815) in his book titled *On the Principles of Political Economy and Taxation* (1817). In his model, labour is the only factor of production, and nations differ only in labour productivity (or differences in technology).[3] By observing different opportunity costs in producing wine and cloth in England and Portugal, he confirmed the mutual benefits of trade. As long as there are different relative efficiencies between nations, trade will take place. Even a nation that has absolute advantages in both goods still can gain from international commerce by specializing in the goods that it can produce most efficiently and trading for those whose production is less efficient. The pattern of international trade is governed by the force of comparative advantage under a free market system.

The perspectives of the classical economists Smith and Ricardo on the relationship between markets, trade and growth had great influence on political parties and economic policy formulation in eighteenth- and nineteenth-century Great Britain. At first their work, which challenged the mercantile doctrines of the time, did not win acceptance, partly because of Great Britain's strained relationships with other nations and partly because of powerful vested interests. For example, Smith's *The Wealth of Nations* was published in 1776, the year of the American Declaration of Independence, and Ricardo's work became available only after the Napoleonic Wars (1804–1815). After the wars, the idea of free trade was still strongly opposed by landlords, as their income from rent would decrease with a fall in the price of grain, which could be brought about by the importing of cheap foreign grains. This, however, was completely distinct from the interests of domestic manufacturers and urban dwellers, who wanted cheaper food and raw materials so as to reduce production costs and raise living standards. Political pressures from the increasingly strong manufacturers grew during the industrial revolution, and the government started reducing tariff protection in 1833. The shift to a laissez-faire regime in Great Britain eventually took place in 1846, when the government repealed the Corn Laws. Alfred Marshall (1920) maintained that trade restrictions in fact impeded the economic development of Great Britain: '[Britain] became the acknowledged leader of the world in massive industries ... through her policy of free trade ... throw[ing] her markets open to the world' (Marshall 1920, book I, ch. 1:18 and ch. 5:64). According to the liberal explanation of history, the pursuit of free trade and a free market policy enabled Great Britain to overtake interventionist France and become a world power in the nineteenth century (Bairoch 1993; Reinert 1994).

Ricardo's hypothesis was continuously tested and used to explain the benefit of free trade, despite unanswered questions as to why trade should be determined by a single factor of production – labour – and what is behind the differences in comparative costs. With the rise of neo-classical economics in the 1920s, new justifications based on Ricardo's explanation were developed.[4] Eli Heckscher and Bertil Ohlin made an important contribution to exploring the underlying basis of comparative advantage. In Ricardo's model, differences in labour productivity between countries were assumed to be the prime source for international trade. Other factors of production were either of no significance or were equally distributed among sectors with a fixed ratio. The Heckscher–Ohlin model introduces the factor-proportions theory to show that factors giving rise to a nation's comparative advantage are in fact determined by that country's factor endowments. Under the assumptions of identical production technology, perfect market competition and intersectoral resource mobility, the model indicates that a country in possession of relatively abundant capital will specialize in producing and exporting capital-intensive goods in exchange for labour-intensive goods from a country that has a comparative advantage in labour. The trade pattern is driven by the differences in the price of productive factors, and a country's specialization should be based on its abundant 'productive factors' (e.g. land, labour, capital) rather than scarce ones in order for it to enjoy welfare gains. Governmental interventions into markets and trade will limit the ability of countries to realize welfare gains.

Much theoretical work expanding the basic Heckscher–Ohlin paradigm followed. The Stolper–Samuelson theorem provides a way to analyse the effects of trade on income distribution. In this model, changes in relative prices of goods have strong effects on relative allocation of resources. Free markets and trade will lead to the international equalization of individual factors. Movements in relative prices create stimulations for merchants to move the factors of production from higher-cost sectors into lower-cost ones until these differentials in factor reward are eliminated. As a consequence, although opening up will hurt import-competing industries which depend on scarce factors, it will benefit those industries with abundant factors and allow the market to allocate resources efficiently, in strong contrast with an autarky, thereby improving welfare (Stolper and Samuelson 1941). According to these theories, the policy prescription for developing countries is to specialize in production to further promote domestic and international division of labour, and the export of primary or labour-intensive goods that they can produce with their most abundant production factors. The theories constitute a good basis for rejecting state intervention in both production and trade.

Both trade liberalization and laissez-faire industrial policy are now said to be 'good practice', or the best way to foster economic development, while protectionism and state intervention of any kind are widely regarded as the source of many economic problems in developing countries. Although policy debate in this field is far from over, current thought on trade and industrial development has moved to a position nearer to the liberal end of the spectrum than it was formerly. Free trade and flow of capital refer to an ideal scenario where countries are able to exchange goods and financial resources without any government restriction or distribution. Laissez-faire policy is a general term for neo-classical economic policy propositions, in particular for a belief in the efficacy of free market economics as an extension of free trade. Knowles (1921) described such policy as meaning that 'the less government intervention there was in any sphere the better'.

To convince developing countries of the vigour of the free market, orthodox neo-liberal theorists rooted in Adam Smith often refer to historical experiences of the developed countries: that of eighteenth-century Great Britain, the first truly industrialized modern economy in the world, followed by the United States and Australia in the nineteenth century, Meiji Japan in the early twentieth century and the East Asian 'tigers' in the second half of the twentieth century. The main common characteristic of these countries is thought to be the establishment of free markets, trade and financial systems during their economic development.

In the view of neo-liberals, it was the heightened economic, social and political tension caused by the First World War (1914–1918) that interrupted free trade and compelled nations to resort to protectionist measures. The US Smoot–Hawley tariff was believed to have aggravated the Great Depression in the 1930s. To prevent nations from repeating the historical mistakes of the 1930s, the General Agreement on Tariffs and Trade (GATT) was established in 1947. It operated on a provisional basis as the International Trade Organization (ITO), whose creation was planned at the 1944 Bretton Woods conference together with that of the IMF and the World Bank Group after the Second World War (1939–1945) for the purpose of promoting international trade and the new financial order.[5] Its preamble clearly establishes trade liberalization as the primary objective:

> Recognizing that [member countries'] relations in the field of trade and economic endeavour should be conducted with a view to raising standards of living, ensuring full employment and a large and steadily growing volume of real income and effective demand, developing the full use of the resources of the world and expanding the production and exchange of goods, ... Being desirous of contributing to these objectives by entering into reciprocal and mutually advantageous arrangements directed to the substantial reduction of tariffs and other barriers to trade and to the elimination of discriminatory treatment in international commerce.
>
> (GATT 1947, preamble)

The GATT policy framers, mostly from developed countries and strongly influenced by US negotiating power in the early rounds of trade negotiations, chose the cosmopolitan version of the free trade theory: comparative advantage. They believed that universal free trade coupled with the market mechanism would guarantee the best use of the world's resources, and that a set of agreed-upon rules would enable contracting parties to benefit from trade. The adoption of this postwar liberal agreement was seen as having been promoted by the interests of developed countries in each other's markets, particularly the United States and Western European countries. Bergsten (1998) observes that the motive behind the United States' initiation of the Kennedy Round in the early 1960s was to reduce the discrimination against American exports that arose with the expansion of the European Common Market from the late 1950s, in addition to defensive reasons. Nevertheless, the United States' embrace of trade liberalization seemed to go beyond American industrial leaders' confidence in their world competitive power or liberal economists' faith in free trade. The US government was motivated more by political expectations of capitalist consolidation, meaning that trade liberalization would enable the countries involved to gain significantly so that Moscow-centred Soviet imperialism would be contained. The cost of trade liberalization was accepted as part of the cost of US security promotion projects such as the Marshall Plan (Nelson 1987).

With the deepening of the Cold War, those economists who favoured protectionism and interventionism sat silently on the sidelines. Their views were rejected both theoretically and politically in advanced capitalist countries. Although macroeconomic Keynesian policy (e.g. full employment and smoothing of the business cycle) largely prevailed during this period, interventionist policies were associated with political aspirations for achieving specific economic goals. They eventually gave way to monetarism and later the neo-liberal agenda in the 1970s as full employment was no longer considered to be the ultimate macroeconomic policy goal. As long as there was price stability, a market-based economy would readily remedy problems and would not require Keynesian interventionist policy to deal with recessions. Neo-liberal thought gained substantial political momentum when heavyweight leaders such as Margaret Thatcher and Ronald Reagan rallied behind it.

On the other hand, protectionist and interventionist theories were widely adopted in developing nations. Since the 1950s, these nations had begun to pursue 'inward-oriented', 'import substitution' interventionist policies to seek development from internal resources. Such policies eventually led to isolation of their economies from the rest of the world. Neo-classical economists often interpret developing countries' policy preferences or their lack of interest in the GATT as equivalent to their inability to see trade as the primary engine of growth or to understand the important role of the free market in economic development.

However, it is also undeniable that early experiences of globalization since the eighteenth century were often accompanied, in the Third World, by unpleasant scenes of colonization, pillage, slavery, and the slaughter of native residents. The real world was not entirely about state intervention and trade protection, which in the eyes of many should be removed for theoretically promised mutual gains in the neo-classical debate. Apart from economic benefits, there are moral issues that require serious consideration. What developing nations were most concerned with was their political, economic and social desire for independence after the Second World War. Their policy objectives reflected local people's nationalist, anti-colonial sentiment against extreme free market and trade policies, which were often associated with imperialism or capitalism.[6]

Interventionist industrial policy also gained credence when political leaders saw the rapid industrialization of the USSR, which was once an economically backward country and yet grew strong enough to defeat German fascism and even drew ahead of the United States in the early space race. Many countries, such as China, North Korea and those in Eastern Europe, became convinced that central planning was no less effective in governing the economy than market mechanisms and might work even better in sectors requiring a concerted effort and large scale at the national level (Chang and Grabel 2004; Ellman 1989). The non-market-based system was adopted mostly by the USSR's allies and satellites, which did achieve impressive advances in industrialization during the 1950s. The success of the state interventionist policy also gave rise to some non-orthodox measures such as nationalization of basic industries and investment planning outside the communist bloc. For example, the UK government opted to nationalize the coal, steel, energy and transport sectors; France nationalized its four biggest banks, the Renault car factories, Air France, etc. and similar measures were adopted in Latin America, Africa, the Middle East and Asia (Chang and Grabel 2004).

Theoretically, Sachs *et al.* (1995) contended that the state-led industrialization and socialist development strategy was supported by a series of misleading 'intellectual beliefs'. The Marxist theories were held by some developing countries to substantiate the claim that the capitalist system has enforced a rigid global division of labour, which caused their own poverty and benefited advanced capitalist countries (e.g. dependency theory). The implication of Keynesian theory that the instability of capitalism calls for governmental actions to direct future investment through nationalization was widely accepted in Western Europe; the 'big push' strategy of Paul Rosenstein-Rodan maintains that the governmental development planning and coordination efforts were essential to reaching the high minimum investment requirement of large-scale public complexes for achieving industrialization; Latin American structuralism or export pessimism (e.g. Raúl Prebisch) argues that trade liberalization distorts the industrialization process of developing countries if their governments cannot play active roles in altering disadvantaged economic structures of product specialization, market structure and technological capabilities. Historical justification is provided by Alexander Gerschenkron (1962) from the industrialization experience of nineteenth-century Europe, when backward countries had relied heavily on the state to allocate resources strategically to enable them to catch up.

The return of most developing countries to international trade and to the GATT negotiating table started after the relaxation of tensions between the two superpowers in the 1970s and flourished in the 1990s. It was interpreted by neo-liberals as a reaction to the failure of conventional import substitution and the planned economic policy of the 1950s to 1970s. Nevertheless, the return was not free but conditional on economic reforms: that they would adopt free trade and market mechanisms and considerably minimize government involvement in resource allocation and trade distortions such as tariffs or barriers, so as to follow the export promotion path. They were told to refer to neo-classical economic theories and the liberal explanation of the historical experience of developed countries for solutions to their economic problems and models for economic development. Moreover, since the early 1980s, the World Bank and IMF have initiated Structural Adjustment Programmes (SAPs) and Stabilization Programmes (SPs), with trade liberalization as a key precondition for the provision of loans. This also serves as political cover for governments to dismantle domestic trade protection measures raised by powerful corporate, environmental or labour interest groups.

The neo-liberal (market fundamentalist) rationales behind the commonly shared themes among policy advice on trade, investment and development, and the reform programmes of the Bretton Woods institutions, were summarized precisely by John Williamson as the 'Washington consensus'. This includes privatization, deregulation and economic liberalization through trade and capital account liberalization, the control of inflation, and the maintenance of tight budgets through a set of macroeconomic policies (Williamson 2000). Finally, the neo-liberal movement reached a peak when the Uruguay Round led to the creation of the World Trade Organization to replace the treaty-based GATT in 1995. The WTO carried forward the aforementioned objective and fundamental principles of the GATT in removing restrictions on imports, reducing discriminations against exports, minimizing or eliminating subsidies, promoting free trade, enforcing intellectual property protection, extending international trade law to the service sector and opening up to foreign investment.

Although the Bretton Woods institutions provided momentum for liberalizing trade and integrating national economies, their management of globalization based on the 'Washington consensus' was by no means beyond disagreement. Developing countries believed that both neo-liberal principles and asymmetry in the multilateral trading regime allow a few powerful developed countries to press many overpopulated developing nations to open their markets universally and withdraw government intervention in the process of industrialization (Subramanian and Wei 2003). Public protests and riots against these institutions have occurred at almost all their major meetings since the 1999 WTO summit in Seattle. These protests have reflected the resentment among many people in developing countries that they have failed to reap the promised benefits of trade liberalization and globalization (e.g. a reduction in poverty and the raising of general living standards). The laissez-faire reform policies and SAPs/SP loan programmes were anticipated to allow market forces to function, channelling resources to countries' more productive sectors. Initially, protected industries might be hurt, but opening up would facilitate technology upgrading, introduce new technologies, improve skills and eventually lead to the creation of new competitive industries.

However, many of these promised benefits appear to have failed to materialize (Stiglitz 2002). There is increasingly worse income distribution both within developing countries and between developed and developing countries. The actual number of people living in poverty (receiving less than $1 per day) has increased by almost 100 million since the 1990s, while the actual total world income has grown at a rate of 2.5 per cent a year (Caprio *et al.* 1998). Second, little has been achieved in terms of the expansion, diversification and upgrading of exports in favour of manufactured goods (deindustrialization – suffering from terms of trade problem) in a large number of low-income countries, including many in Africa and Latin America that have actively embarked on structural reform and trade liberalization since the 1980s (Katz 2000; Shafaeddin 2005; UNCTAD 1999; UNDP 2001, 2004). Third, the financial and economic crisis in the late 1990s as a consequence of rapid trade and financial liberalization in Asia and Latin America threatened the economic stability not only of developing countries but also of the world as a whole. Fourth, the introduction of 'shock therapy', or overnight market-oriented economic reform, in former communist countries has demonstrated a far less satisfactory result. For example, Russia's transition has not generated the promised long-term benefits, but rather has led to an unprecedented increase in poverty (Stiglitz 2002).

So if in many cases the actual benefits of market and trade liberalization during globalization have been far less than its advocates anticipated, where does the fundamental problem lie in the present industrial and trade policies recommended by neo-liberals? The next section, looking at criticism of universal free trade and markets ('market fundamentalism'), argues that as far as developing countries are concerned the deficiency lies within the cosmopolitan version of free trade and market theory itself and in the very principle of comparative advantage. Trade liberalization creates opportunity for development, but the liberal proposition on its function in advancing universal prosperity and welfare remains very much an open question. Historical records demonstrate that even the developed countries did not pursue a free trade policy until their industrial base had gained considerable strength. The neo-liberal doctrine adopted to support rapid universal trade liberalization and withdrawal of governmental intervention happened to ignore the varied levels of industrial, technological and institutional capabilities among the nations. It leaves the weak exposed to competition from the strong, which furthers the developed countries' advantage (Chang and Grabel 2004).

Criticism concerning universal free trade and market liberalization

The neo-classical justification of comparative advantage is often used to persuade developing countries to adopt laissez-faire and trade liberalization policy. Liberals claim that the 'good theory' of comparative advantage is often misapplied and 'harnessed to erroneous stylized facts' by some economists to support trade and market interventions (Krueger 1997). However, the 'good theory' itself is in reality not only challenged by many historical records and empirical tests, but also arguably based on unrealistic assumptions

Revealing the real 'catching-up' story from history: justification for List's infant industry theory

Much classical and neo-classical literature has argued about the problems of mercantilism and the benefits of free trade as an extension of free markets resting on Ricardian comparative advantage. In disagreement with the Ricardians, Friedrich List (1789–1846), often recognized as the forefather of the 'infant industry' argument, published *The National System of Political Economy* in 1841. The infant industry argument was developed at the time when the United States and Germany had fallen behind Great Britain in terms of industrialization. List argued that Smith's proposition of universal free markets and free trade with economically underdeveloped countries was largely based on British interests at that time. Today his idea is also used to criticize the interests underlying developed countries' advocacy for market and trade liberalization.

Revisiting historical lessons from medieval and Renaissance Europe and nineteenth-century North America, List pointed out that infant industry promotion policy was behind the development process of many countries' economic prosperity, and England was in fact the first country that wisely practised this principle before its rise.[7] For example, in order to develop the English wool cloth industry, King Edward III (reigned 1327–1377) launched a number of infant industry promotion policies, including investing in weaving machineries, centralizing trade in raw wools and banning the importation of woollen cloth. He also decided to wear only English cloth so as to set an example for the rest of the country to follow. His policies were further developed and reinforced in the Tudor dynasty. A century later, in Henry VII's reign, the English woollen cloth industry grew considerably under state promotion and protection and successfully led England to transform itself from a country exporting raw wool to one exporting woollen cloth (List 1841; Chang 2002).

Prior to the early 1700s, the English 'catching-up' strategy was mainly about capturing trade routes.[8] After 1772, the British Parliament had begun to introduce new legislation to promote manufacturing industries intensively. Measures included lowering, waving or rebating import duties on raw materials for export-oriented manufacturing activities, abolishing export duties and subsidizing most manufacturers, raising significantly import duties on foreign manufactured items or superior goods, and introducing quality control on manufacturing industries for reputation building (Chang 2002). Interventionist and protectionist policies had been continued throughout the period of the industrial revolution (1760–1830).[9] After more than two centuries of state promotion and protection, Great Britain developed far more rapidly than other countries. For example, its population reached 8–10 per cent of the total European population, production of pig iron increased from 29 per cent of the European total in 1800 to 45 per cent in 1830. During the same period, the per capita industrialization achieved by Great Britain was even more remarkable, exceeding that of the rest of Europe by 110–250 per cent (Bairoch 1982). Unsurprisingly, British domestic manufacturers with leading production capabilities aggressively lobbied the government to promote a free trade system for them. In the 1860s, following the Anglo-French Trade Treaty (the Cobden–Chevalier Treaty signed by Napoleon III in 1860), Great Britain began its trade liberalization on a large scale and promoted free trade and market doctrine to other countries and its colonies.

List precisely described the free trade strategy of developed countries and argued eloquently with historical evidence in opposition to Smith's 1776 proposition:

> It is a very common clever device that when anyone [meaning Great Britain] has attained the summit of greatness, he kicks away the ladder by which he has climbed up, in order to deprive others of the means of climbing up after him. In this lies the secret of the cosmopolitical doctrine of Adam Smith, and of the cosmopolitical tendencies of his great contemporary William Pitt, and of all his successors in the British Government administrations…Any nation which by means of protective duties and restrictions on navigation has raised her manufacturing power and her navigation to such a degree of development that no other nation can sustain free competition with her, can do nothing wiser than to throw away these ladders of her greatness, to preach to other nations the benefits of free trade, and to declare in penitent tones that she has hitherto wandered in the paths of error, and has now for the first time succeeded in discovering the truth.
>
> (List 1841)[10]

Strongly influenced by Alexander Hamilton,[11] Henry Carey, Henry Clay and Daniel Raymond, List developed his infant industry theory to defend the principle of interventionist policies against universal free trade while resident in the United States from 1825 to 1832. To elucidate his principle, List proposed five different stages of economic development that countries need to go through: (1) the savage or primitive stage (hunting and fishing), (2) the pastoral stage, (3) the agricultural stage, (4) the agricultural united with manufacturing stage, and (5) the agricultural–manufacturing–commercial (services) stage. Free trade policy might enable a country to progress from a state of 'barbarism' to the agriculture stage. Upon reaching stage 3 and getting ready to industrialize, a country needs an appropriate protectionist policy because such a transition would not happen by itself through market forces. Since there is a 'competence gap', free trade is only mutually beneficial to those countries that are at a similar stage of development. For example, when economically backward countries are moving to the stage where they are able to exchange manufactured products instead of agricultural goods, competition from more developed countries might destroy their newborn industries and consequently slow or stop their industrialization (List 1841). Even neo-classical economists had to agree that 'it would be foolish for nations with immature industries to adopt England's [free trade] system pure and simple' (Marshall, cited in Keynes, 1926: 392).

The British 'wisdom' of trade protection and industrial subsidies policies was widely practised during the American industrialization process. British free trade doctrine prevailed in Europe following the 1860 Anglo-French Trade Treaty (the Cobden–Chevalier Treaty) during the first half of the nineteenth century. However, at about the same period, from 1866 to 1883, the United States started import substitution and raised tariffs by as much as 45–50 per cent on average, three time more than that of continental European countries for manufactured goods (Bairoch 1996). By 1913, the per capita industrialization level of the United States was almost twice that of five world-leading economies combined: the United Kingdom, Belgium, Switzerland, Germany and Sweden.

Conceding leadership to the United States and motivated by the 1930 US Smoot-Hawley Tariff Act, the United Kingdom reintroduced tariffs on a large scale since 1931 when its current account balance moved into deficit. The free trade era had by then come to an end (Bairoch 1996). The US protectionist policies remained in place until the end of the Second World War. Similar stories of state intervention and trade protection for industrialization can be found from the experiences of the Netherlands, Switzerland, Germany and Sweden to the rise of Japan, South Korea and other Asian 'tigers'. Major industrialization movements were accompanied by relatively higher tariffs each time: the first industrial revolution, in Great Britain, lasted from around 1770 to 1830, the second one, in North America, from 1873 to 1914. Freer trade lasted merely for a short period from around 1860 to 1880 when many European countries reduced tariff protection substantially, following the free trade practices practiced within the British empire and with 'independent countries' that were subject to its unequal treaties. Tariffs then went up dramatically during the two world wars and went up further in the 'late' industrialization period from 1950 to 1995. Just as List had argued from historical evidence, rich countries began to push developing ones into adopting neo-liberal policies only after they had climbed to the top of the 'ladder' (Chang 2002).

However, a careful reader must notice that List was not against market and trade but against the 'cosmopolitical' version of unregulated and universal free trade and market doctrines that classical and neo-classical economists proposed. His work provides a fundamental theoretical framework, based on historical records, to explain the necessity of protectionism and interventionism for building strong industries in developing countries. It thus has many implications for the problems of trade and industrialization in developing countries, which is why this book highlights his propositions. In contrast to the British classical tradition, he saw economic development as a dynamic rather than a static process and one in which the state needs to play a key role. Although there is literature misperceiving the infant industry argument as equivalent to import substitution and mercantilist doctrines (e.g. Little *et al.* 1970; Krueger 1978), List was against neither trade nor the expansion of exporting. Instead, he recommended selective but not across-the-board protection for new (manufacturing) industries in late-industrializing countries (Mehdi 2000). He argued that protection should be temporary and removed when the industry become mature (attained stage 5).

> A nation which has an agrarian economy and is dependent upon foreign countries (for its manufactured goods) can … stimulate the establishment of industries by means of a protective tariff. Such a country may well sacrifice much 'exchange value' [i.e. material capital] for the moment, if its new workshops produce expensive goods of poor quality. But it will greatly increase its productive power in the future … This is our main argument in support of a protective tariff and in opposition to the doctrine of free trade.
>
> (List 1938: 35–36)

This is because protection is neither an incentive nor a determining factor in enhancing a country's 'productive power', which is what differentiates economically advanced from economically backward countries. In essence, his theory regards protection as a partial means to achieve infant industry development. According to List, the crucial source of 'productive power' is from the indigenous capital of mind (mental capital) on top of the other two sources: the capital of nature and the capital of matter (material) which can be exchanged from trade.

> The nation derives its productive power from the mental and physical powers of the individuals; from their social, municipal, and political conditions and institutions; from the natural resources placed at its disposal, or from the instruments it possesses as the material products of former mental and bodily exertions (material, agricultural, manufacturing, and commercial capital).
>
> (List 1841: XIX.1)

In the context of the great many nations in the world, the main roles of each state in terms of economic management are to protect and augment its 'productive power', and to create adequate conditions for development (e.g. fostering human capital through education and investing in infrastructure). In today's economic terminology, it is about state-directed capability in upgrading technology and innovation, and improving competitiveness (Levi-Faur 1997).

Structuralist dependency theory: import substitution argument

After the First World War, almost all countries began to impose tariffs, raise existing ones and set up quotas on foreign imports in order to protect their domestic industries. The Great Depression soon came along and rapidly spread from the United States to Europe and other industrialized areas of the world.[12] In the wake of these historical events, developing countries in the post-Second World War and Cold War era had great doubts about the benefits of free trade and markets, and considered heavy reliance on trade a danger to their development. Governmental interventions in the management of industrial growth and substituting imported goods were regarded as increasing independence and thus conducive to national security.

The underlying principle for such across-the-board protectionist trade and interventionist industrial strategies adopted by developing countries was often thought to be based on structuralist/Marxist dependency theory. The theory was developed by Raúl Prebisch, an Argentinian economist at the United Nations Commission for Latin America and later at the United Nations Conference on Trade and Development (UNCTAD) in 1950 (Prebisch 1950; Singer 1950).[13] He contended that economic growth in the 'core' may not necessarily lead to growth in the periphery and could contribute to the underdevelopment of the peripheral countries. Such a possibility was not predicted by neo-classical theories, which often assume that economic growth is a result of further international division of labour and will bring benefits to all, although these may not be equally shared.

The theory hypothesizes that the developed nations are the industrial 'core,' which consists of the majority of manufacturing producers, while the developing countries are the 'periphery', which comprises many makers of primary goods. Income growth in the periphery could stimulate a larger demand for imported manufactured goods as the fruits of technical progress and increased productivity in the 'core', and could thus boost the economies of the industrialized countries. However, because manufactured goods are noted as having relatively higher price elasticity of demand compared with those for primary products, income growth in the 'core' may not generate greater demand for commodities imported from the peripheral countries.

In other words, if developing countries follow this new order of international division of labour, which is unnatural and shaped by power relations in the 'world system', they will never be able to earn enough from the production and export of primary commodities to pay for their imports of manufactured goods and thus will be unable to raise their standards of living.[14] Developing countries must achieve industrialization in order to close the gap between them and the advanced industrialized countries because of the secular deterioration of the terms of trade for the primary goods and slower growth and inelasticity of world demand for these goods (Prebisch 1958). They should not follow the neo-liberal comparative advantage which dictates that they continue to import industrial goods even if they have a future comparative advantage in the production of industrial products.

Inspired by Prebisch's idea, developing countries reached a broad consensus in the 1950s and 1960s that the best way to achieve industrialization was for the state to advocate an import substitution strategy, promoting relatively higher income-elastic goods produced locally in order to replace imports. However, the developing countries misunderstood and applied Prebisch's idea wrongly. Many developing countries in Latin America, Middle East, North Africa and Asia imposed across-the-board trade restrictions from the Great Depression to the post-Second World War period and suffered significantly from their tight import controls.

Prebisch was not in fact against trade, nor did he support across-the-board protection. He did not suggest that excessive import substitution should be a permanent feature of industrial policy, but advocated it only for specific periods when a developing country had an underdeveloped industrial infrastructure and external market conditions were unfavourable for the export of manufactured goods (Shafaeddin 2005). In the mid-1960s, he explained the adverse effects that 'inward-looking industrialization' practices involved. For example, national markets in developing countries were not large enough for them to achieve scale economies in their manufacturing industries, cutting down production expenses and improving productivity to keep their prices relatively lower than those of industrialized countries. In the 1970s, he further contended that a gradual reduction in protection is needed in order to introduce competition. He also argued that industrialization programmes need to be selective and cover both production promotion and export subsidies in order to reduce cost differentials with the 'core' industrialized countries. A strategy that mixes export promotion and import substitution is necessary to increase the domestic added value in exports (Prebisch 1984; Shafaeddin 2005).

Prebisch's work of course has drawbacks. For example, many 'centre' countries are also major producers of some primary products (e.g. the United States Canada, the Scandinavian countries, Australia, New Zealand). His argument often assumes that the mechanism for the difference derived only from the supply conditions of primary and manufactured goods. Farmers always produce the same amount of primary goods without considering the price changes while manufacturers can always adjust production capacity according to changes in demand. In fact, developing countries are very different from one another in economic performance, and their differences are increasing.

Empirical tests: unrealistic assumptions and irrelevance to developing countries

At roughly the same time as import substitution argument was formed, empirical tests on the universal validity of comparative advantage quickly developed. A Russian-born American economist, Wassily Leontief, first conducted an empirical test on the Heckscher–Ohlin (HO) model in 1953. His findings provided a paradoxical result and significantly challenged the neo-classical model. By definition, the United States was regarded as a capital-abundant country in the world at the time. Capital and labour were the two factors considered to differ between the United States and the rest of the world. According to the model, one could expect that the United States would export goods that were relatively capital-intensive and import labour-intensive goods. However, by way of analysing the 1947 data, Leontief unexpectedly found that the United States appeared to be a capital-importing and labour-exporting nation. The capital intensity in production for import substitution was higher than that for exports (Leontief 1953).

Leontief then undertook another study using the data of 1954 in response to criticism from Swerling (1954), who argued that 1947 was an atypical year for both the United States and the rest of the world as the world economy was still in recovery from the Second World War. Once again, Leontief's research showed the same result as in 1947 (Leontief 1956). Baldwin (1971) later carried out another study, which confirmed that the Leontief paradox continued to exist in the United States in 1962. A number of attempts were also made to apply Leontief's study to other countries. For example, Tatemoto and Ichimura (1959) found that Japan, a less developed labour-abundant country, exported capital-intensive goods to the United States in the 1950s. Bharadwaj (1962) revealed that India's exports to the United States were also capital-intensive while imports from the United States were labour-intensive in 1951. Faced with unexpected empirical 'evidence', a number of economists conducted further investigation to refute the paradox. A study carried out by Stern and Maskus (1981) revealed that the paradox vanished from US trade in 1972 if the measure of a capital:labour ratio based on industrial wages were used. Later, Leamer (1980) argued that Leontief's approach, which compares the capital:labour ratio in trade, was inappropriate. By using an alternative method to compare the capital:labour ratio in net exports with that in consumption and production, he declared the paradox to be non-existent.

The empirical tests of Ricardian–HO comparative advantage theory demonstrated a mixed set of results. On the one hand, these tests proved that the Leontief paradox suffers from difficulties with empirical validation in seeking to refute the HO model completely. On the other hand, the tests revealed that the two-factor assumption of the HO theory is highly restrictive and cannot statistically explain precisely how comparative advantage can strengthen a country's economy and determine its specialization in real-world circumstances. No empirical evidence that can be found is strong enough to support the universal validity of the HO theory. Although Leamer regarded the Leontief paradox as a mere result of conceptual misunderstanding, he stated:

> What about the facts? Don't they matter? Sorry, they do not matter very much. One important reason why the facts do not matter much is that the Heckscher–Ohlin model (and every other model in economics) is both factually correct and factually incorrect. We have not developed an intellectual culture that can deal with the complexity and ambiguity of real economic

phenomena. We teach ourselves a naive methodological parable of hypothesis formulation, empirical tests, rejections, and reformulations. Not even in whispers do we admit it, but we do know that our models are neither true nor false. They are useful sometimes, and not so useful other times.

(Leamer 1993: 436–437)

The assumptions of the theory are primarily made for the purpose of illustrative simplicity and academic clarity. They are not realistic in real-world circumstances. Ohlin was also aware that factor proportions were only one of the simplified explanations of trade. He stressed in his work that trade is also influenced by other factors such as location and transport costs, economies of scale, technology, innovation, skills, product differentiation, and quality and income distribution as well as a country's political, legal and administrative capability (Ohlin 1933). The following briefly outlines the main assumptions contained in HO's simplified, static two-country, two-commodity, two-factor production model.

1   Countries are assumed to use homogeneous technology in the production of the same goods. Firm-specific knowledge or technology cannot constitute an entry barrier. However, although technologies are identical, prices of factors can be different in each country. There is no reason why a country should use more capital than labour while another uses more labour and less capital in producing the same goods.
2   Goods differ in their factor intensities at all factor prices and are not reversible. That is, goods are either labour-intensive or capital-intensive. The theory assumes that there is no possibility for technological progress between countries over time and that learning-by-doing and other technological externalities do not exist.
3   There is perfect competition in all markets. No single company, consumer or trader possesses the power to influence product price or output; there are no barriers to entering the market; and perfect information is available concerning demand, supply, present and future prices of goods, and all production factors.
4   Factors are not mobile between countries but move freely and costlessly within each country from one sector to another.
5   The production function for each good is homogeneous. Production structure retains constant returns to scale. The output of a firm increases by the same amount that inputs (of capital and labour) increase. The theory implies that the firm size does not have effects on the long-run saving of production costs.
6   Both trading countries are similar in all respects apart from factor endowments (e.g. identical preferences and tastes towards products). The theory simply implies that countries are developed at the same level and there are no differences in technological and institutional capability, infrastructure, cultural influence, etc.
7   There are no pre-existing distortions such as trade barriers or transport costs. The real-world conditions are significantly different from the ideal

model. International trade and the division of labour between countries are often subject to trade restrictions and to transport and other costs incurred during transactions.

Imperfect competition and increasing return of scale: the size of firms and industries

Highly sceptical about the neo-classical economic rationale that neo-liberalists proposed for universal free trade and markets, the modern (new) trade and development theorists began to modify, expand and reject some of the conclusions of the conventional comparative advantage doctrine. However, as political and economic thinking was still dominated by neo-classical notions at the time, they could not reject the neo-classical theory altogether. Rather, they conceded that across-the-broad trade liberalization is generally beneficial, although not always so. The main focus of their research became identifying the circumstances under which free trade enables countries to truly gain and acts as an engine for economic growth. In doing so, they needed first to explain why empirical studies contradicted the neo-classical theory.[15]

The first issue concerns the role of firms in industrial development and international trade. As discussed earlier, neo-classical theories often assume that a perfect and well-functioning market prevails and can be established overnight. They also assume that there is a constant return of scale. Under pure competition, the market comprises a large number of firms, of which the average size tends to be small. No one firm has significant cost advantages over others and thus no one firm has any influence in market price setting. Firms are said to be 'price takers', accepting the prices determined by supply and demand of market forces. They are passive and have no role in influencing price and trade. New trade economists pointed out that the crucial limitation of the neo-classical doctrine is that actual world competition is imperfect. Only if this assumption is set aside could theorists consider the strategic behaviour among firms and their possibility of making positive profits above or beyond the constant return deriving from production factors and externalities. Their research demonstrates the failure of the neo-classical comparative advantage (CA) theory to explain trade and industrial growth based on differences in factor prices, technology and resource availability.

Emerging from the microeconomic notion of increasing returns, theorists began to develop new frameworks, incorporating new elements of economies of scale, the possibility of product differentiation and imperfect competition into the neoclassical theory to explain the phenomena we have been discussing. The introduction of new factors into the classical model enables theorists to adjust the comparative advantages and to show that specialization could take place in a particular industry.

Internal economies of scale

When internal (static) economies of scale (EOS) prevail, firms involved in trade can play active roles as average costs fall and their output increases. The determinant of whether countries have an advantage in trade becomes the size of their firms and not that of their industry. Large firms tend to have a cost advantage over small firms when increasing returns are prominent in production. The larger the firm size, the more its output and the lower its average cost. The existence of internal EOS in the domestic market eventually leads to a collapse of perfect competition where the market is dominated by one (monopoly) or several (oligopoly) firms. Pure monopoly in reality rarely exists as high profits attract many new entrants into the sector. The number of firms that can coexist (the equilibrium point) until monopoly profits are competed away is determined by the size of the market. The bigger the market, the larger the number of big firms that can be accommodated, each of which can achieve larger scale and lower average cost. Trade could increase market size by creating an international integrated market bigger than any individual country could offer and support more firms and varieties than an autarkic market could do.

Putting forward ideas different from the HO theories, Brander and Krugman demonstrated that the gains from trade arise from competitive effects in their mode of oligopoly, and that trade can take place in the absence of comparative advantage. Countries can gain mutual benefit even if they do not differ in their resources or technology. International division of labour can be explained if there is an increasing return of scale; unit cost falls as output increases. Trade can enable countries to specialize in a limited range of products that they can produce at larger scale, becoming more efficient in comparison to a situation in which countries produce everything for themselves. Trade will enlarge the market and therefore ensure that countries benefit from EOS, which in turn provides incentives for countries to exchange goods even in the absence of a comparative advantage (e.g. factor endowment or technologies). Furthermore, local monopolies lose their market power when opening up brings competition. Trade can be seen as 'reciprocal dumping' that forces firms to raise their output above the autarky level, thereby reducing the price below the one in the autarky situation (Brander and Krugman 1983). As a result, consumers in each country would be better off, expanding their consumption possibilities with a fall in average prices and enjoying greater varieties of goods than in an autarky.

This monopolistic competition combined with the concept of differentiation can also be used to shed light on the phenomena of inter-industry and intra-industry trade. Inter-industry trade refers to a situation in which countries trade different products from different industries. It could be explained by following the traditional thought of CA that a country's gains from trade are largely based on different factor endowments. Conversely, the intra-industry trade model does not conform with the CA doctrine. The Helpman–Krugman model shows that countries' gains from trade do not have to reflect comparative advantage, but stem from product differentiation. Even if countries have identical factor endowments and capital:labour ratios, they still trade differentiated products from the same industry in order to satisfy the variety of consumer tastes in different countries (Balassa 1967; Grubel and Lloyd 1975; Helpman and Krugman 1985).

Furthermore, as products are differentiated, individual firms could retain some market power as a result of their strategic actions towards one another in price setting. Differentiated products in early product life-cycle stages often enable firms to enjoy some degree of monopoly power (Vernon 1966). They could limit the number of participants and give a monopolistic character to the industry structure (Helpman and Krugman 1985; Krugman 1990). This is particularly true in today's international market, where multinational firms based in developed countries can achieve internal EOS in production, distribution, procurement and marketing, and also have the capability to differentiate products to gain monopoly power. In some industries, the number of participants is very small (e.g. the aircraft manufacturing industry).

Having seen the roles of EOS and imperfectly competitive markets, 'strategic' trade and development economists argued that protections and subsidiaries in some industries are necessary for firms to gain strategic advantage. This is because it might be too expensive and risky for latecomers to begin production in today's oligopolistic international markets, facing technological barriers such as intellectual property rights on patented technologies, operational barriers such as marketing and distribution channels, and the EOS that multinational corporations from the developed countries have already achieved (Lall 2004; Stiglitz and Charlton 2005).

External economies of scale

External EOS occur outside (external to) a firm but within (internal to) an industry. They are consistent with some neo-classical CA assumptions: the decrease of average firm production costs depends entirely on the size of the industry's output rather than on firms' own output. Firms could still be characterized by constant return to scale. Hence, large firms do not have significant advantages over small firms. The situation of absent internal EOS leads to a relatively perfect competitive market structure where average firm size tends to be small. A country is regarded as being capable of specializing in making a few products and still maintaining a competitive domestic market structure for these products. Strong external EOS tend to confirm existing patterns of inter-industry trade and offer more possibilities for efficiency gains than trade based on comparative advantages.

The theory of Marshallian external economies has long indicated an important implication for gains from trade at the national level (Marshall 1920). When one or more geographically concentrated 'industrial districts' (the origin of Michael Porter's cluster theory) can form a large national industry, or, in other words, when a country has a large production volume in a particular industry, that nation will be very likely to show more efficiency gains than countries with smaller industries. Producing goods in large quantities will enable the country to lower its production costs. Consequently, in the presence of trade, domestic firms could undercut their foreign rivals with an obvious cost advantage (Krugman 1991a). The country would then enter into a no-turning-back process of specializing in the industry.

Historical or accidental factors have played a major role in determining in which industry a country can specialize. First movers at the time of achieving early cost advantages can often accumulate production knowledge through their experiences (learning-by-doing) (Burenstam-Linder 1961; Vernon 1966). From a dynamic point of view, this knowledge is a self-reinforcing factor that continuously generates competitive advantages enabling countries to advance their positions in the world industry over time. Lacking technological capability and facing huge start-up costs, latecomer countries would find it hard to establish businesses in this sector even if they had potential comparative advantages (for example, if they were well endowed with the necessary production inputs). They will be 'locked in' to undesirable patterns of specialization and could not benefit by following the CA theory on universally free trade when developed countries have already built strong external economies and are able to skew the terms of trade in their favour.

The underlying issue of protection and subsidies for firms is that the composition of trade becomes more important than mere trade volume when differences in demand elasticity (the Prebisch–Singer theorem) and knowledge (including technology) are taken into account. High-tech industries are often cited as an example, as they are often said to yield direct positive externalities to a country's economy, generating higher productivity and higher-income jobs. The development of such industries requires heavier investment in R&D and involves greater risk than 'traditional' industries. Domestic firms from developing countries thus face difficulties in financing these costly R&D projects, bearing the risk of market failure, sharing the 'fruits' of risky and non-reimbursed ventures with domestic 'free riders', and competing with well-established and technologically advanced foreign multinational companies.

The implication of external EOS lends support to the strategic trade policy argument and the interventional role of the state in aiding some capital-intensive high-tech sectors. Protections such as tariffs, quotas, and subsidies for R&D can motivate and help firms to break the barriers in order to enter the high-productive sectors. These implications have also been seen as the theoretical foundation for the governments of developing countries to target certain industries, to form large industries and to implement clustering strategies in response to increasing trade liberalization. The new trade theories provide some intellectual justification for interventionist industrial policies, but they are too simple to be policy guidelines (Krugman 1987). For example, Krugman emphasizes that intra-industry trade occurs more often in sophisticated manufactured goods than in primary goods sectors between industrialized countries that have similar levels of economic development. Intra-trade will not result in serious income distribution effects or significant reallocation of resources. The behaviours of oligopolistic firms are less well known and unpredictable. The government support to domestic firms and technical externalities cannot be analysed, nor can it easily be measured.

Although new trade economists admitted that government interventions could be beneficial, they still shared the neo-classical view that the free market and free trade will lead to efficiency gains that are beneficial to all countries. Paul Krugman also argued that the new trade theories challenged only the traditional view that CAs enable all kind of trade and not the mutual benefits of free trade. The introduction of increasing return of scale and imperfect competition to trade models demonstrates gains from trade in addition to benefits resulting from complementary differences in resources and technology. Free trade creates larger markets for countries to achieve EOS and to reduce imperfect competition by allowing foreign firms to enter into domestic markets. Increasing competition can reduce rent-seeking pressure imposed by special interest groups and avoid trade wars and other political economic conflicts. In his words:

> International competition does not put countries out of business. There are strong equilibrating forces that normally ensure that any country remains able to sell a range of goods in world markets, and to balance its trade on average over the long run, even if its productivity, technology, and product quality are inferior to those of other nations. And even countries that are clearly inferior in productivity to their trading partners are normally made better, not worse, off by international trade.
>
> (Krugman 1991b: 811)

Full employment of resources

Going further from Krugman's argument, Stiglitz and Charlton (2005) rejected neo-classical propositions and pointed out that the modern trade arguments date back to Paul Samuelson (Samuelson 1938, 1939, 1962), for the benefits of trade liberalization are based on efficiency gains rather than growth. Trade liberalization may improve a country's average efficiency and contribute to higher growth in GDP for a brief period but might not be able to increase the long-term rate of growth (Thomas *et al.* 1990). This is because the neo-liberal policy prescription is substantially restricted in its assumptions and has difficulty in capturing the relevant issues that developing countries urgently need to solve.

As the neo-liberal theory claims, when a country engages in trade, its resources will be reallocated from protected low-productivity and high-cost sectors into efficient and low-cost export industries, according to international comparative cost advantages and prices (Bhagwati 1998). In other words, trade liberalization under the market mechanism can lead some domestic export sectors automatically to become competitive and efficient, while protected and less productive industries will be replaced by foreign imports. Countries exposed to the international market may lose jobs in inefficient sectors but will increase employment opportunities in their productive industries.

However, the nineteenth-century global trade pattern that orthodox economists used to develop comparative-cost theory was misleading in a historical setting, and inapplicable to developing countries. The extension of production in Western Europe from subsistence agriculture to plantations and mining for exports was mainly caused by a surplus of labour. Breakthroughs in transport, communication and new mining locations improved the total quantity of production resources, but not overall productivity. The expansion of exports was not the result of reallocation of resources and did not cause domestic subsistence output to contract. All production was still based on conventional fabrication techniques. The main cause of the expansion was 'vent-for-surplus' – the employment of hitherto unused or surplus resources (labour in the above example) into export production (Myint 1958).

Neo-liberals (Heckscher–Ohlinians) simply suppose that the resource redeployment process will work in a textbook manner such that factors are perfectly mobile among sectors without any time delay or cost, yet by no means so between different countries. They also assume that developing countries have already established a reasonably flexible economic and social welfare system that can help them to adjust the production methods required for combining new varieties of supply factors after opening up. Moreover, neo-liberals presuppose that a competitive market mechanism will always enable job creation for all who need a job. Free trade would not cause any overall job losses. However, in reality the unemployment rate remains high in developing countries. Surplus labour as a surplus factor emerges from the losing sectors after opening up, and cannot be automatically and fully absorbed by local exporters as they may not have developed the necessary supply capability to expand or to create new and productive jobs. It may also be difficult to reallocate surplus production factors to mining and agriculture, as in the nineteenth-century case, because of inelastic external demand for agricultural goods and the limited nature of land and mineral resources (Myint 1958; Shafaeddin 2005).

The neo-liberal theories also fail to explain how developing countries that specialize in primary commodities and face inelastic demand for their exports might be able to develop competitiveness in other productive sectors such as manufacturing industries, so as to absorb a surplus of labour. It is very unconvincing from an individual and social standpoint to suppose that new opportunities (new jobs and industries) created by trade liberalization will be superior to those lost behind protectionist walls. Questions concerning neo-liberal thought are also raised on the question of how to compensate those groups and sectors that lost ground during trade liberalization. The neo-liberal argument is that the problem of unequal income distribution is only a temporary phenomenon. It will be automatically and naturally resolved since the increasing income of those who gain from the change will eventually generate sufficient governmental revenues in the form of tax to compensate the losers. Such compensation unfortunately rarely happens in reality.

Tax on trade, accounting for one-quarter or more of total state income, was the main source of government revenue in developing countries in the late 1950s. It was probably the best revenue-raising device because the cost of collection is much lower than for income or commodity taxes (Chang and Grabel 2004; Corden 1974, 1997; Dasgupta and Stiglitz 1974). When trade liberalization sharply reduces tariffs and other trade taxes, the availability of this source for the compensation scheme becomes very questionable. Kuznet (1977) thus emphasizes the role of the state as the mediator of political conflicts between the winners and losers in the process of growth, structural changes and opening up. Interventionist industrial and trade policies designed to create manufacturing or other productive activities and to compensate losers are required until developing countries have developed the productive capability to absorb surplus labour.

Market versus government failure

Yet another central argument in free market and trade theories and interventionist industrial and trade policy is embedded in the general debate on market and governmental failure. Neo-liberals promote their laissez-faire policy on the basis of 'market fundamentalism', whereby the market and its competition mechanism work perfectly. There is no, or only a minimal, role, in any form or fashion, for state intervention in trade and industrialization (Haberler 1950; Krueger 1978). To the critics of neo-liberalism, markets will never work in a textbook manner: market failure may present in a situation where markets cannot function to allocate resources optimally as expected.[16] Developing countries will encounter market failure frequently and require state interventions, which are perhaps the best or the only way, to improve social welfare. State intervention is needed because the market on its own will be inadequate for developing countries to fulfil their catching up objectives, achieving self-sufficiency and industrialization, and gaining competitiveness for export expansion of manufactured goods. This view has dominated state-led industrial and trade policy in the post-war period. Import substitution industrialization (ISI) strategy, financial 'control' policy, overall planning and state ownership strategies have produced some successes while failing on other occasions.

In exploring the failure of the state-interventional trade and industrial policies we have discussed, neo-liberals often refer to the 'getting the price right' argument: the price will provide coordination for all and generate allocative efficiencies in free markets and trade. Getting the 'right' price in the home market, it is suggested, will deregulate products and factor markets; at the international level it acts to free up trade and deregulate exchange rates. As long as the 'right' price is set by market forces, developing countries would follow their comparative advantage so as to gain a suitable place in the international market through using their resource endowments efficiently. The 'right' price provides an incentive to export, and for production for domestic markets. This is because the market itself is competitive when trade is unrestricted, contracts are enforced, macroeconomy is relatively stable and property rights are protected.

This neo-liberal proposition, however, suffers from several shortcomings. First, there might be collective inefficiency as a result of individual rational decisions in response to price signals (Schotter 1985). In practice, markets in developing countries are often absent or underdeveloped, and price is not able to perform its function. Second, as was discussed earlier in the section on economies of scale, international markets are imperfect and consist of monopoly and oligopoly power. Internationally, prices could be influenced by various factors; multinational corporations from developed countries have advantages, for example economies of scale in production, procurement, R&D, marketing and transfer pricing. Unfettered trade makes the prices for the output of domestic firms, especially in small economies, irrelevant to total domestic output but significantly affected by world markets. Firms in developing countries will experience variable income and prefer to avoid risk by investing in lower-return but lower-risk and less variable activities. Their total output will decline (Stiglitz and Charlton 2005; Stiglitz and Newbery 1984).

Under such circumstances, the socially optimum allocation of resources would be hard to obtain in developing countries. The state's role in late industrialization needs to be to mediate market forces or coordinate the needs of various individuals by creating multiple prices through a managed financial system to make profitable investment opportunities available. This would enable developing nations to direct their investment towards long-term growth rather than short-term resource allocation efficiency. It is important to ensure that non-tradable intermediate goods sectors are not over-invested in order to support the creation of some high-end industries. Finally, East Asian countries such as Japan and Taiwan, which have got the relative price 'wrong', also empirically proved the success of violating market principles and the price mechanism for long-term growth. The process of their industrialization does not fit in with the neo-classical models that draw on neo-liberal observation of eighteenth-century Great Britain and the nineteenth-century United States (Amsden 1989; Wade 1990, 2004).

Neo-liberals continue to defend market failure. They argue that the market can cope efficiently with market imperfection if property rights are appropriately reassigned (Coase 1960). As secure property rights reduce transaction costs, property holders, who generally have higher expectation of profit from their 'stock of capital', will be encouraged to develop their property further, and thus efficiently allocate resources for economies to grow. The notion of market imperfections and market failure is somewhat ambiguous. It is indeed a 'normative judgement', and no theory can prove it analytically (Stigler 1975); even if market failure may exist, there is no guarantee that government intervention can do any better (Dahlman 1979; Wolf 1979). Neo-liberals maintain that 'governmental failure' may prevail as a result of political and administrative distortions, which have already become evident in the downfall of Keynesianism. The 'rent-seeking' activities of powerful interest groups will run counter to public interest and will eventually result in 'directly unproductive profit-seeking' (Bhagwati 1982; Krueger 1974). Hughes (1993) argues that Wade (1990) and Amsden (1989) paid insufficient attention to the costs of rent-seeking activities imposed by private sectors and governmental officials during the East Asian industrialization process. 'Neutral' policies were implemented as reformers were not politically strong enough to remove protections and to introduce competitive market policies. The liberal part of the policy definitely offset the cost of interventionist industrial and trade policies, and contributed significantly to the success of those countries.

Posner also argues that 'the economist recognizes that government can do some things better than the free market can do but he has no reason to believe that democratic processes will keep government from exceeding the limits of optimal intervention' (1987: 21). Some scholars went even further to argue that the risks associated with market failure always tend to be lower than those involved in government failure (Johnson 1975); the additional cost of rent-seeking activities would occur when the trade interventions exceed the welfare costs of the tariff equivalent. Hence, state intervention should be avoided even if the market fails (Bauer 1984).

Neo-liberals also believe that government failure in developing countries is most often attributed to the low capacity of the state, namely as a result of corruption and incompetence on the part of governmental officials. Johnson, Winters and Krueger all argued that the second-best interventionist trade and industrial policies should be avoided at all costs. The implementation of such policy calls for the very best economists to be able to interpret research results and put them into practice (Johnson 1970; Krueger 1997; Winters 2003). To prevent governmental failure, one should limit the state's roles by (1) reducing the size of public administration, (2) reducing the size of the public sector, (3) insulating the state from private pressures, (4) relying on rules rather than allowing discretionary decisions, and (5) delegating decisions subject to dynamic inconsistency to independent bodies that have no incentives to yield to political pressure (Przeworski 1998).

In criticizing these neo-liberal views, Chang (2003a) calls attention to the definition of 'free market' or 'intervention'. He argues that it is pointless to suggest removing all state intervention in order to let markets function. Markets could not be totally free and are subject to some state interventions that people have already accepted as basic social order and business rules. For example, the state regulates who can or should participate in the labour market: it bans child labour, immigrant labour, and slave labour, even though firms would find it more profitable to employ children, immigrants or slaves; banking laws regulate the range of assets and business that banks can run in order to prevent fraud; company and industrial licensing laws regulate firms' service or product lines for national security, customer safety, environment protection, etc. There is no distinctive free 'market' in reality but various institutional arrangements that have different consequences for 'markets'. The other criticism of neo-liberal views is related to perfect information and information externalities. Stiglitz (1994) argues that:

> the standard neo-classical model – the formal articulation of Adam Smith's invisible hand, the contention that market economies will ensure economic efficiency – provides little guidance for the choice of economic systems, since once information imperfections (and the fact that markets are incomplete) are brought into the analysis, as surely they must be, there is no presumption that markets are efficient.
>
> (Stiglitz 1994: 13)

When markets are absent, prices cannot reveal the profitability of resource allocations or opportunity costs that have not yet been discovered or priced (everything is given a price in neo-classical equilibrium theories). Such information imperfection leads to a lack of investment in new activities, owing to uncertainty over the returns.

Hausmann and Rodrik (2003) point out that such potential market failure in developing countries is a result of the absence of entrepreneurship in addition to information externalities. Diversification of production into new activities often calls for entrepreneurs to go through a process of 'discovering' the cost structure of their national economy. Firms need to overcome market information asymmetry on an experimental basis to discover new activities that are remunerative and can be produced at a low enough cost to be profitable in their home country. It is random attempts at self-discovery, rather than comparative advantage, that may thus cause countries with nearly identical resource and factor endowments to have different patterns of specialization.

Although this discovery process provides the first mover with some market-competitive advantage, the initial risks involved are not shared by its market followers; only information provided by the market and the social gains of the discovery are shared. The first mover bears the full cost of its discovery as well as failures in adapting existing foreign technologies or production processes to domestic conditions. The gain that it can keep for itself is very small because the new activities (newer to the country) discovered have already been established or widely mastered in foreign countries. The 'discovering' process is different from launching new products or adopting processes as an outcome of innovation and R&D, which can be protected under intellectual property right laws or through restrictions against the entry of market followers. In this case, the state's role in providing rents seems necessary for entrepreneurs to undertake a self-discovery venture, to back up those who fail during this process through government compensation and to coordinate long-term investment for firms (e.g. through trade protection, industrial licensing, the provision of venture capital, and the provision of subsidies for technology acquisitions and learning) (Wade 2004; Hausmann and Rodrik 2003).

Some failures do occur, and there are indeed many examples of failed industrial and trade-industrial experimental policies. For example, Westphal (1990) demonstrated several mistakes when governments of East Asian countries intervened in heavy industry and the chemical industry as well as other infant sectors, all at once during the 1970s. Nevertheless, these failures did not come as surprises. The government does not possess perfect information, and nor does the private sector. Investment coordination failures may arise when the profitability of new industries is dependent on the simultaneous development of the industrial value chain or when economies of scale and non-tradable inputs are required (e.g. cluster theory and the big push model) (Rodrik 1996). However, ignorance of, and firms' risk-averse reactions to, new activities as a result of outside information, undeniably suggest a need for government intervention even if the state possesses worse information than private firms.

The argument on the competence of governmental officials in managing trade and industrial policies to promote growth is, in fact, not sound in the case of the East Asian industrialization experiences. Some government interventions can unambiguously increase average social returns based on a wide range of state projects (Rodrik 2004). Finally, Amsden (2001) argues that low transaction costs and secure property rights are necessary but not sufficient conditions for a developing country to catch up. Even if market information is perfect, the essential capability of understanding and using 'knowledge' may incur higher production costs for latecomers than incumbents. This is often referred to as the dynamic learning argument.

Dynamic gains through learning

The focus of most free trade theories has been on static efficiency gains. The long-term effects of trade liberalization, however, are determined by its impact on the rate of economic growth. Some neo-liberal research has acknowledged the impact of endogenous changes on growth and presented many policy implications for developing countries. Moreover, in many developed countries, output and employment growth are increasing faster in high-technology and science-based sectors than the manufacturing averages, as are rates of productivity and real wages (OECD 2000, 2003b, 2004b). This phenomenon has convinced many policymakers in developing countries that technology nowadays plays an important role in improving economic performance.

Optimistic economists contend that technology will flow into developing countries and their economies will grow faster as long as they liberalize trade and investment markets, create 'market-friendly' environments and invest in both infrastructure and education. Opening up to the world will provide access to the latest knowledge and higher technologies (Atiyas *et al.* 1992; Coe and Helpman 1995), enlarge human capital (Romer 1990) and create spillover effects (Sala-i-Martin and Barro Robert 1995). The larger the markets, the greater the returns on investment in technological upgrading and R&D, the more production specialization for learning by doing, and the larger variety of inputs a country can have for both efficient production and a faster pace of innovation. For these reasons, market and trade liberalization is particularly favourable to developing nations in gaining the economic potential to catch up and improve overall technological capability (Bell and Pavitt 1993, 1995; Ernst *et al.* 1998; World Bank 1993).

Under the neo-liberal global regime, multinational enterprises that are attracted by the lower cost of production in the developing nations will transfer technologies and business operations to those nations (Arndt and Kierzkowski 2001). Increasing competition in both domestic and global markets could provide incentives for local firms to imitate new technologies and lead to innovation (Balassa 1988; Grossman and Helpman 1991). Again, there is no need for government intervention – or even if there is, it should be minimal and focus on the liberalization of trade and investment markets, providing a stable macroeconomic environment, improving the legal enforcement of market rules and private property protection, and investing in both infrastructure and education. This neo-liberal belief shows that technological change is an unpredictable evolutionary process in which only financially and technologically strong firms will survive. No one has superior knowledge or is absolutely certain about the future course of technological changes. State intervention is unnecessary because it will distort the natural selection mechanism of the market (Burton 1983).

Criticizing this neo-liberal view, Chang (1994b) argues that neo-classical theory is misleading in suggesting that static allocative efficiency will naturally bring about dynamic efficiency. The neo-classical static equilibrium theory indeed assumes that the costs or benefits of firms are independent of each other at any point in time – that economies are static. It takes little or no account of the learning process going on between them in what are actually dynamic economies with decreases in cost per unit with accumulated learning and experience over time), although some neo-liberal scholars have noticed exogenous changes. From his study of several East Asian economies, Wade emphasizes that the neo-classical theory is not relevant to developing countries and the research focus should be centred on dynamic rather than static analysis (Lall and Teubal 1998; Wade 2004). Learning, knowledge and human capital are all important for developing countries to upgrade their product structure.

However, technological progress is not a simple process whereby firms purchase foreign technologies and apply them to production. It calls for prolonged experience of production and a complex institutional arrangement to assist in the process of mastering foreign technologies. The requirements for mastering or creating technologies also vary with different new skills and knowledge. This apparently simple task is in fact difficult and costly and cannot be achieved by relying heavily on markets when both technological and institutional capabilities are weak or absent in developing countries (Lall and Teubal 1998; Nelson and Pack 1997; Teubal *et al.* 1996).

In terms of innovation, firms will not always move away from imitation even though liberalization brings the possibility of accessing a wide range of external knowledge (Arrow 1962; Dahlman *et al.* 1987; Dosi *et al.* 1988). Under open economic conditions, imitators have to compete directly with the original inventors in addition to complying with relevant patent legislation while international rules become stricter, and so face difficulties in generating positive profits and investing in R&D (Grossman and Helpman 1991). Schumpeterians would go further and argue that the market function of allocation efficiency would reduce the possibilities for monopoly profit, which works as the incentive for firms to innovate, and consequently hinders the process of 'creative destruction' for dynamic industrial changes and growth (R. R. Nelson 1987; Schumpeter 1942). Innovation capability in a firm is therefore determined by its historic knowledge accumulation and again depends on its host country's physical, human and institutional supporting network (Furman and Stern 1999). Rather than automatically enabling technology upgrading and progression from late to higher stages of the product life cycle, market liberalization is more likely to lead to specialization in primary goods and the more labour-intensive lower-tech industries in which developing countries normally hold comparative advantages.

Foreign direct investment (FDI) has been very important in developing economies for technological learning, but not as important as it is often thought to be if it is unregulated. Multinational enterprises (MNEs) often move on a regular basis from one developing country to another in search of politically and economically secure profit as a result of the current complex and unsteady global economic environment. They are more volatile and generally do not share the long-term development objectives of the host country (Wade 2004; Shafaeddin 2005). Moreover, for high-growth activities, the cost advantage in labour in developing countries becomes irrelevant or less attractive to foreign investors. Multinationals are not likely to bring state-of-the-art technologies because of the poor supporting environment, with deficiencies ranging from inadequate physical infrastructure to a lack of sufficient intellectual property protection. The experiences of the newly industrialized East Asian countries (NIEs) show that governmental interventions for the purpose of directing multinationals to export and highly dynamic growth sectors on a selective basis are necessary (Wade 2004).

Finally, regarding the market's natural selection mechanism, Chang responded that this concept in economics is very different from its origin in biology. Species' genes change in adaptation to changes of environment so as to enhance survival, whereas firms can change both themselves and the external environment in a dynamic sense. Hence, economic evolution is a result of people's intentions, based on their experience and their ability to change as a result of learning by observing each other's behaviours. This metaphor of a biological concept cannot be used to support the idea that markets will definitely pick up the right high-return industries and technologies for developing countries (Chang 1994a). Drawing upon the early work of Weber (1946), Myrdal (1968) and Gerschenkron (1962), statist scholars proposed the development state paradigm, which emphasizes the interventional and visionary roles of the government in industrial success (Breznitz 2005; Lall and Teubal 1998). These researchers argue that market mechanisms are not perfect, although they remain a powerful force; governmental intervention is required to improve market output and adopt technological changes, which neo-liberals could not reject (Amsden 1989; Evans 1995; Fransman 1986; R. R. Nelson 1987; Pack 1987; Lall and Kraemer-Mbula 2005; Chang and Grabel 2004).

Conclusion to Part I: China in the theoretical debates

The current fast-growing body of literature regarding the debates on the role of the government in international trade, as well as in the process of industrial development, has provided a rich theoretical framework for this book to investigate how China established itself in the high-tech ICT sector. In essence, the central theme of this book falls within the broadest debates on how we think of the role of government in economic development. The neo-classical policy propositions to developing countries are that the best developmental approach is to rely on market forces and the private sector. There is no role, or at most a minimal one, for the government to play in the whole process of industrialization. The historical experiences of today's developed countries are not useful guides for developing nations because truly competitive conditions did not exist in the past. With the development of the new international division of labour, the market competition mechanism is going to be well established and trade will soon work as promised (Bhagwati 2002).

However, no empirical evidence has been found to prove conclusively that openness is always good for economic growth.[17] Contrary to the neo-liberal view, statists see unrealistic assumptions underpinning neo-liberal policy propositions to developing countries. They advocate strategic state intervention to help domestic firms overcome learning costs and coordination problems, and to build up the necessary institutional capabilities such as in finance and R&D beyond simply providing a stable macroeconomy and ensuring intellectual property rights and the enforcement of market rules in developing countries (Chang 2003c; O'Riain 2004; Rodrik 2004). These intellectual arguments also reflect several major shifts in advice for policy reform to developing countries during the post-war period, namely import substitution in the 1950s, export promotion in the 1960s and 1970s, outward orientation in the 1980s and endogenous growth and economic geography in the 1990s.

These changes of policy prescriptions have raised the question of how in practice latecomers in transitional economies should achieve an optimal degree of governmental intervention or market liberalization. Policies are likely to shift between statist and neo-liberal approaches and eventually lead to economic disputes in the situation where domestic firms lobby the state to protect or provide subsidies, while developed nations under the WTO rules put political pressures on the latecomer governments to liberalize their markets, readjust their economic structures and minimize intervention. The theoretical arguments and political thought have significantly influenced China's policy designs, but what exactly China has done to promote a particular high-tech industry is still less well understood. For example, how does China promote the ICT industry in the face of formidable challenges from neo-liberal thought under the WTO and Information Technology Agreement (ITA) rules?

By exploring the nature of the development of the Chinese ICT industry, this book aims to provide a specific observation of a specific industry, while drawing general theoretical lessons. It investigates the changes of the governmental roles in China against the background of its rapid technological and industrial development, in the hope of extending our understanding of the literature that emphasizes the interventionist roles the state has played in the newly developed East Asian countries (Amsden 1989; Amsden and Chu 2003; Hobday 1995b; Hobday *et al.* 2001; Mathews and Cho 2000; O'Riain 2000, 2004; Sung 1997). In the next few chapters, this book explores the key issues surrounding China's intentions to emulate the industrial policies of its East Asian neighbours to promote the targeted industries in response to the increasing degree of economic liberalization.

It seeks to contribute novel ideas and new insights into the ongoing theoretical debate on the state's role in economic development, to show how China's industrial development strategies evolved over time in response to economic liberalization and to comply with the WTO agreement. Further investigation of these issues will enhance our understanding of China's complex economy, which will facilitate diplomatic efforts to resolve the inevitable future trade disputes and political conflicts as China becomes an increasingly bigger player on the world stage as a major economic superpower. It suggests that people should rethink China's industrial emergence with the new perspective on catching up in the WTO era, which may provide valuable insights for policy designers in other developing countries. On the basis of these theoretical settings, a framework for understanding China's high-tech industries from socialist reform to the WTO era can then be sketched out, followed by a conclusion in Part IV together with an indication of the theoretical and policy lessons gained from this research.

Part II

The development pathway of the ICT industry, 1949–1993

Creation, reform rationales and development context

> To revitalize our country's economy, information and communication technology is a very effective multiplier ... [The government] needs to vigorously promote the application of ICT and regards it as a vital strategy [for economic development]. [If we let] ICT exert its multiple effects on the economy, we can then improve national productivity, reduce wastage, and use our existing scale economies in iron, coal, electricity and oil resources to generate GDP several times more than now.
>
> (Jiang Zemin 1989; president of the PRC, 1993–2003, and minister for the electronics industry, 1983–1985, Jiang 1993)

> Informationisation is the main trend of global economic and social development today. It is also a crucial part of industrial upgrading, industrialization and modernisation in our country. [We] must set national economic and social informationisation as our developmental priority. [We need] to endeavour to realize a leap forward in the development of our country's information industry by following the development of the world information technology industry, facing market demand, and promoting system reform and innovation.
>
> (Zhu Rongji 2000; prime minister of the PRC, 1998–2003)

China today is undertaking a remarkable process of transformation from a planned to a market economy and a broadly defined social, economic and institutional revolution. Chapter 2 reviewed the theoretical debates underpinning trade and industrial strategies as well as historical experiences of advanced countries in economic development. The following chapters apply this debate to China's experience of industrialization since 1949. This part of the book explores the question of whether an interventionist policy was a significant factor in China's industrial performance. Of particular interest as proposed by this book is how China has managed to develop its ICT industry. The study concentrates on three crucial policy shifts in the development of China's ICT sector, which resulted from China's responses to the political and economic changes of the outside world: the military-driven developmental stage from the 1950s to the 1970s, the export-led stage in the 1980s, and the 'strategic' developmental stage since the 1990s, which aims to facilitate the industrial upgrading of the whole economy. At the micro level, the investigation focuses on the evolution of a specific set of unorthodox industrial policies that China designed, based on the East Asian model, in order to support the growth of a 'national team' of ICT enterprise groups during and after the early 1980s. These strategies have been carried forward after WTO accession. It was hoped that these strategies would enable China to catch up with leading developed countries as well as to compete directly with their global enterprises. The entire development process of China's ICT sector in fact provides an ideal historical case to show how international integration has impacted upon domestic institutional changes and to test the propositions of the East Asian state-led growth models in China's ICT sector.

3 Creation of the electronics industry

Military-driven development, 1949–1978

We cannot just follow the beaten track traversed by other countries in the development of technology and trail behind them at a snail's pace. We must break away from conventions and do our utmost to adopt advanced techniques in order to make China a powerful modern socialist country in not too long a historical period.

This is what we mean by a giant stride forward. Is this impossible of attainment? Is this boasting or bragging? Certainly not.

It can be done. It is neither boasting nor bragging. We need only review our history to understand this. In our country haven't we fundamentally overthrown imperialism, feudalism and capitalism, which were seemingly so strong? Starting as we did from 'poverty and blankness', haven't we scored considerable successes in all fields of socialist revolution and socialist construction after 15 years of endeavour? Haven't we too exploded an atom bomb? Haven't we wiped out the stigma of 'the sick man of the East' imposed on us by westerners? Why can't the proletariat of the East accomplish what the bourgeoisie of the West has been able to?

Early this century Dr. Sun Yat-Sen, the great Chinese revolutionary and our precursor, said that China would take a giant stride forward. His prediction will certainly come true in the coming decades. This is an inevitable trend no reactionary force can stop.

(Mao Zedong 13 December 1963 [Mau 1977a])

Phase 1, 1949–1952: initiation

In the latter part of the twentieth century, the ICT industry was often referred to as the electronics and telecommunications industries (see Appendix 1). Although China's ICT industry actually took off in the mid-1990s, its origin can be traced back to 1949 when the Chinese Communist Party (CCP) assumed power. The initial development of the industry in the early 1950s was somewhat complicated. It was a result not only of China's responses to international conflicts, but also of its social and economic reformation. During the early economic restoration period from 1949 to 1952, the government aimed to build a 'neo-democratic society with all social classes collaborating'.[1]

This decision was made largely based on Sun Yat-Sen's philosophy of state-led development. Sun's philosophy was a market socialist one and highly sceptical towards Chinese capitalists. It advocated a Russian-style economic policy for 'state control of capital, state ownership of profits and state operation of industries' because state control was necessary to build a 'practical and reliable system' and could prevent the private sector from controlling or manipulating the national economy (Wang 1966). The philosophy allowed for the existence of private capital in the national economy, but sought to keep it out of key industries that were large-scale and often had significant effects on the national economy (e.g. all major transportation, mining, banks and manufacturing industries). During communist China's early development, Mao supported Sun's philosophy as he was concerned that rapid socialization would make more 'enemies' for China. Wider configuration of classes in society could encourage industrial production and investment (Mao 1950). As for when to totally adopt socialist policies and abolish private property, both Mao and Politburo member Liu Shaoqi agreed to postpone the change for at least 10 to 15 years (Liu 1993). With the application of Sun's market socialist philosophy to the state working plan, China's economy began to recover. Although the communist government did not intend to build a closed economy, the country was diplomatically recognized by just 25 countries in 1952, and a Western embargo was in full force.

Against this background, the electronics industry as a dual-use sector for both civil and military purposes was closely linked with national defence and considered a fairly high priority. The history of the Chinese electronics industry began with the establishment of the Telecom Administration Bureau under the supervision of the Temporary Military Committee in July 1949. At this time, the industry consisted of a few private firms and damaged military plants taken over from the Nationalists (Kuomintang or Guomindang) after the civil war. The industry was capable of producing only a small volume of light bulbs, electronic tubes and simple radio devices (CASS 1987).[2] The total number of employees was around 4,500, with about 1,000 units of production equipment, while the total output of the industry was about RMB 4.95 million, accounting for 0.05 per cent of China's total industrial output (Yu 1989). With the intention of restoring the industry, the communist government established a new Bureau of the Telecommunications Industry as a part of the Ministry of Heavy Industry in May 1950, but under the direct administration of the Central Military Commission (MII 1999).

The outbreak of the Korean War in October 1950 soon drew China into a major international conflict. For the industry, the war generated a huge demand in a very short time for military electronic devices, especially field radios. In order to support the army logistically, the government assigned a large number of technicians to convert and fix the electronic devices available from the existing electronics plants. Nevertheless, China's production relied heavily upon the importation of radios, vacuum tubes and many components from the USSR and Hungary (Cao 1994). Driven by the war, the industry grew dramatically. By the end of 1952, the total industrial value had risen to RMB 65 million, 13 times bigger than in 1949. The number of central state-owned factories rose to nine, with 4,080 workers, while the number of local small factories increased to 748, with 5,633 employees (see Table 3.1). The industry also made some impressive progress in military field radios, telegraph transmitters and broadcast devices. Industrial production expanded from virtually none to 16,200 radios, 5,990,000 loudspeakers, 222 electronics application devices, 151 electronic measuring instruments, 745,000 electronic tubes and 2,800 components. For the first time, China was no longer entirely reliant on imports for electronic products and components (CASS 1986).

Phase 2, 1953–1957: the formation of new development principles

After the Korean War ceased in 1953, Mao became convinced that a radical instead of a gradual reform towards a socialist society was best for China. From the early 1950s, he began to propagate his view that China needed an independent and integrated industrial system as a solid base for its transformation from a backward agricultural country to an advanced industrialized state and from Sun's neo-democratic society to a socialist country (Li Z. 1997; Zhao 1995). Massive investment should be directed into 'goods-producing sectors' (heavy industries) so as to maximize industrial production and strengthen China's military capability as quickly as possible. Mao believed that the agricultural sector was the main source of finance for China's industrialization. The government should take control of the sector and establish a monopoly over grain distribution and supply. In doing so, the state could raise funding through profiting from the difference between the buying and selling price and generate a sizeable volume of agricultural goods for export (Mao 1955). Politburo member Chen Yun, who was in charge of economic development at that time, explained Mao's thoughts in a speech:

> If we continue to allow free purchase and supply [of grain], the central government would become a beggar. All the money will be used to import food. There would be nothing left to import machineries. We would never be able to achieve industrialization.
>
> (Chen 1953: 208–11)

Agricultural collectives were established in order to control the peasants and to facilitate the sharing of the means of production, such as land, tools and draught animals. While individual households disappeared in the countryside and the market mechanism was replaced by state control, the existence of privately owned businesses became meaningless. At the 1955 National Industry and Business Conference, Mao proposed that it was time to 'get ready and directly advance to communism'. The 'socialism conversion' programme was soon launched to nationalize private enterprises or transform them into state–private joint ventures. The programme significantly raised the level of state ownership, from 21.3 per cent to 92.9 per cent of the economy by 1957, enabling China to run a Stalinist-style centrally planned system (NDRC 1949–2005). Apart from Mao's influence,

Table 3.1 Thirty-five-year development of the electronics industry measured by numbers of factories, employees and industrial output

	Restoring period, 1949–1953	1st FYP, 1953–1957	2nd FYP, 1958–1963	Adjusting period, 1964–1965	3rd FYP, 1966–1970	4th FYP, 1971–1975	5th FYP, 1976–1980	6th FYP, 1981–1986
Total number of factories (unit, 1) #	**757**	**377**	**225**	**460**	**2,500**	**2,701**	**2,834**	**2,294**
Central government	9	40	57	141	176	176	178	178
Local government	748	337	168	369	2,359	2,525	2,656	2,114
Total number of employees (unit, 10,000)	**0.97**	**8.54**	**20.7**	**25.2**	**55.2**	**85.6**	**123.8**	**134**
Central government	0.41	6.90	13.5	14.9	19.3	29.1	33.7	37.8
Local government	0.56	1.64	7.2	10.3	35.9	56.5	90.1	96.2
Total value of industrial output (billion yuan)	**0.065**	**0.560**	**4.280**	**2.330**	**10.600**	**33.800**	**76.800**	**172.200**
Central government	0.044	0.41	2.46	1.34	4.32	8.10	15.00	34.60
Local government	0.021	0.15	1.82	1.00	6.28	25.70	61.80	137.80
Average growth rate (%)	**79.6**	**49.5**	**15.1**	**38.1**	**31.4**	**12.9**	**14.6**	**23.3**

Source: *Yearbook of the Electronics Industry*, 1986–1988.

Note: industrial value is at constant 1970 prices. FYP, Five-Year Plan. # the total number of electronics factories is different from the total number of centrally and locally owned enterprises due to duplicaed ownerships among these enterprises.

the radical reform was made possible by three crucial factors. First, Chinese officials had to rely on state control and ownership to channel available resources to the heavy and military industries. Second, Chinese economists and governors were convinced by their Russian advisers' forceful view that central planning was how the economy should be run. Third, the market approach to economic development was not politically acceptable because it was often associated with imperialism, colonialism and capitalism. Under the centrally planned system, trade was seen as a tool for exchanging goods that could not be produced in China (Wu 2003a; Zhao 1995).

Mao's radical strategy for realizing socialism was implemented throughout the first Soviet-style Five-Year Plan, which lasted from 1953 to 1957. It emphasized both the priority development of heavy industries and the nationalization of private assets. During this period, the electronics industry was mainly considered to be of military rather than economic importance. The principal objective for its growth was set to 'combine the civil and military development of the industry during both peace and wartime'. Accordingly, direct administration over the Telecommunications Bureau was transferred from the Ministry of Heavy Industry to the Ministry of the Second Machinery Industry (the Ministry of Defence) in April 1953. The bureau was then renamed as its 'tenth bureau'. Nevertheless, the government made very little effort to initiate the growth of the electronics industry. The amount of investment allocated to the sector accounted for only 1.1 per cent of the total of all industries. About 11 out of 156 national projects launched were related to the sector (MII 1999).

During the entire initiation period, assistance from the USSR and East Germany (the German Democratic Republic) played important roles. Nine of the 11 projects were aided by the USSR through direct technological support, consultation or human resource training. These projects led to the establishment of a number of enterprises in the fields of radar, components, electronic tubes, telephone switches and artillery-controlling devices. For example, a self-designed radio broadcast transmitter project under the technological guidance of Russian experts led to the creation of Huabei Broadcast Device United Enterprise. Through a project for manufacturing broadcasting devices, aided by East Germany, the Huabei Broadcast Device Enterprise was formed. Other self-initiated projects included the Beijing Electronics Tube Enterprise, the Beijing Broadcast Device Enterprise, the Beijing Cable Device Enterprise, the Baoji Changling Machinery Enterprise, the Chengdu Xinxing Instrument Enterprise, the Hongming Broadcast Device Enterprise, the Jinjiang Electronics Machinery Enterprise, the Guoying Dazhong Machinery Enterprise and the Huang River Machinery Enterprise. To ensure the supply of military electronics devices, the government relocated many industrial plants to inland regions, instead of making improvements to existing plants near the eastern coastal areas of Shanghai, Tianjing and Nanjing. The government also funded a number of new institutes to foster human resources. These included a polytechnic college, the Number Ten National Research Institute, six technical secondary schools and seven electronics technician schools (Lou 2003). By the end of the first Five-Year Plan (FYP),

China had completed 'socialist conversion' and achieved nationalization of the whole electronics sector. The industry continued to expand at a relatively high average annual growth rate of 49.5 per cent (Table 3.1). A range of radars, navigation instruments, broadcasting transmitters and a few consumer products constituted the greater part of the industry's production (see Table 3.2).

Phase 3, 1958–1965: the Great Leap Forward

Towards the end of the first FYP, Mao was no longer sure whether the Soviet socialist development model was suitable for China. He became very critical of Khrushchev's reversal of Stalinist policies as well as his international orientation, which he believed to be seeking 'peaceful coexistence' with Western capitalism. Mao believed that China should explore its own path to communism and no longer follow the current Soviet model. At a 1956 Politburo meeting, he made a report on 'discussion of ten relationships', which outlined his ideas of economic system reform (Mao 1977b).[3] The central idea behind his proposition was that China's massive supply of cheap labour could allow it to stop importing large amounts of heavy machinery. China could do better and achieve socialism much earlier and more quickly than the USSR. At the beginning of the second FYP (1958–1962), he announced a new economic programme, the 'Great Leap Forward', which aimed to increase both industrial and agricultural production rapidly in the hope of surpassing the United Kingdom within three years and the United States within ten years.[4] To achieve this goal, Mao called for a further round of collectivization to form larger 'giant people's cooperatives' (communes). However, his objective was never accomplished and its results were disastrous (Wang 2001). While China was in internal turmoil, its relationship with the USSR deteriorated after 1959. Clashing views emerged on the Great Leap Forward programme and several international events.[5] Since 1960, the Soviets had not only

Table 3.2 Production capacity of the Chinese electronics industry in units produced, 1952–1957

Products	1952	1957	Percentage increase
Radios	1,620,000	26,630,000	1,540
Loudspeakers	599	8,033	1,240
Gramophones	2,150[a]	26,041	1,100
Recorders	None	1,054	–
Electronic tubes	74,500	6,210,600	8,240
Electronic components	2,800	40,555,000	1,448,400
Measuring instruments	151[b]	2,399	1,490
Application devices	222	2,550	1,050

Sources: Guo and Cao (1994); MII (1999).

Notes: [a]Figure for 1954; [b]Figure for 1953.

begun to withdraw all personnel and financial assistance, but also restricted the flow of technological information to China.

The development of the Chinese electronics industry was greatly compromised and disrupted by these international political events and economic reform programmes. In 1956, the State Council launched the Scientific and Technological Long-Term Perspective Development Plan, which lasted from 1956 to 1967 (*Kexue Jishu Yuanjing Jihua*) and hoped to build up the top-priority sectors in several fields, such as computers, radio, high-frequency electronic instruments and controlling devices. The development of civilian products focused on television broadcasting and devices for the telecommunications industry. Unfortunately, the plan was interrupted, owing to rapid deterioration of China's international relations. The development priority during the second FYP was reassigned to sectors that could facilitate the military development of nuclear, missile and aviation technologies. The decentralization reform promoted in the wake of the 'Great Leap Forward' further compromised the implementation of the plan. Enterprises under the administration of the bureau of the Third Machinery Industry were put under the authorities at the provincial and city level, or reassigned to military authorities in different regions. These authorities were given the right to allocate resources, allocation, manage enterprises and carry out local economic planning. They did not have to follow the procedure set out in the FYP plan, but were asked to achieve a quantitative target. Under huge pressure from the central authorities to surpass the USSR, the United Kingdom and the United States in production quantity, they often found themselves with no alternative but to compete with one another in announcing seriously inflated results (Li Z. 1997).

The situation became even worse when Lin Biao was appointed to the Party's Central Military Committee. In 1959, he launched a campaign for 'more constructions, more experiments; less production, less sale'. In the FYP system, projects were normally scheduled and the amount of investment already decided for a five-year period. During Lin's term of office, not only did state investment rise 30 per cent more than planned, but also the number of national projects increased from 48 to over 50. This left the relatively small-scale electronics industry deprived of the capability to support numerous projects that were launched simultaneously in 1960. When the USSR withdrew all personnel and no longer provided key electronics materials and production equipment, the production of the industry came to a complete halt owing to lack of electronics materials, human resources and finance (MII 1999; Yu 1989). During the second FYP as a whole, the actual growth of the average industrial value slowed down to 15.1 per cent (Table 3.1).

The initial experience of the Great Leap Forward reform was discussed at the 1959 Lushan party conference. Mao admitted that failure in finding the equilibrium point for his agriculture–industry parallel development strategy was the main cause of the policy disaster. It was decided that the central government should balance the relationship between economic factors itself and centralize economic rights that had earlier been conferred on local authorities (Wang 2001). In 1963, the Ministry of the Fourth Machinery Industry (Ministry of Radio and

Electronics Industry) was established as an autonomous ministry, providing a central plan, coordinating production for the whole electronics industry, and directly supervising enterprises owned by either the central government or local authorities. While some administrative power was reassigned to the ministry, much daily decision making and operation remained in the hands of the military authorities. Five years after restoring centralized control, production started to show signs of recovery. The MII report shows that the total industrial value of the electronics sector rose from RMB 21,599 in 1960 (a 71 per cent decrease compared with 1957) to RMB 56,827 in 1965, an increase of 160 per cent (MII 1999). In the period between 1963 and 1966, the industry's average annual growth increased to 38.1 per cent, doubling its average growth rate during the second FYP (Table 3.1). Helped by the early technological assistance of the USSR, China had made progress in several fields. These included 408-style radar, black-and-white television sets, 10-frequency TV broadcasting stations (which first appeared in 1958), computers for nuclear weapons experiments (which first appeared in 1958 and 1959) and integrated circuits (which first appeared in 1965) (Lou 2003). By all accounts, the government put very little emphasis on the development of consumer electronics products.

Phase 4, 1966–1976: the 'Third Front' construction and the 'Great Proletarian Cultural Revolution'

The third (1966–1970) and fourth (1971–1975) FYPs were again disrupted by both China's internal political struggles and external military threats. In the wake of the Great Leap Forward's catastrophic failure, Liu Shaoqi replaced Mao to become chairman of the People's Republic of China in 1959. Along with the Party's General Secretary, Deng Xiaoping, Liu reintroduced many policies used prior to the Great Leap Forward in the hope of restoring living standards, developing agriculture and increasing production of consumer goods for economy recovery. Their economic thoughts emphasized that China's economic development had to rely on technology, education and the bourgeoisie. These ideas posed a serious challenge to Mao's communitarian vision. Mao exhorted the public that 'the bourgeoisie [in a socialist country] is right inside the Communist Party itself' and declared a revolution to 'bombard [its] headquarters'. In 1966, Mao launched the Great Proletarian Cultural Revolution against Liu and Deng's 'capitalist development approach'. During this period, the government's economic plan was suspended. The vast majority of Chinese people were drawn into class struggles and called upon to overthrow the established government (Naughton 1995; Wang 1998; Wu 2003a).

While the Cultural Revolution ravaged the country, China's international environment became even worse. The early Sino-Soviet confrontation turned into military conflict when the USSR increased troop deployments along the north-western and north-eastern Chinese borders. The confrontation soon exploded in a skirmish on the Manchurian border in 1969. On the other side, China was drawn into the Vietnam War after the Gulf of Tonkin Incident in 1964, threatened by US military power. In response to these international events, Mao called for an inland defence emergency plan, the so-called Third Front Construction Plan, to prepare for possible war against both the United States and the USSR. As nearly all of China's contacts with the rest of the world were cut off at the time, the plan focused on the creation of large-scale 'self-reliant' and 'self-sufficient' industrial base areas as strategic reserves in case the war spread further (Naughton 1988). Development priorities were given to four 'basic industries' in the defence (nuclear and electronics), metallurgical, energy machinery and railway sectors.

To make China more resilient to attack, Mao advocated relocating existing factories and research institutions from coastal urban regions to the remote regions in western and south-western China. The initial 'Third Front' geographical focus was on the south-western and north-central provinces of Sichuan, Guizhou, Yunnan, Shaanxi and Gansu, and later extended to the central and western provinces of Henan, Hubei, Hunan, Qinghai and Ningxia, as well as Guangdong and Guangxi (Cao 1994; Wang 1998). In the electronics industry, the previous development principle of 'combining civil and military production' was substantially altered to ensure military production. In 1970, 33 enterprises under the direct administration of the Fourth Bureau were transferred to central and local military authorities. Factories and research institutions were 'strategically redistributed' to the 'Third Front' regions in 'widely dispersed and covert locations' near mountains, in caves or underground. The programme was immensely costly for the weak Chinese economy at the time. Table 3.1 shows that from 1966 to 1970 (the third FYP) the total number of electronics factories increased from 460 to 2,500, while centrally owned enterprises increased fractionally in number from 141 to 176 (95 were built under the Third Front plan) and the locally owned factories dramatically expanded in number from 369 to 2,359 (533 sizable enterprises were established under the 'mini'-Third Front plan).[6] Moreover, over 120 large-scale national projects were initiated. Investment and the limited supply of production inputs and technicians were spread over an excessive number of projects, some of which had been repeatedly launched by local authorities throughout the third and fourth FYPs. The average percentage of technicians/researchers in the factories decreased from 15.07 per cent in 1966 to 9.12 per cent in 1976. Eventually, the Chinese leaders found these programmes very difficult to accomplish (CASS 1987; Lou 2003; MII 1999; Wei 2001). Although overall industrial output doubled and that of the third FYP and reached RMB 10.6 billion, most of it came from military production. The average industrial growth rate declined from 38.1 per cent during the second FYP restoration period to 31.4 per cent in the third and 12.9 per cent in the fourth FYP (Table 3.1).

4 The 'opening up' reform and state-led growth, 1978–1993

> We must actively develop relations, including economic and cultural exchanges, with other countries. . . . After several years of effort, we have secured international conditions that are far better than before; they enable us to make use of capital from foreign countries and of their advanced technology and experience in business management. These conditions did not exist during Comrade Mao Zedong's lifetime.
>
> (Deng 1978b: 127)

> The key to the Four Modernizations is the modernization of science and technology. Without modern science and technology, it is impossible to build modern agriculture, modern industry or modern national defence. Without the rapid development of science and technology, there can be no rapid development of the economy. . . . Only if we make our country a modern, powerful socialist state can we more effectively consolidate the socialist system and cope with foreign aggression and subversion; only then can we be reasonably certain of gradually creating the material conditions for the advance to our great goal of communism.
>
> (Deng 1978c)

By the early 1970s, Mao realized that China was too strategically isolated and vulnerable to confront both the USSR and the United States at the same time. As the Soviets were geographically close and were thus potentially the greater threat to China, Mao decided to seek an accommodation with the United States in order to confront the USSR. The worst period of confrontation between China and the United States finally ended when the US President Nixon visited China in 1972. After Mao's passing and the purge of the 'Gang of Four' in 1976, the chaos of the Cultural Revolution subsided and China began to look outward again. The dynamism of the East Asian newly industrialized economies undoubtedly caused the Chinese leaders to have second thoughts about the capitalist development approach, and to reflect on China's disappointing growth record since the first FYP and the problems associated with duplicating the Soviet model. At this development stage (1978–1993), the Chinese leaders' attention was primarily on overall industrial restructuring. There were no specific promotion strategies launched for the electronics industry. This chapter therefore discusses the major impacts of broadly applied restructuring policies that are relevant to the development of the electronics industry.

The reorientation of development strategies

During the late 1970s, the leadership became very critical of the 'leftist' policy, which was believed to be a cause of serious damage to the Chinese economy. Although still quite conservative, the government revived those readjustment policies that Deng and Liu had attempted to introduce in the 1962–1965 period. At the pivotal 1978 Third Plenum of the Eleventh Central Communist Party Congress, Deng came to power and declared a shift in the Party's focus from political class struggle to economic construction. He proposed a more radical economic reform with the aim of raising the real living standards of the Chinese people. The reform placed greater emphasis on the development of consumer goods than on that of heavy industries (Wang 2001). Deng believed that the fundamental task in achieving socialism is to develop 'productive forces' faster and to a greater extent than can be done under the capitalist system. Socialism does not mean poverty, but the elimination of poverty.

The ultimate objectives of China's industrial strategy are therefore to enable the country to regain its pre-eminent historical status, to ensure its economic and technological autonomy, to attain the frontier of international competitiveness and to advance its national defence in the twenty-first century. A more practical and quantitative goal of 'Four Modernizations' was set: achieving US$1,000 GNP per capita and a *xiaokang* (middle-class) society by the end of the twentieth century.[1] No policy should be rejected merely because it was not associated with Maoism or was similar to Western capitalist policies: 'It doesn't matter whether the cat is black or white, as long as it catches mice'. Deng's pragmatic interpretation of Chinese socialism stresses the need to 'seek truth from facts' and emphasizes that the success or otherwise of economic policies is determined by their empirical effectiveness rather than by ideology (Deng 1978a).

The reform was characterized by informal, experimental and decentralized gradualist approaches. Typically, the central authorities laid down overall policy objectives, which were often visionary blueprints, instead of announcing any national programme. Local officials then implemented these ideas on an experimental basis in a particular economic sector or across all local industries. There was neither clear strategy beforehand nor a planned sequence of reform measures. In Deng's dictum, this reform style was described as 'crossing the river by feeling for the stones underfoot', a metaphor meaning that further reform is dependent on the result of previous reform. If pilot policies proved successful, the central leaders would then adopt them in a piecemeal way throughout particular provinces. In some cases, if the policy outcomes contradicted socialist thought, the central authorities would either keep these experiments informal or formalize them as 'Chinese characteristics' within socialist thought (Steinfeld 2004).

Apart from the need to improve social well-being, the reorientation policy launched at the 1978 plenum was in reponse to three main emergent issues that occurred simultaneously in China: an energy crisis that resulted from the collapse of petroleum, the short supply of agricultural goods, and rising unemployment. By shifting away from energy-intensive heavy industries to labour-intensive consumer industries, China could release resources for the agricultural sector, improve the consumption of consumer goods and provide job opportunities, and thus raise living standards without increases in energy supply (Naughton 1995; Wu 2003a; Zhao 1995). Although it occurred slightly later, in the mid-1980s, the perception by most Chinese leaders of an easing of international political tensions facilitated China's industrial restructuring process.[2]

The electronics industry, however, is not just a simple civilian sector, but a vital strategic sector for national defence. Throughout the early development stages, the Chinese government had given priority to the technology-intensive and defence-related electronics sectors. After the 1978 plenum, China's industrial strategy shifted towards building up indigenous capabilities in mastering and developing cutting-edge information technology while focusing on the development of consumer, labour-intensive light electronics sectors. The following sections demonstrate four crucial changes that took place simultaneously in the electronics industry against the background of China's overall reorientation reform.

'*Junzhuanmin*': conversion of military production towards civilian-oriented manufacturing

After the Cultural Revolution, the structure of the electronics industry became very fragmented. The industry was subject to the administration of various local, ministerial and military authorities. In order to promote the expansion of consumer production more effectively, the central government first introduced more organizational coherence to the industry. The Broadcasting and TV Industry Bureau (BTIB) and the Computer Industry Bureau (CIB) were formed in 1978 and 1979, respectively, under the direct supervision of the State Council. The temporary administration of the industry was delegated to the Fourth Ministry of Machine Building.

However, China's electronics industry was initially built as a part of the military-technology production system. Large majorities of electronics enterprises and R&D institutions were established for military production during the 1960s 'third front' construction. They were under the command of the National Defence Department and decentralized to various military and local authorities. Table 4.1 shows the dominant position of military electronics production in the industry from the mid-1960s to the early 1970s. As the reform had no clear framework or strategy, military officials assumed that their enterprises did not fall within the scope of the reorientation reform. When investment was shifted away from heavy and military industries to light and agricultural sectors in the coastal areas, they often found it difficult to maintain production, owing to a sharp decline in the

Table 4.1 Industrial output of the electronics industry from 1966 to 1975

	1966	*1967*	*1968*	*1969*	*1970*	*1971*	*1972*	*1973*	*1974*	*1975*
Centrally enterprises (total)	0.97	0.65	0.49	0.94	1.27	1.64	1.42	1.44	1.60	–
Civilian production	0.23	0.16	0.11	0.22	0.39	0.47	0.27	0.31	0.32	2.09
Military production	0.74	0.49	0.38	0.72	0.88	1.17	1.15	1.13	1.28	–
Locally owned enterprises*	0.66	0.66	0.83	1.39	2.75	4.03	4.44	4.41	5.06	7.97
Total industrial output	1.63	1.32	1.32	2.32	4.03	5.67	5.84	5.84	6.65	10.06

Source: *Yearbook of the Electronics Industry*, 1987.

Note: At 1970 prices, in billions of RMB. *total mixed civilian and military production

number of orders for military electronics devices. Even when defence production was significantly slashed and excess capacity showed everywhere, military officials were afraid to make political mistakes by converting military equipment to civilian production purposes (CASS 1987; Yu 1990).

In 1982, on a military commission meeting, Deng expressed more explicitly the government's intention to use the technologies and equipment of the defence industries and the excessive capacity of military enterprises for consumer production once they had fulfilled their targets for military production. He explained that producing and selling civilian goods to gain profits was the best way to finance the advancement of the defence industries. This is known as the '16-words guideline' for reforming the national defence industry (Deng 1984a). Following Deng's guideline, Chinese planners improvised a specific and gradualist strategy to reform the electronics industry. In 1980, the Fourth Ministry was hived off from direct supervision of the central military committee to be under the supervision of the Machinery Industrial Committee of the State Council. Subsequently, in 1982, the BTIB, CIB and the Fourth Ministry were merged to form the Ministry of the Electronics Industry (MEI) in order to reflect the industry's new goal of increasing production towards civilian goods and goods for export. This institutional restructuring made production of civilian goods ideologically and politically acceptable for military enterprises and allowed the newly created ministry to revive the development principle of 'combining civil and military production' that had been implemented previously.

In 1983, Jiang Zemin, who would later become president of the PRC, was appointed minister of the electronics industry to preside over Deng's 'military conversion' blueprint. A 'production transformation' investment programme was launched during this reform stage. Investment was granted primarily to existing factories to convert from military production to the production of civilian and

Table 4.2 Percentage of civilian production in
military electronics enterprises,
1971–1992

1971–1975	15% ~ 22%[a]
1979	20%
1981	50%
1985	62%
1992	97%

Sources: Cao (1994: 79); Yu (1989: 10).

Note: [a] An estimated figure shown in the *Yearbook of
the Electronics Industry*, 1987.

export goods. From 1979 to 1984, 54.2 per cent of the total investment in the electronics industry was allocated for this purpose. The percentage of civilian production over total industrial output rose from 22 per cent in 1980 to 43 per cent in 1984. In the military enterprises, the percentage of civilian production rose significantly from 20 per cent in 1979 to 62 per cent in 1985 and 97 per cent in 1992 (see Table 4.2). Military enterprises also took significant shares in the total output of China's main consumer goods during this period. For example, their production accounted for 30 per cent of the total output of TVs, 50 per cent of the production fridges for export and 30 per cent of the top 100 enterprises by size, based on sales (Cao 1994; Lu 2002; Yu 1989).

The reorientation programme, however, primarily emphasized the conversion of existing factories for civilian purposes rather than relocation. Most electronics enterprises, about 70 per cent of the total, were established under the Third Front plan in inland regions. The cost disadvantage of inland industrialization soon became the key issue that impeded the development of the industry. Not only were the majority of factories too distant from industrial centres to take advantages of 'cluster economies', but also their remote locations made it difficult to reduce transportation costs.[3] In 1985, Deng announced a reduction in army personnel.[4] Accordingly, a rectification plan was formed to restructure and relocate Third Front enterprises from mountain valley areas to coastal 'open' cities. Many small factories were permanently abandoned. Although the specified number of factories covered by the plan was unknown, Chinese officials reported that 64 electronics enterprises (possibly centrally owned) were designated for relocation in 1985, and 53 of them had completed this relocation process by 1990 (Lu 2002). By the end of the sixth FYP in 1985, the electronics industry consisted of 178 centrally owned and 2,114 locally owned enterprises. Chinese records previously showed that there were 95 centrally owned and 533 locally owned enterprises established under the Third Front plan (Development Phase 4). These figures indicated that there were 42 centrally owned and many locally owned factories still in operation at their original sites. These factories were certainly sizeable and presented a significant obstacle to further industrial restructuring.

Enterprise autonomy, industrial restructuring and non-state-owned enterprises

While industrial geographic relocation policy was in place, Chinese leaders needed simultaneously to turn electronics factories into financially independent and managerially autonomous business enterprises. The main critique of Mao's economic policies often challenged centralized state management of enterprises.[5] In 1978, the Party secretary of Sichuan, Zhao Ziyang, who later became premier of the PRC (1983–1987) and general secretary of the CCP (1987–1989), conducted the first 'enterprise autonomy' (*qiye zizhu*) experiment in Sichuan, using six selected state-owned factories. The experiment proved to be very popular as it allowed profit retention for individual enterprises. Officials believed that the outcome of the experiment showed an increasing level of efficiency and productivity in enterprises (Qian 1999). Shortly afterwards, in the early 1980s, the experiment was adopted at the national level.

The MEI accordingly initiated its own 'rectification' plan, which covered 1,606 electronics SOEs, accounting for about 56 per cent of the total number of enterprises in the industry. Among them, 160 were centrally owned and 50 were locally owned large enterprises. The plan conferred upon enterprises the right to sell output in excess of planned quotas, and specified the percentage of profits they could retain; military and profitable enterprises could retain 25 per cent, unprofitable Third Front enterprises could retain 80 per cent, and small and non-centrally-owned enterprises could retain 40 per cent. Enterprises were allowed to vary their prices by 20 per cent to 25 per cent from the plan price, except for the price of televisions and military goods; they could also purchase inputs across geographical and administrative regions. Factory mangers were given the right to form their own management teams, subject to approval by governing authorities, and to hire and promote employees (CASS 1986; Lou 2003).

The main problem of the enterprise autonomy reform is that it took place when most market institutions were yet to be established. In the early 1980s, the development reorientation policy rapidly shifted central state investment away from heavy and military industries to consumption industries and agriculture. As a result, household incomes started rising and soon grew by more than the production of consumption goods.[6] Pulled by massive demand and pushed by the short supply of energy, inflationary pressure began to build up. The government responded by cutting down further the central investment budget for large construction projects, production plants and heavy industries. The macroeconomic imbalance was fuelled, however, by the financial decentralization reform, which was launched in 1986 in the hope of adjusting industrial spending through bank lending, and provided more incentives and financial resources for enterprises. However, in order to reduce short-run employment problems, local governments often assisted enterprises to obtain bank loans for scale expansion. Enterprise investment had increased at almost the same speed as central state investment had declined (Wang 1998). Additionally, owing to the lack of a coherent reform approach there was unnecessary duplication of facilities and technology importation in almost all industries.[7] These costly, irrational projects and unregulated enterprise borrowing had put huge pressures on monetary expansion. Before long, Chinese leaders had to face similar financial chaos to that they had experienced during Mao's decentralized 'Great Leap'.

A group of economists and reformers (price reformers) argued that the policy failure was primarily caused by the partial market reform. As the plan apparatus remained unchanged and functioning, price was not associated with demand and supply, and could not provide signals for autonomous enterprises to adjust their production and investment plans (Wu 1985; Xue 1982). Conservative leaders claimed that the policy failure was the disastrous consequence of rapid market reform. Informal relaxation of price controls would always lead to macroeconomic imbalances and cause open inflation. As a consequence, aggregate demand for material and agricultural imports would increase. Foreign currency reserves used for the upgrading of technology would be drained away. The government therefore had to place great emphasis on perfecting the existing planned economic system. If necessary, the market could be used as a supplementary channel to the plan for allocating some goods (Wu J. L. 1985, 2003a).

When the efforts to gradually introduce market elements into the centrally planned economy were overwhelmed by command sectors, Deng decided to start his reform from the countryside.[8] In the early 1980s, collective communes were rapidly replaced with a 'contract responsibility' system by which peasants were allowed to retain surplus agricultural yields for 'market' sale after fulfilling specific production targets and financial obligations. This led to a doubling of agricultural output, subsequently generating more domestic consumption and releasing labour into non-agricultural pursuits (Qian and Xu 1993). Township and village collectively owned enterprises soon appeared and grew significantly in many industries (Chen *et al.* 1994). The successful experiences in the countryside created further political support for economic reforms in the city. Beginning in 1984, a renewed market reform strategy was launched to limit the scope of planning while expanding markets to allow autonomous enterprises to respond.

The reform approach was associated with the thought of 'enterprise reformers'. They argued that price adjustments were simply unfeasible, given the current dysfunctional and bureaucratic command economic environment. Moreover, the state would have to pay huge costs to enterprises if floating prices were allowed. For example, enterprises might not be able to continue operation if there were a sudden increase in prices of production inputs. Enterprise reformers believed that the reform should take on two tiers. This is also known as the 'dual track' approach. In the first tier, the state needed to focus on providing adequate incentives for enterprises to maximize production and improve efficiency, such as by converting state-owned enterprises (SOEs) into joint-stock companies or expanding contract responsibility, while gradually reforming the command economy system. In the second tier, the government should create a 'market' with an uncontrolled price system to stimulate enterprises to trade their above-plan production output (Li Y. 1986).

In practice, the enterprise reform approach mirrored much of the rural reform. It turned the 'contract responsibility system' into a 'profit responsibility system' to manage enterprises' profit retention schemes. Rewards or penalties were determined according to enterprises' profit compared with previous years.[9] Urban enterprises could procure inputs and retain a share of their profit by producing and selling goods outside the plan at market prices. Goods produced under the plan were allocated at state-controlled prices. This 'dual price' or 'dual track' reform created markets for SOEs to exchange goods and non-state-owned enterprises to grow out of the plan (Naughton 1995).

China's decentralization reform was accompanied by a political relaxation of non-state ownership restrictions. The driving force was the pressing problem of urban unemployment since 1978. Millions of young people born after 1962 were about to reach working age. In addition, a large number of 'educated urban youth' (*zhishi qingnian*) who had been sent to the countryside during the Cultural Revolution started returning home. Official statistics showed that the urban unemployment rate reached 5.3 per cent by the end of 1978 (Wang 1998).[10] The growth of the 'non-state' economy in labour-intensive sectors was thought to be able to absorb the excess labour force and facilitate industrial restructuring. In the early 1980s, household-based individual businesses (*getihu*) were permitted, with a maximum of eight employees.[11] When a market channel was established to coexist with the command plan system, the government then introduced legislation to confer legal status upon the private sector at the 1988 Seventh People's Congress (Lin *et al.* 1996).[12]

Following the urban enterprise reform blueprint, the MEI embarked on its own policy experiments derived from the 1980 'rectification' plan. In July 1985, an experimental reform package was introduced to 59 selected enterprises in targeted cities such as Sichuan and Beijing. These included a 'profit responsibility system' and 'factory managers' rights and responsibility mechanisms'. To help local leaders to implement the reform plan, ten experienced ministerial officials were assigned to 18 provinces in November and December. Besides decentralization of enterprise management rights, the MEI engaged in the task of transferring administration of ministry-owned enterprises to municipal and provincial governments for the purpose of fitting them into the local development plan and adapting to local economic conditions. In 1986, the administration of 172 out of 198 ministry-owned enterprises was transferred (excluding factories selected for policy experiments such as for foreign technology transfer and foreign joint ventures) (Yu 1990).[13]

By withdrawing itself from the daily administration of enterprises, the MEI aimed to concentrate on the role of offering administrative guidance and coordination between different governing authorities and enterprises at the industry level. In fact, the withdrawal allowed the MEI to centralize and strengthen its power over the planned production and the management of industrial restructuring across regional and administrative authorities. This can be vividly seen in the state-led industrial reorganization programme, the 'Horizontal Industrial Integration and Economic Cooperation' of 1980. The policy was originally implemented to reverse Lin Biao's strategy in building a local 'wholly integrated production system'. It aimed to close down unprofitable and unnecessarily duplicated Third Front factories as well as to encourage a greater specialization of enterprises across the country. The first cooperative-run enterprise, the Nanjing Wuxiandian Company (Nanjing Broadcast and Radio, later renamed the Panda Company) was created on 12 July 1980 by merging 38 electronics enterprises in Nanjing across different administrative authorities. This policy experiment was later adopted at the national level as the big business strategy (see Chapter 5).

Like most industries in the 1980s, the electronics industry was dominated by SOEs. It was clear under the 'dual track' system that the MEI promotion policy mainly targeted SOEs and military-owned factories (covered by the plan). Non-state-owned electronics enterprises were only allowed to grow as spillovers of the urban economy. 'Commune and brigade enterprises' (also called 'township and village enterprises', TVEs) outside the plan were generally organized to take over some labour- and process-intensive production on a small scale. Even so, the expansion of the non-state electronics sectors was striking and unanticipated. Although statistical archives were not available, a Chinese electronics official recorded that the number of TVEs rose from virtually none in 1980 to 2,426 in 1986 with production output that accounted for about 17 per cent of the total industry (Yu 1989). Another figure provided by the Ministry of Agriculture shows that the number of TVEs (with less than RMB 5 million of assets) increased to 12,002 in the field of electronic machinery and devices, and 4,536 in electronic telecommunications equipment, with a share of 37 per cent and 13.9 per cent respectively of the total electronics output (Cao 1994). Industrial output of the non-wholly state-owned electronics sector in total increased from RMB 2.48 billion (22.6 per cent of the total industry) in 1982, to 26.1 billion (24.2 per cent) in 1992 (see Table 4.3). Rapid and vigorous growth of non-state sectors was comprehensible to all as a response to early economic liberalization. It was also crucial evidence that supported Chinese reformers in enlarging the market's horizon in larger selected areas.

Management of trade and investment

Trade and investment liberalization was another important aspect of China's economic reform. With the perceived international political relaxation in the late 1970s, Deng decided to move China's development strategy away from Mao's policy of extreme self-reliance to one of economic cooperation. At a hearing in September 1978, Deng said:

> We must actively develop relations, including economic and cultural exchanges, with other countries ... After several years of effort, we have secured international conditions that are far better than before; they enable us to make use of capital from foreign countries and of their advanced technology and experience in business management. These conditions did not exist during Comrade Mao Zedong's lifetime.
>
> (Deng 1978b: 127)

Table 4.3 Industrial output of the electronics industry by type of ownership, 1982–1992

	Total industrial output (billion RMB)	SOEs	Collective	Joint SOE/ collective	Foreign-invested enterprises	Joint-stock companies
1982	11.0	76.1%	19.3%	3.3%	1.3%	
1983	14.3	76.2%	19.7%	3.8%	1.6%	
1984	21.4	74.3%	17.0%	4.9%	3.8%	
1985	28.6	73.8%	17.8%	5.0%	3.0%	
1986	30.0	74.0%	16.6%	4.6%	4.6%	
1987	42.7	72.4%	16.0%	4.6%	6.8%	
1988	59.9	68.8%	16.1%	4.4%	6.2%	
1989	63.4	69.4%	15.6%	4.6%	6.9%	
1990	69.8	67.2%	14.0%	4.4%	9.7%	
1991	88.6	63.4%	14.4%	9.3%	12.9%	
1992	108.0	55.7%	14.2%	3.3%	15.6%	6.7%

Source: *Yearbook of the Electronics Industry*, various years 1986–1993.

Notes: The values of industrial output before 1990 were at constant 1980 prices and later years were at constant 1990 prices. 'Joint-stock companies' (*gufenzhi qiye*) refers to firms with a mixture of state, collective or non-state ownerships and with an 'autonomous' Western style of management (Wang 2001). The companies are formed by the individual contributions of a group of shareholders and with registered capital of at least RMB 10 million (the Company Law of the PRC 1993). SOE, state-owned enterprise.

Deng believed that external political and economic circumstances had changed and China could take this opportunity to step up the 'Four Modernizations' through 'opening up'. As of 1980, China had established trade relations with more than 170 nations and signed trade agreements with more than 80 of these countries. Between 1984 and 1995, official statistics show that the annual growth rate of nominal exports was about 22 per cent and the volume of foreign trade increased from 7 per cent in 1978 to 25 per cent of China's national income in 1987 (China Statistical Yearbook 1986–2006).

China's early opening to the outside world was indeed cautious and gradual. Import restrictions were widely applied across sectors. The basic viewpoint of the state was to mirror the domestic 'dual track' reform by establishing two different economies, namely one dominated by the centrally planned system, in inland China, and the other market and export oriented, in coastal regions, used to attract foreign capital and reduce political obstacles in promoting an export-led growth strategy. In doing so, the state could not only avoid domestic political and ideological opposition, but also keep disturbance to the centrally planned system to a minimum (Chow 2002; Segal 2002). The initial liberalization strategy had selected a few coastal areas, with minimal connections to the domestic economy, to attract foreign investment for export-oriented activities. These areas were so-called Special Economic Zones (SEZs), where foreign-invested firms were granted special tax concessions, private property and expanded land-use rights, independent trade activities, and market-oriented institutional supports. Guangdong and Fujian were the first two provinces chosen for policy experiments in July 1979, in consideration of their geographical proximity to Hong Kong, Macau and Taiwan. In 1980, the three SEZs of Shenzhen (near Hong Kong), Zhuhai (near Macao) and Shantou (a major home of overseas Chinese and a treaty port established for Western trade in the late nineteenth century) were set up in Guangdong, and one SEZ was established in Xiamen (opposite Taiwan). After a short time, rapid economic growth and higher incomes were observed in Guangdong and Fujian Provinces. Geographical proximity as well as common language and culture have been seen as the most compelling factors for cross-border capital movement from Hong Kong to Guangdong, and Taiwan to Fujian (Chow 2002; Wang 1996).

The success of the four SEZs led to a great step forward towards further economic liberalization in China. In 1984, Deng expressed his intention to 'get some areas rich first' by extending the SEZ experiment to more cities (Deng 1984b). In the same year, the central government announced an additional 14 coastal open port cities (*duiwai kaifang gangkou chengshi*). These included Dalian, Qinhuangdao, Tianjin, Yantai, Qingdao, Lianyungang on the Bohai Rim, Nantong, Shanghai, Ningbo in the Yangtze Delta, Wenzhou, Fuzhou, Guangzhou, Zhanjiang and Beihai. Three coastal areas (the Pearl River Delta, the Southern Fujian Delta and the Yangtze River Delta) were subsequently created in 1985 as 'Open Economic Zones' endowed with preferential policies similar to those for SEZs. In 1988, Hainan Island was given provincial status and designated as the fifth SEZ. In 1990, the central government established the Shanghai Pudong Development Zone. All these coastal regions were conferred with favourable terms and special legal status for market- and export-oriented activities. Domestic enterprises in these zones, regardless of ownership, were encouraged to obtain export licences and given special treatment. For example, they could retain a share of their foreign exchange earnings, and receive special loans or tax reduction.

All in all, Wu Jinglian, a senior Chinese economist, argued that China's export strategy during this period was a combination of export-led growth and import substitution. This was partly because the central government still kept a high average tariff rate of 43.5 per cent between 1985 and 1992. Many of the export production activities were indeed for the domestic market and misrepresented in trade data (Wu 2003a). It was also partly because local officials were confused by the export-oriented and import substitution policies. When the economy became overheated by expansionary policy, which happened around 1981, 1985 and 1989, the Chinese central government imposed tight control on the imports of heavy industries and repeatedly launched import substitution policies. Decentralized local authorities were given import rights to meet local demand for capital goods, but import restrictions were still widely applied across sectors.

In the electronics industry, the MEI followed the central 'blueprint' and formulated its own trade promotion plan with a view to reflecting the features of the 'dual' system. In the plan-dominated system, military electronics enterprises were restructured towards civilian and export activities according to the national development reorientation policy. Although domestic non-state sectors were permitted, they were treated as 'outside-the-plan' activities and had received very little policy attention in the early stage of economic liberalization. Their growth was tremendous but they remained small in size. The creation of SEZs certainly provided an opportunity and environment for non-state-owned enterprises and former Third Front SOEs reallocated in the costal areas to expand. The MEI policies for enterprises in 'outside-the-plan' areas came in two forms: the first was the state arrangement for joint venture business. In 1981, the first MEI-organized joint venture (JV), Fujian Hitachi Limited Company, was set up by the government of Fujian and the Japanese firm Hitachi in 1981. Nevertheless, foreign JVs or cooperative JVs were still kept to a small scale by 1992. The earliest available data from the MEI show that in 1983 the output value of JV production represented 1.6 per cent of the total industry. This figure increased to 4.6 per cent in 1987, 9.7 per cent in 1990 and 15.6 per cent in 1992 (see Table 4.3).

As the impact of FDI was fairly small before the 1990s, foreign trade production was primarily carried out by domestic-owned electronics enterprises with a focus on '*sanlai yibu*' (three come-ins and one compensation): processing, assembling, original equipment manufacturing (OEM) and compensation trade activities. The enterprise relocation and promotion policy had led to higher industrial output in coastal SEZ areas. Table 4.4 shows a shift of the top ten electronics manufacturing regions from inland to coastal areas and their increasing shares of the total electronics output in 1982, 1986 and 1992. The total export of the electronics industry increased more than ten times, from RMB 0.648 billion in 1986 to RMB 6.876 billion in 1992. The share of product exports (original design manufacturing, ODM, and own brand manufacturing, OBM) was slightly larger than that of processing activities (see Table 4.5). The dramatic decline of processing

Table 4.4 The top ten electronics manufacturing regions in selected years by industrial output (in billions of yuan)

1982		1986		1992	
Shanghai	2.2	Jiangsu	5.1	Guangdong	23.9
Jiangsu	1.7	Shanghai	4.5	Jiangsu	18.2
Beijing	1.0	Guangdong	3.4	Shanghai	8.4
Liaoning	0.6	Beijing	1.9	Beijing	6.9
Tianjing	0.6	Tianjing	1.6	Sichuan	6.3
Guangdong	0.5	Liaoning	1.6	Fujian	6.3
Sichuan	0.5	Zhejiang	1.4	Zhejiang	5.2
Hubei	0.4	Sichuan	1.3	Shanxi (western)	4.9
Shandong	0.3	Shanxi (western)	1.1	Tianjing	4.3
Zhejiang	0.3	Fujian	1.0	Shandong	4.2

Source: *Yearbook of the Electronics Industry*, various years.

Table 4.5 Export activities of the electronics industry, 1986–1992 (in billions of US dollars)

	1986	1987	1988	1989	1990	1991	1992
Product exports	0.32	0.66	1.02	1.58	2.64	3.16	4.09
Processing activities	0.33	0.55	0.89	1.07	1.15	1.30	2.78
Total	0.65	1.21	1.92	2.65	3.79	4.46	6.87

Source: *Yearbook of the Electronics Industry*, 1986–1993

Note: Data concerning other *'sanlai yibu'* activities are not available for this period.

Table 4.6 Planned foreign reserves (in billions of dollars) for imports, substitution made possible by domestic production and actual state spending in the electronics industry, 1986–1992

	1986	1987	1988	1989	1990	1991	1992
Planned foreign reserves for imports	1.16	1.72	1.23	1.84	1.67	1.94	2.34
Substitution by domestic production	0.02	0.24	0.28	0.16	0.19	0.19	0.06
Actual spending	1.14	1.48	0.95	1.68	1.49	1.76	2.29

Source: *Yearbook of the Electronics Industry*, 1986–1993.

activities in 1989 and 1990 reflected the impact of the Tiananmen Square political event on FDI. These time series figures confirm Wu's argument that the industry was highly protected and state intervention was intensive. While export incentives were intensified, import spending through the use of foreign exchange was tightly regulated by the central government. Table 4.6 shows that the state had attempted to maintain the spending of foreign reserves below US$2 billion each year, while encouraging import substitution.

In 1987, the State Council issued the first list of 'permissible' electronic import items. The list covered 22 broadly defined industrial categories, about 129 different kinds of electronics products. These included transport control devices, television broadcasting equipment, navigation telecommunications equipment, metrological and hydrographic equipment, industrial automatic control systems, electronic measuring equipment and industrial specializt devices. The approval mechanism for the import list was perhaps the most important instrument used by Chinese planners to protect newly established industries (see Chapter 7). Nevertheless, the Chinese leaders found the mixed result that labour-intensive manufacturing activities flourished, but the industry did not diversify very much. Table 4.7 shows that by 1992 China's primary electronics exports mainly consisted of a large number of video and audio consumer products and components, such as televisions, radios, walkie-talkies, television tubes and computer-related

Table 4.7 The main electronics export products in 1992

	Number of exports	Value of exports (10,000 US dollars)
Colour TVs	335.9	45,584.0
Black-and-white TVs	430.2	16,319.6
Car stereos	1,063.3	13,711.6
Radios	9,655.2	26,726.2
Sound recorders	8,067.8	10,7151.9
Recorder components		10,788.0
Telephones	4,539.6	34,438.8
Walkie-talkies	293.7	2,969.1
Colour TV tubes	119.6	7,447.2
B&W TV tubes	53.4	595.3
Computer and related		49,996.0

Source: *Yearbook of the Electronics Industry* 1993.

accessories. The Chinese leaders felt that China needed to upgrade its industrial technology structures as soon as possible in order to further expand exports and increase gains from international trade. The dilemma they faced, however, was whether the country should rely on its existing military technological bases to meet a substantial portion of its need for export production, or obtain foreign technologies through FDI in a similar way to its East Asian neighbours.

Technology leverage

One of the main goals of Deng's reform was to master modern technologies in order for China to regain its pre-eminent historical status as a technologically advanced and powerful state:

> The key to the Four Modernizations is the modernization of science and technology. Without modern science and technology, it is impossible to build modern agriculture, modern industry or modern national defence. Without the rapid development of science and technology, there can be no rapid development of the economy … Only if we make our country a modern, powerful socialist state can we more effectively consolidate the socialist system and cope with foreign aggression and subversion; only then can we be reasonably certain of gradually creating the material conditions for the advance to our great goal of communism.
>
> (Deng 1978c)

Technology imports

Through the re-establishment of diplomatic relations with the United States in 1979, China gained an opportunity to access foreign technology and aid from the West.

The initial technology importation projects were carefully chosen to focus on possible US participation in developing mineral resources, particularly petroleum, and so to prevent an energy crisis. With the implementation of the reorientation policy, the Chinese leaders became increasingly aware of the need to raise China's technological capabilities in order to make its light and export-oriented industries more competitive. In the electronics industry, the initial attempt to import technology was made in 1972 when a group of Chinese officials from the Fourth Machinery Bureau were sent to Japan to assess the possibility of importing television tube production equipment. In 1974, the government began to approach the US RCA Company and several firms from Japan and France. However, no final agreement was reached, because of political interruption by the 'Gang of Four'.[14] Then, in April 1980, the government established the Electronics Technology Trading Company to manage technology trade, and the industry was able to import foreign technologies on a substantial scale. From 1979 to 1983, China imported three colour television assembly lines; tube manufacturing technologies and equipment; 18 television component and material production lines; two electronics transformer, two frequency tuner and eight speaker production lines; one printed circuit, five black-and-white television-tube production lines; six radio and recorder assembly lines; and three recorder and one magnetoresistive head production lines (MII 1999).

The decentralized reform approach towards technology importation suffered greatly from a lack of policy coherence, however. At a 1983 meeting of China's Machinery and Electronics Industrial Technological Progress, the central government announced a decision to permit local authorities to approve technological projects and sign technology agreements with foreign parties. This decentralization reform enabled lower-ranking officials, government administrative departments and a wide range of public institutions besides the central government and the MEI to import technologies and launch research projects according to their own financial budgets. However, what often happened in practice was that when local officials perceived a growing demand for certain electronic products, they simply instructed and financed subordinate enterprises to purchase foreign technologies to enter the targeted sectors. Constrained by their abilities to analyse and understand the technologies, local leaders and enterprises' managers often rushed into the import of technology-embodying machinery and production lines in order to get into what they believed were the 'newest' and 'potential' sectors. Not only were similar and less advanced technologies repeatedly imported, but also enterprises could hardly gain any technological spillover effects from this kind of technology importation. Duplicated construction became very common in the industry. From 1983 to 1985, more than 1,800 foreign technology transfer agreements, worth about US$1.4 billion, were signed in only a few areas: colour TV production lines (113 projects); television tubes, components and materials; telecommunications, navigation and optical fibre production devices; and semiconductor and electronic circuit production equipment (CASS 1987; Yearbook of the Electronics Industry 1986–2001). By 1988, 27 out of 32 provinces had their own television production lines, but manufacturing capabilities varied greatly. For example, whereas Guangdong's annual TV production reached 2,030,000 units in

1988, provinces such as Henan and Shanxi (in western China) could produce only 50,000 units or less per year (Wei 2001).

Moreover, uncoordinated technology importation often led to shortages of supply in manufacturing input. For example, the importation of 113 colour TV production lines enabled the industry to have a manufacturing capacity of 15 million televisions per annum in 1985. At the same time, it also generated a huge demand for television components at the lower end of the production chain. However, the television component sectors did not receive much policy attention. Their output could only meet the production needs for about 1 million televisions. In order to keep enterprises in production, Chinese officials had to use extra foreign exchange, beyond what their budget allowed, to import the rest of their production supplies. As many MEI officials proudly announced the great achievements of their TV technology importation projects, most TV production lines were left totally idle. In the mid-1980s, the central government had to reclaim its coordinating and goal-setting roles in order to improve policy coherence across all sectors. In doing so, the State Economic and Trade Commission was created, with the aim of managing technology importation projects, which now focused on the technological upgrading activities of existing SOEs instead of new plant construction (Cai 1998). The involvement and influence of the central government and ministries had since become strong in the selection of foreign technology importation projects, especially in the 'high-tech' field, although local officials could still approve individual FDI-related cases under their own financial budget.

Foreign investors at this development stage were restricted to export activities only. The central government regulated domestic market access in a monopolistic way, by which it hoped to gain bargaining power over foreign technology suppliers. Access to domestic markets was granted to foreign investors only after the nature of the technology in the proposed production has been assessed on a case-by-case basis by the relevant authorities. This strategy was used to press foreign investors to increase investment and to bring more technologies into China's targeted sectors. For example, both AT&T and Nortel were completely kept out of the domestic telecommunications equipment market by the Ministry of Posts and Telecommunications because of their lack of commitment to technology transfer and production investment. Conversely, in exchange for substantial technology commitments from ITT Belgium (subsequently acquired by Alcatel), the government not only guaranteed domestic market access for its Shanghai Bell joint venture, but also allowed it to sell imported telecommunications switches in China (Naughton and Segal 2003).

Building up indigenous technological capabilities

The most pressing policy dilemma that Chinese leaders faced was not the decentralization or centralization of technology importation. It was whether China's industrial modernization should rely on foreign technology associated with the expansion of FDI, or rather develop indigenous technological capacities. Given their concerns over national security and the political desire to regain

China's historical status, Chinese leaders had undoubtedly chosen to focus on building up indigenous technological capabilities. China's technology policies therefore contained elements that were able to interact with or stimulate the development of defence-related military technologies. Its policy objectives were fundamentally different from those of East Asian latecomers. The Chinese government was more willing to bear greater economic costs in order to retain a high level of technological and economic independence.

During the 1950s and 1960s, the government had paid significant attention to science and technology and achieved remarkable success in the fields of strategic defence technologies such as computers, semiconductors, jet propulsion and nuclear technologies. In the electronics industry, China had developed more than 200 military-owned factories and 50 military research institutes, with about 60,000 technicians and 400,000 skilled workers, during the same period (Wei 2001). When Sino-American relations developed from economic, scientific and security cooperation in the late 1970s, Chinese scientists had opportunities to access technological information from the West (Feigenbaum 1999). From both academic and governmental contacts, Chinese scientists and leaders realized that China's technological infrastructure had in fact fallen very far behind international standards.[15]

Chinese officials believed that the key issue lay within the fragmented structure of China's science and technology (S&T) system. This consisted of a large number of institutions funded and governed by several different authorities: the Chinese Academy of Sciences, the Ministry of Education, the Ministry of Defence and many industrial and local authorities. Under the old Soviet-style S&T system, the central and local governments often completely controlled and determined industrial research objectives and treated funding allocation to R&D institutes as a matter of annual appropriations. All governing authorities were decentralized and given a budget to operate their own autonomous research activities, with great emphasis on increasing quantitative output rather than on the quality, technological intensity, or economic and social desirability of the products (Kong and Xing 2005). Additionally, R&D institutions were widely scattered in inner China follwing the Third Front construction plan. R&D activities were not only carried out in remote and diffuse locations, but also without any coordination and connectivity between them. The Chinese Academy of Sciences, which was created initially as a supervising agency, could hardly function across a large number of authorities to coordinate research projects. By the early 1980s, R&D and technological learning activities were still carried out on the basis of 'whoever needs, develops' (MII 1999).

To ensure that the S&T system could facilitate industrial growth, the Chinese central government issued 'the Decision of the Central Committee of the CCP regarding the S&T System Reform' in March 1985. This measure aimed to reform the R&D system in notable ways: the fund allocation reform was launched and led to a drastic cut in regular state budgets for research institutes in the hope of forcing them to shift towards market-oriented R&D activities and seek revenues through the spinning off of commercial ventures; research institutes under the control of ministerial and local governments were either merged into existing enterprises or converted into autonomous enterprises. The measure also had several other objectives, such as creating technology markets; promoting cooperation between research institutes, universities and enterprises; encouraging contacts with foreign countries for training and research; and freeing scientists from political interference (Li M. 1997).

An even greater S&T reform took place after four renowned Chinese military scientists wrote directly to Deng Xiaoping in March 1986 to urge China's need to 'trace the development of world strategic high technology and develop its own high technologies' (Liu 2004: section 4).[16] Their appeal was a response to two major policy shifts: the changing focus of domestic policy from military to civilian production for economic growth, and the external changes in international military development and economic competition in the early 1980s, for example Japan's technology promotion initiatives, Europe's EUREKA technology programme and the US Strategic Defense Initiative ('Star Wars'). The scientists argued that the development of high technologies would change the stakes of global competition. From a long-term development perspective, China must gain a position on the 'battleground of world high-tech sectors' to ensure its national security and economic competitiveness. The process of technological advance calls for a significant reconfiguration and development of domestic institutions and infrastructure. The Mao-era technology policy, based on a simple spin-off concept and self-reliant techno-nationalist ideology, could hardly bring China to the technological frontier. China's S&T system was far too underdeveloped to keep pace with the rapid technological development led by industrialized countries. Chinese leaders noticed that military technological advances had come about in the West primarily through civilian processes of innovation. The best technology development model perhaps was to combine the US 'dual use' approach with the Japanese techno-nationalist model.

Two days after receiving the military scientists' appeal, Deng noted that 'Action regarding this matter [the high-tech development strategy] must be taken immediately and it can not be held over' (cited in Liu 2004: p. 4). In the following six months, more than 200 scientists were gathered to draft a large-scale national plan, the High-Tech Research Development Programme (863).[17] The programme aimed

> to pool together China's best technological resources over 15 years in order to keep up with the development of the world high tech industries, to narrow the technological gap between China and other countries, and to make breakthroughs in areas in which China has advantages so as to form a basis for China's economic development and national security in the late 20th and early 21st centuries.

> (863 plan, www.863.org.cn)

Unlike the previous national projects, the 863 plan sought 'dual use' development in leading-edge technology fields. It attempted to combine technological development of both defence and civilian industries and to link them to the long-term national goals in improving military strength and economic competitiveness. The initially targeted areas included automation, biotechnology, energy, information technology (the electronics industry), lasers, new materials and space technology. The 863 plan introduced the concept of peer review and a mixed method of project selection, which primarily focused on allocation of funds to applied science. Chinese planners were quite aware that in the Western model private enterprises were the main driving force throughout the whole innovation and technological upgrading process. Given the extent of China's backwardness, the lack of required resources and the political difficulty of promoting private firms, the Chinese leaders decided to continue relying on state-owned enterprises, and state planning and target-setting methods to promote the growth of high-tech industries such as the electronics sector (Li M. 1997).

Apart from the 863 plan, the government launched a series of national projects according to long-, medium- and short-term plans derived from the visionary central blueprint. Figure 4.1 shows that China's technology projects were classified into four main functions: basic R&D, technology commercialization, dissemination and the absorption of foreign technology. For example, the 'Torch Plan' was launched in 1988 to commercialize high technologies in SOEs. It was the first plan that aimed to guide rather than command enterprises, research institutes and relevant authorities to carry out R&D activities. The direct allocation of funds from central government for the Torch Plan was limited. The majority of funding was either raised by enterprises themselves or came from various channels such as Chinese high-tech bank loans and local governments. The governing authorities of the Torch High Tech Centre were under the direct control of the Ministry of Science and Technology and played a role more like a fund-raiser and broker for SOEs.

Chinese planners also incorporated their policy experiments with geographic concentration into the Torch Plan. The High-Technology Development Zones (HDTZs), which replicated the Silicon Valley model, were established to support high-tech enterprises. It was hoped that enterprises could benefit from being geographically close to universities and research institutions, as well as from crucial supporting infrastructure, preferential tax and finance policies, human resource policy and special international trading rights available in the zones. In July 1985, the first HDTZ was created in Shenzhen. Subsequently in 1988, the Zhongguancun (Beijing's Silicon Valley) was created by the central government in the Haidian District of Beijing. HDTZs soon extended to Shanghai, Guangzhou and many other coastal opening areas. By 1993, the total number of HDTZs approved by the Chinese State Council had reached 52.

Have these technology strategies and plans been successful in upgrading China's technological structure when they were carried out in the next two decades? Chapter 7 examines their impact on the electronics industry when more specific plans were drawn up by the Chinese leaders.

Conclusion to Part II

Several points stand out from this review of China's policy towards the ICT/electronics industry prior to 1993.

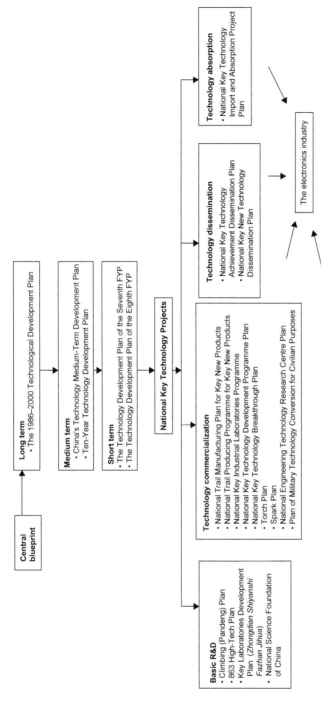

Figure 4.1 Structure of China's technology development plan.

Source: Adapted from Gao (1993: 24).

First, China's ICT policy has been characterized by intensive direct government involvement. Ever since the industry began, its development objective has been closely linked with defence. Government investment was driven to meet military needs in response to the changes in the international political environment. Additionally, the establishment of a centrally planned Stalinist system in the late 1950s determined the predominance of state ownership in the industry and the planning role of the government for all aspects of its development. The close state–industry 'collaboration' was fundamentally different from the Western sense of 'crony capitalism'. It is perhaps best understood as a command–obedience relationship within the context of the centrally planned system and the control of military authorities in the early period of development.

Second, the growth of the industry in the early post-Mao reform period was associated with the reorientation policy, which shifted the development priority from heavy and military industries towards consumer production. Visionary and less coordinated decentralization reform had proved problematic as most market institutions were absent and the governing capacity to carry out the reform at local level was fairly weak. The central government had to undertake significant administrative restructuring and to use investment reallocation as the key policy instrument to direct industrial restructuring in both geographical and production terms. Given the existing centrally planned economic system, the policy instrument was pretty much a command entirely based on Chinese leaders' perceptions and preferences. It threatened to penalize any enterprise that did not follow the plan. Incentives were introduced much later, when more liberal economic policies were adopted to limit the scope of planning and to allow the coexistence of market forces.

This leads to the third point: the creation of a 'dual' system by the state. For the electronics industry, the 'dual' system meant more than just 'dual track' (market and plan); it also meant a 'dual' ownership system, a 'dual' geographical economic system and a 'dual use' system. The 'dual track' system was established as a compromise between reformist and conservative bureaucratic parties. While the compulsory plan for production and resource allocation remained in operation, a market channel was created to ensure that above-plan transactions could take place and be guided by relatively market-oriented prices. The state-run enterprises were given sufficient autonomy to expand production beyond the plan in order to receive incentives, which came proportionally from the sales of the volume in excess of the plan. A 'dual' ownership system permitted the non-state-owned enterprises to grow within the state ownership-dominated planned system and to support the market system outside the plan, as well as to introduce competition. Although growth of the non-state sector was tremendous, the government attempted to keep its size small at this stage. It mostly involved the labour-intensive part of the electronics industry, absorbing the excess workforce. The 'dual' geographical economic system, such as the special economic zones, high-tech zones and export processing zones, worked in two ways: on the one hand, it kept disturbance to the centrally planned system to a minimum and avoided domestic political opposition. On the other hand, it could provide preferential policies to enterprises within the designated areas and attract

Table 4.8 Percentage of industrial output of the electronics industry in the total manufacturing and agricultural sectors and all industries, 1988–1992

	Total value of industrial output (billions RMB)	Percentage of the manufacturing and agricultural sectors	Percentage of total industries
1988	59.92	2.4	4.1
1989	63.42	3.2	4.9
1990	67.27	3.2	4.9
1991	88.63	2.4	3.1
1992	18.98	1.3	2.2

Source: *Yearbook of the Electronics Industry*, various years.

foreign investment for export-oriented activities. As with the non-state sectors, the impact of foreign investment remained small at this stage. In fact, from 1986 to 1992 the total production and export of the electronics industry represented on average only 3 per cent and 5 per cent respectively of China's total. Because of its small economic contribution to the national economy and industrial size in this period, the 'dual use' system was encouraged primarily to focus on military modernization though civilian applications.

Fourth, Chinese officials did not, perhaps, have a very ambitious vision and did not realize the full economic potential of the electronics industry, given its small size at this stage. Table 4.8 shows that the industry accounted for an average of only 2.5 per cent of China's total output for the manufacturing and agricultural sectors and an average of 3.8 per cent of all industries in the period 1988–1992. Frequent and repeated splitting up and merging of administrative authorities showed that the development focus of the industry was still unclear at this stage. In April 1988, the MEI was merged with National Committee of Machinery Industry to form the Ministry of Machine Building and Electronics, with the goal of integrating electronics devices and technologies into machinery production. Policy emphasis was placed on the development of machinery rather than the electronics sector.

In 1993, the central government decided to restore the MEI by splitting up the ministry. Policy launched by the MEI indeed reflected only the large general trend of recentralization, regulation and restructuring that prevailed in China's economy as a whole. No specific strategies had been formulated to promote the electronics industry and improve its international competitiveness at this stage. The early trade and investment policy was based on the infant industry strategy, and was primarily used to obtain foreign technologies. The trade promotion strategy enabled the expansion of China's electronics exports in the early 1980s. Chinese officials perhaps believed that a mixture of import substitution and export promotion strategies would enable China to develop a number of stronger and more independent industries at that time. The next part of the book looks at the specific strategy that the Chinese government adopted to promote the ICT industry after the early 1990s.

Part III

Making the ICT sector a 'pillar' industry

China's catching up strategies since the early 1990s

> [We need to] revive the electronics and machinery, oil and chemistry, automobile manufacturing and architectural industries, and make them become the pillar industries for China's national economy. Losing no time to develop new high tech industries …
>
> (Jiang Zemin 1992)

So far, this book has explored the development of the Chinese ICT (electronics) industry prior to the early 1990s. It has revealed a general trend of gradualness, discontinuity and unevenness in China's industrial reform. A 'dual track' system was eventually adopted to reconcile the different development visions and political concerns held by the conservatives and the reformers. Many structural problems remained in the economy even though the reform had achieved, to some degree, an expanding of market forces, improvement of incentives, an increase in autonomy for SOEs, and a liberalization of foreign trade and investment. Structural problems frequently broke out during the 1980s and 1990s. As conservative leaders had believed, the price reform could not immediately create a market mechanism that enabled uneven factor distribution to self-correct, given the inherited shortages in the bureaucratic economy. China's leaders supported the reform of enterprises and pushed forward an expansionary monetary policy in 1986 to provide more incentives and resources for entrepreneurs, and hoped to correct the amount of industrial spending at the macroeconomic level by adjusting bank credit lending (Li Y. 1986). Unfortunately, decentralized expansionary policy enabled massive irrational and uncontrollable credit expansion. Inflationary pressures continued to build up and eventually erupted in 1988.[1] Together with growing corruption issues associated with the 'dual price' system and a sharp decline of real incomes in 1989 after the launch of the austerity policies, stalling reform progress eventually turned into fierce social, economic and political crises in 1989.

The renewed reform

Conservative leaders claimed that the main cause of the inflationary outbreak and structural imbalance was a loss of control over the economy since the beginning of the reform in 1978. They were also critical of market reform, claiming that it would abolish the plan and turn China from a socialist state to a capitalist country (Wang 1990; Wu 2003a). After strengthening their political power during the Tiananmen crisis, they were able to launch a three-year rectification programme, attempting to restore control of the economy and limit the 'dual price' system through a number of macroeconomic austerity, recentralization and reallocation policies: tight controls on fixed investment and bank credit were applied, price controls were re-established, wage increases were held down, permission for above-plan production was cancelled, and 'industrial policies' were adopted to replace the coastal development strategies and to reallocate resources towards priority heavy and energy industries.[2] The rectification programme reduced inflation and aggregate demand, but led the economy into recession. It also increased resource allocation in heavy industries while slowing down the growth of sectors that demanded products from the heavy industries. Moreover, when inflation persisted, households tended to stock up on durable and non-perishable consumer goods to hedge against future uncertainty. In response, conservative leaders adopted an indexed saving deposit measure (*Baozhi Chuxu*) to raise interest rates equivalent to the inflation rate. Household income was drawn away from consumption spending to bank deposits, which were dramatically increasing at about 40 per cent per annum by late 1989 (Wang 1998).

When demand for both consumption and investment goods sharply declined, inventories of unsold commodities began to build up. Factories responded by reducing production and laying off workers. Urban unemployment increased considerably and could not be absorbed by rural enterprises because of the tight credit control imposed on their expansion. The profitability and efficiency of large SOEs eventually collapsed when interest payments were raised and unsold output accumulated. Unlike what conservatives had expected, SOEs were unable to make contributions to the state budget and turned out to be a financial burden even if they received a large amount of credit. As the policy's failure became evident, conservative leaders had to suspend the recentralization programme and look for more practical reform measures.

Deng's southern tour in 1992 marked a watershed in rolling back conservative policies. In October, his idea of building a 'market socialist economy' was ratified by the 14th Congress of the CCP as a new reform agenda, one that provided a basis for accelerating a more comprehensive and programmatic market reform. The most fundamental achievement of this renewed reform was the creation of a functioning market. The plan was significantly reduced and price controls were widely dismantled from energy to the sensitive consumer and agriculture sectors. While market prices were strengthened, in 1993 the government began to consolidate market institutions and introduce various measures to cope with rising inflation. These included a unified and centralized tax system that could be more equally applied to enterprises with different types of ownership across different sectors to solve revenue distribution problems; reform of the banking system to separate the central bank from commercial and policy-lending banks so as to concentrate on monetary policies; abolition of a dual exchange rate by establishing a united market rate; enterprise reform to restore the autonomy reform and withdraw Communist Party bureaucrats from management under the 1993 enterprise law; the allowing of private ownership and, on a small scale, privatization of SOEs; and restoration of the coastal development strategies to promote the inflow of FDI. The government also declared that its main function was no longer to control the economy or industries, but to maintain macroeconomic stability and to ensure market allocation of resources. In addition to these reforms, the austerity policies launched by the reformist vice-premier Zhu Rongji began to function and eventually, in 1997, brought inflation and macroeconomic imbalance under control.

Formation of the pillar industry strategy

Although China underwent a significant shift towards a more radical and less controlled economic system, that does not mean that China was heading towards the neo-liberal version of free trade and a free market. While announcing a socialist market reform at the Fourteenth Party Congress, Chinese leaders frequently reiterated Deng's 'three steps in socialist construction'. In more quantitative terms, the overall economic objectives were to double the GNP of the 1981–1990 period in order to provide people with adequate food and clothing as the first step; to double GNP again in the 1991–2000 period to reach *xiaokang* (a middle-class society) as the second step; and the third step was to raise GNP per capita to the level of a medium developed country and also to accomplish modernization by the first quarter of the twenty-first century. Chinese leaders believed that the country needed to strengthen its agricultural sector and promote some 'new' industries to keep up with the changes in consumption structure when moving from one step to another. Leaders began to stress the crucial importance of developing some 'pillar industries' because these industries could not only upgrade China's overall industrial and economic structure, but also support its rapid economic growth and 'bring [China's development] to a new level' every few years. The withdrawal of state control from economic activities therefore only meant that the government would limit its commands and intervene in the market to promote selected strategic sectors in a similar fashion to the East Asian latecomers.

Jiang's statement at the Fourteenth Party Congress clearly denoted a number of 'pillar' industries:

> Agriculture is the basis for national economy … while placing the development priority on agriculture, we need to accelerate the development of infrastructure industries such as transportation, telecommunications, energy, crucial materials [e.g. steel and non-ferrous metals], water resources, etc. … [We need to] revive the electronics and machinery, oil and chemistry, automobile manufacturing and architectural industries, and make them become

the pillar industries for China's national economy. Losing no time to develop new high-tech industries …

(Jiang 1992)

Together with the oil, chemistry, automobile manufacturing and architectural industries, the electronics and machinery sectors were chosen to be the 'pillar' industries. These industries were assumed be important in a number of ways. They could create spillover effects for other industries, accelerate China's industrialization to move from labour- to capital- and technology-intensive sectors, provide highly sought-after products that could increase the varieties of available consumer products in order to improve people's living standards, contribute significantly to GNP through their high value added nature, and improve China's export competitiveness and so increase foreign reserves (Hu 1996). The areas targeted for industrial development in Jiang's statement were identical to Zhao Ziyang's, which had been announced at the Thirteenth Party Congress in 1987. The government renewed the 1987 development strategy, and was about to launch a set of more specific industrial policies.

The ICT industry

Although the idea of promoting the ICT industry was discussed prior to 1986, central leaders' vision of the rapid development of the industry became clear only in the early 1990s. The central leaders and ministers began to speak frequently of 'making the industry a big and growth-accelerating industry' in order to catch up with the world development trend. More specific promotion strategies were formed and launched thereafter. At the fourth plenary session of the Eighth People's Congress in 1993, the state council restored the MEI by separating it from the Ministry of Machine Building and Electronics. Hu Qili, a former standing committee member of the Politburo and secretariat member of the CCP's Central Committee, was appointed as the new minister to carry out the electronics promotion strategies.

On the establishment meeting of the new MEI, Hu Qili announced a '16-word' development strategy:

to make the ICT industry market oriented, to link the domestic to international markets, to stimulate the internal growth through external [foreign] factors, and to accelerate the growth above the pace of national economic growth *(shichang daoxiang, neiwai jiehe, yiwai cunei, jiasu fazhan)*.

(Hu 1993)

In addition to consolidating and extending the industrial policies of the 1980s, this strategy specified three main areas in which the government would play an important role: the creation of large-scale businesses, integration of China's domestic market into the world economy, and the building up of technological capability. These guiding principles extended many development thoughts and approaches previously proposed by the former MEI ministers Jiang Zemin (1983–1985) and Li Tieying (1985–1988). Their development thoughts were highly influential and have dominated the policy regime in the ICT industry since they first appeared in 1986. Even today, in the early twenty-first century, officials from the Ministry of Information Industry (MII) are still renewing and extending policies based on these guiding strategies.

What exactly were the strategies China used to 'accelerate' the growth of the ICT industry during its socialist market transformation reform? What kind of economic theories did Chinese bureaucrats refer to when they were designing their promotion strategies? To what extent did China refer to other countries' experiences? How were China's new strategies carried out and evolved from this point to the WTO era? What kind of role did historical factors play in the policy implementation? This part of the book explores the evolution and implementation of Hu's guiding strategies, which were used to make the ICT industry the pillar industry for the national economy from 1993 to the WTO era. As leaders repeatedly mentioned the development experiences of four 'Asian tigers' of the 1960s and 1980s in their speeches, this part of the book also analyses China's strategies in light of the development paths of Korea and Taiwan. Chapter 5 discusses China's ICT Big Business Strategy and Small and Medium Firm Strategy. Chapter 6 analyses China's ICT 'attracting in' inward FDI attraction policy and 'walking out', export promotion and outward FDI internationalization strategy. Chapter 7 looks at the selective targeting strategy, the 'breaking through' strategy, which was aimed at leading state-owned and state-controlled enterprises into some 'strategic' sectors such as semiconductors.

5 The big business strategy and the small and medium-sized enterprise strategy

One of Hu Qili's development approaches at the enterprise level was the big business strategy. It was believed that a 'pillar' industry must be supported by a number of large 'backbone' enterprises. This strategy in fact was not totally new, but appears to be a resumption and extension of the enterprise reform of the 1980s. This policy prescription was largely based on the East Asian development models of the 1960s–1980s, in which government intervention was used to promote industrial and economic development. Has China successfully emulated the East Asian model, given that it has very different economic and historical conditions as compared with the East Asian countries? Nevertheless, after China had formally joined the WTO in 2001, Chinese officials attempted to maintain the 'national champion' strategy while promoting 'small giants' (small and medium-sized firms) in chosen sectors. The policy implementation faces many challenges because China is prevented under the WTO rules from fostering nationally controlled industries through the various governmental support mechanisms utilized extensively by East Asian latecomer countries such as Korea and Taiwan to catch up during the 1960s to 1980s. Can China still implement a large-firm strategy to improve its technological capabilities and to 'catch up' with leading countries in high-tech industries while complying with the new WTO requirements? Could this mixed policy or the shift towards promoting SMEs represent a more satisfactory alternative for China? What will be the new role for the government as markets open up?

The following sections attempt to explore the role of the Chinese government in creating particular sizes of firms in the ICT industry during the economic liberalization process. The aim is to extend our knowledge of the development of China's ICT high-tech industry and to show how policies evolved over time in response to market-oriented reform and economic liberalization, and to comply with the WTO and Information Technology Agreement (ITA) rules. This examination is made in the light of the development paths of Korea's big business and Taiwan's SME strategies, which Chinese policymakers are keen to follow. The following sections demonstrate that the state had played an important role in creating and supporting firms' growth, but policy implementation that artificially focuses on particular sizes of firm cannot significantly bring benefits, because of China's different economic and historical conditions. The following sections begin with an examination of the basis of China's strategies from a historical perspective and the historical conditions of China's responses to economic liberalization compared with those of Korea and Taiwan; it then discusses whether China should adopt the development strategies of these two countries.

A historical perspective: differences in economic conditions

Since the early 1980s, MEI officials had begun to make frequent visits to foreign countries to look for a 'suitable' development model and to invite potential investors from outside China. Initially, visits were made to Japan, the United States, Western Europe (France and West Germany) and some East European countries (Bulgaria, Hungary, Czechoslovakia, East Germany). Among these trips, Hu Qili's visits to Japan (from 29 November to 7 December) and Korea (7–11 December) in 1993 were made especially to gain an understanding of the Japanese–Korean big business model. Hu believed that South Korea had developed an independent indigenous electronics industry by actively learning from and adopting Japanese and US technologies as well as through extensive import substitution. He also saw that the large and highly diversified group companies had significantly contributed to Korea's success (Hu 2001).

Korea and the large-scale firm strategy

Korea's large-firm model undoubtedly influenced China's big business strategy to a great extent in the 1990s, but Korea's decision to promote *chaebols* was strongly associated with local historical and economic conditions that Chinese officials may not have been aware of, namely the Japanese colonial culture and the availability of local private capital. Korea was a Japanese colony during the Second World War. It was considered by Japan to be a military-industrial base for its control of Manchuria. When Korea's independence was restored in 1945, the remaining Japanese assets still accounted for 80 per cent of Korea's total national assets (Kuznet 1977; Woo 1991). Although a small proportion was sold by the US military government during the Korean War, the rest were passed over to the Rhee government in 1948 and privatized by 1957. Rich local entrepreneurs became the beneficiaries and purchased large amounts of confiscated Japanese-owned assets at a very low price. These tycoons also acquired the knowledge of how the Japanese operated *zaibatsus* (large-scale Japanese family-owned businesses) during the war (Sung 1997). Large firms thus become a main ready resource for the post-war reconstruction and catching up policies.

In the electronics industry, Korea followed the path of the Japanese development model (*zaibatsu* type), with heavy, direct government intervention during the 1960s and 1970s.[1] It formed a close state–firm relationship and aimed to establish large-scale and large-scope conglomerates such as Samsung, Goldstar, Daewoo and Hyundai to battle in international markets. Moving away from import-substituting to export-oriented policies in the 1960s, the government began to encourage the entry of foreign investment for initial technology inflow.

At this stage, policies were still very restrictive in general. Little technological diffusion occurred as foreign firms mainly transferred labour-intensive activities to Korea to take advantage of lower labour costs.

In the 1970s, the government decided to make a big push to develop heavy industry, including electronics as a sub-sector. With respect to indigenous technological upgrading, the government first established advanced goal-oriented science and technology institutes for both private and public firms, and fostered human resources through training and education institutes.[2] Second, it intensively used government procurement to steer domestic demand and promote exports. Third, the government imposed domestic content requirements and assisted domestic firms to negotiate with multinational enterprises (MNEs) concerning technology transfer and local content agreements. Fourth, it subsidized huge amounts of credit directly to *chaebols* through the national banking system (Amsden 1989; Hobday *et al.* 2001; Nolan 2002; Wade 1990, 2004). Interventions declined only gradually in the 1990s as a result of the economic crisis led by over-investment in and expansion of heavy industry and the chemical industry, pressure from international organizations (e.g. the IMF and the World Bank) and Korea's main trading nations, the United States in particular, and the growing economic and political power of the *chaebols*. The Korean ICT industry now focuses on scale- and process-intensive hardware and has become the world leader in DRAM chips (Hobday *et al.* 2001; Mathews and Cho 2000; Sung 1997).

Taiwan and the small and medium-scale enterprise strategy

Taiwan's SME strategy that China in 2002 became keen to use to promote 'small giants' also has its local historical and economic roots. Like Korea, Taiwan (China) too was a Japanese colony from 1895 to 1945. However, it was treated mainly as an agricultural base during the Japanese colonial period. *Zaibatsus* did not expand their production to Taiwan, and their influence was not as strong as in Korea. After the war, the Kuomintang government established an independent state–firm relationship in order to prevent corruption by separating politicians from business communities. Accordingly, policies were designed to broaden its support base to include the general public and small businesses, as opposed to just a few large corporations (Sung 1997). Unlike in Korea, privatization of confiscated Japanese assets was prohibited and there were few local wealthy entrepreneurs who could create the foundations of large firms. Taiwan thus did not choose big-business strategies but looked instead to promote SMEs because of the lack of pre-existing knowledge of Japanese-style big business, limited private investment capital and the different governing ideologies.

In the Taiwanese electronics industry, governmental interventions at firm level in general were fewer than in Korea since the 1960s start-up period.[3] This does not mean the government did not intervene in the technological learning activities of domestic firms. As in Korea, when gradually shifting to export-oriented strategies in the 1970s the government set up various incentives (e.g. export economic zones) to attract foreign firms so as to increase technology inflow. As a result, export assembly activities for foreign producers dominated industrial production. In the mid-1970s, the government started working on the further development of the industry. Like Korea, it invested heavily in human capital and research institutes.[4] Industrial parks were established to encourage foreign companies to locate and to attract overseas-educated Chinese engineers to return to Taiwan.[5] It also provided a stabilized macroeconomic environment, promoted export-led growth strategies and used tariff deductions for the importation of technology and capital goods.

Unlike Korea, it provided only financial incentives such as low interest financing and tax relief, rather than huge amounts of direct credit for business operating. This later became one of the main reasons that it was less affected by the 1997 Asian financial crisis (Dahlman *et al.* 1993; Hobday 1995a,b; Sung 1997; Wade 1990, 1998, 2004). As Taiwan lacked concentrations of capital from the private sector, the government used SOEs as a means to provide technological spillover to private firms and boost demand for targeted infant sectors. Domestic firms focused on scale-intensive PC sectors and specialized in many niche markets (e.g. computer boards and integrated circuit design) (Hobday *et al.* 2001; Sung 1997).

China: moving from a large-scale firm strategy to a strategy promoting both large firms and 'little giants'

The historical and pre-reform economic circumstances that China faced were fundamentally different from the Taiwanese and Korean ones. Unlike these two latecomers, China was not a colony of any country, and the war left only a few damaged industrial plants. The Chinese government gave development priority to the electronics industry because of its significance for defence. In 1949, China started restoring the electronics industry with assistance from the USSR. Government investment was largely driven by military needs during the Cold War in response to international conflicts, namely the outbreak of the Korean War in 1950 and the Sino-Soviet confrontation and the Vietnam War in the 1960s. The industry primarily focused on the development of military telecommunication devices during the Korean War. After splitting with the USSR in 1960, China became isolated from both the Western and the Eastern blocs. The concerns about national security led to a 'war on two fronts' against both the United States and the USSR. In 1964, the Chinese government initiated the 'Third Front Construction Plan', which aimed to create large-scale 'self-reliant' or 'self-sufficient' strategic industrial bases in inner China in case the war spread further. This plan not only led to the allocation of an enormous amount of resources and scientists to the sector, but also changed the primary focus of the development target from military communications to novel weapons systems (see Chapters 3 and 4).

Additionally, China's economic system was different from those of the two latecomers. This led to a different industrial structure and policy focus. In the mid-1950s, China adopted a Stalinist-style centrally planned system that aimed to substitute the administrative plan for competitive markets, and to abolish social class inequality by nationalizing production. Capitalism was regarded as the anarchy of the free market accompanied by class inequality caused by unequal ownership of the means of production (Nolan 2004). Under this system, the state was responsible for the development of all sectors and decided all aspects of enterprises' operations, for example product range and scope, investment, prices, wages, suppliers and purchasers. Enterprises were required to concentrate not on profit making, but rather on fulfilment of the production plan. Industries were dominated by SOEs in cities and communes in the countryside, with no private ownership permitted (Five Year Plan 1986–2004).

This situation changed dramatically with the implementation of the development reorientation and opening up strategy in 1979. The government began to get enterprises previously involved in the production of military goods to convert to the production of civil goods. The development priority was set for consumer electronics in order to accumulate capital and stimulate the growth of components and integrated circuits (Li 1981). Foreign capital was highly selectively introduced into the sector to enable technology inflow. Polices to encourage exports were launched, and many export-oriented economic sites were established to facilitate trade. During the 1986–1992 reform period, China started promoting four targeted sectors: integrated circuits, computers, telecommunications equipment and software. Industrial polices were designed to extend enterprises' autonomy over management and administration, invest in R&D and education, and encourage technology importation (Five Year Plan 1986–2004). However, enterprise and market-oriented reform were carried out at a time when the bureaucratic economic apparatus remained dominant. Macroeconomic imbalances frequently emerged and led to open inflation. The reform was also associated with capitalism by conservatives, and encountered political resistance. China has thus since the mid-1980s been undertaking a gradualist approach to move towards a 'socialist' market-oriented economy that emphasizes a predominance of state ownership in the economy.

China's big business strategy in the ICT sector

Against such a fundamentally different economic and political background, China launched the 'grasping the large and releasing the small' strategy. It was intended to build state enterprises into vertically integrated and international competitive giant companies in pillar industries, including the electronics/ICT sector. The big business strategy implemented by Hu Qili in the electronics industry largely extended the enterprise reform experiments conducted by Li Tieying. As Chapter 4 shows, the MEI started the policy experiment of 'economically integrated units' (*jingji lianheti*) in 1980. In 1984, the central government adopted this policy at the national level and reiterated that the mergers and acquisitions (M&A) between enterprises would be voluntary and horizontal, and would preferably take the form of cooperation and alliances between large and medium-sized SOEs in the form of joint-stock companies (JSCs). The measure was launched in the hope of achieving three things: to strengthen the market so as to increase economic convergence through breaking down of the bureaucratic and geographic barriers imposed on the local economy under the command economic system; to increase coordination among different regions in order to avoid repeated construction and production; and to prevent firms from attempting to achieve fully vertical diversification without realizing scale economies. The government also expected that M&A could create some 'fist enterprises' (*quantou qiye*) to produce internationally competitive products.

In response to this central 'blueprint' and the enterprise autonomy reform, Li Tieing in 1986 announced a development strategy of 'applying theories of economies of scale and building China's IBM, Hitachi, and Siemens' in order to 'catch up' with leading countries. He emphasized that enterprises should develop greater self-initiatives and 'competitive consciousness' (*jingzheng yishi*) that could alter their attitude towards the new reform strategy from 'I am asked to integrate' to 'I want to integrate' with other enterprises to improve performance (Li T. 1986a). Although enterprises were given decision-making rights, they were treated as subdivisions of local hierarchical bureaucracies and in practice were required to respond to the command of governing authorities. Enterprises' M&A decisions were very unlikely to be based on their own initiatives, but rather were the choice of the MEI, which gained more centralized decision-making power, or of local governments, which during the reform were given the authority to administer local enterprises directly. Stemming from the MEI's announcement in 1987, 150 'horizontally integrated economic units' were established by provincial, city and ministerial officials. Of these, 26 were group companies and 13 achieved nationwide status.

In terms of how to group enterprises in the electronics industry, Li Tieying (1986a) provided the following guide.

- M&A within existing industrial bases. Enterprises were grouped in existing industrial bases, for example established industrial centres in Beijing and Shanghai, coastal cities (Jiangsu and Guangdong), and old military bases in Sichuan, Shaanxi and Guizhou. It was believed that this grouping method could enable firms to utilize the established local infrastructure to achieve scale economies quickly.

- M&A according to similarities of technology and production and the existing market power of enterprises. It was hoped that groups of firms formed through this method could gain cost advantages and achieve scale economies in production volumes by sharing production equipment, materials, human resources, brand images and service providers. For example, the Guizhou Zhenhua Group Company was formed by grouping enterprises with products linked to each other vertically in the field of machinery and agriculture electronics devices. Beijing Great Wall Computer was created to bring firms that specialized in services (sales and R&D design) together with those in manufacturing so as to complement each other in the production chain, and Nanjing Broadcast Group was founded by grouping a number of enterprises specializing in television and radio products for which there was strong demand. Rainbow Group companies were merged with the sixth bureau of the MEI and the Shaanxi Yellow River TV Factory, the Haiyan TV Factory and the Inner Mongolia Factory to increase the production scale of the well-known Rainbow-brand TVs.

- Cooperation regarding distribution channels. The local authorities grouped together enterprises that could share the same distribution network. For example, the Beijing local government coordinated a product sales and exhibition network for 11 local electronics instrument enterprises.
- R&D cooperation between research institutions and enterprises. Jiannan Broadcast and Radio Enterprise was created jointly by the Sichuan Solid Electro-circuit Institute and the Jiangnan Factory of Radio and Broadcast Devices to share their expertise in radio and broadcasting technology and production. Legend (later known as Lenovo) was created by the Chinese Academy of Sciences.
- Commercialization of national projects. For each national R&D project launched, the state had created at least one large state-controlled group company to absorb and localize its technological outcomes. It was hoped that this method would allow the national R&D project to generate greater technological spillover effects. For example, Huawei and Huaxin group companies were initially establizhed to turn ATM technologies into large-scale production. Huaxu Group Company was created to absorb integrated circuit card technologies.
- Economic cooperation across geographical and administrative borders, and industrial sectors. For example, 117 enterprises and local authorities were involved in the creation of the Shenzhen Electronics Industrial Group Company. The Zhenhua Group Company was establizhed by 32 enterprises and local authorities in Guizhou Province.

In the 1987 enterprise reform, large enterprises were granted a number of rights to operate with substantial autonomy outside the plan activities. They were allowed to hold foreign trade rights, to decide the scope of sales, technology imports and upgrading, to diversify production, to establish financial subsidiaries, to raise funding from local banks and the public, as well as to facilitate fund transfer within the group. They were often aided by top political and military officials and encouraged to operate internationally. The enterprise autonomy reform of large enterprises was retrenched when the austerity policies were adopted in the late 1980s. In 1991, when conservative policies were rolled back, the government was able to designate the first 55 group enterprises to receive support and preferential policies. Prior to 1993, enterprises directly related to the electronics industry in the machinery and electronics industry were Great Wall Computer, Changjiang Computer and Zhenhua Electronics Group. The number of firms was later extended to seven in 1997 by the MEI (see Table 5.1).

A further enterprise reform was declared by Jiang Zeming at the Fourteenth Party Congress in 1992. The focus of the reform was on the operation mechanisms for large and medium-sized enterprises. The government decided to replace

Table 5.1 Selected large enterprises for the big business experiment in the eighth and ninth ministerial Five-Year Plans

---

1991: the Ministry of the Electronics and Machinery Industry

- China Great Wall Computer Group Company
- Changjiang Computer Group Company
- Zhenhua Electronics Groups Company

1997: the Ministry of Electronics newly extended group companies

- Rainbow Group Limited Company TV
- Sichuan Changhong Group Company TV
- Legend Group Company
- Beijing Beida Fangzheng Group Company
- China Hualu Limited Group Company
- Shanghai Guangling Limited Group Company
- Panda Electronics Group Company

By 2005

- Zhongshan Group Company (until 2000, 2001)
- Putian (Potevio) Information Group Company
- China Electronics Corporation Group Company
- China Electronics Technology Group Company (since 2002)
- Tianjing Electronics Group Company
- Changbai Computer Group Company
- Shenzhen Saige Group Company
- Shanghai Guangdian Group Company
- Shanghai Changjiang Computer Group Company
- China ZhongCi Device Company (until 2002)
- Gansu Electronics Group Company (until 2002)
- Shanghai (Yidian) Electronics Development Holding Group Company
- Shanghai Aviation Group Company

Sources: the State Council, State Planning Commission, State Economic and Trade Commission, and State Reform Commission, 'Opinions and Notice regarding Further Large Group Enterprise Experiments', no. 19970429; State Council, State Planning Commission, State Production Commission, and State Reform Commission, 'Instruction Notice regarding Selecting a Number of Large Enterprises for Policy Experiments,' no. 19911214; and *Yearbook of the Electronics Industry* (various years).

the 'tax for profit' incentive regime with a 'modern enterprise conversion' pro-gramme in order to substantially withdraw bureaucratic administration from enterprise management and to allow them to respond to the market. As is discussed at the beginning of this chapter, China's development strategies in the ICT sector were inspired by the Japanese and Korean models to support a team of national ICT group companies with a wide range of statist industrial policies.

These include:

- Domestic market protection through tariff and non-tariff barriers.
- Demand pull and supply chain building through government procurement and local content requirements.

- Technology upgrading through direct governmental subsides for R&D technology transfer and selection of domestic firms to enter into foreign joint ventures.
- Financial subsidies and incentives such as the purchase of production inputs on preferential terms, tax relief, preferential loans from the state-owned banks.
- In 1992, two stock exchanges in Beijing and Shanghai were created. The intension was to allow these large group companies to raise more funding so as to diversify their ownership and to set up a modern Western-style management enterprise in the form of limited liability joint-stock companies.

The strategies were experimental. Tight control was imposed in order to maintain the primary state ownership in the industry. The Ministry of Information Industry (MII) was set up in 1998 by merging the Ministry of the Electronics Industry with the Ministry of Posts and Telecommunications to 'make an overall plan for the industrial development, to rationally allocate resources for R&D and production, and to avoid the overlaps of construction projects by various ministries'.[6] Most importantly, this administrative reform saw the new ministry become more unified and centralized than before, serving a similar function to that of the Ministry of International Trade and Industry in Japan, to coordinate and extend production networks from manufacturing to service sectors (MII 1998). In 2001, the State Council reinforced the big business strategy and the policies discussed earlier during the Fifteenth FYP by issuing 'instructional opinions regarding developing international competitive large multinationals'. In the same year, the MII chose the top 100 ICT enterprises in order to focus on promoting them. (Appendix 4 lists these firms.) In summary, the state attempted to create a number of large state-owned pillar enterprises that could assist industrial restructure, improve efficiency and accelerate the pace of technology and product innovation in order to enhance China's international competitiveness.

China's policy of promoting both large ICT firms and 'little giants' in the WTO era

While Li Tieying launched the big business strategy in accordance with the central blueprint in the late 1980s, he also proposed the small and medium-sized business promotion strategy: 'while promoting collectively the large enterprises, we also need to develop a number of small, new, specialist small and medium size companies in order to complement the development of the large firms' (Li T. 1986b: 31). This policy was not implemented in 1993. The 'grasping the large and releasing the small' policy rather let the local authorities deal with small and medium-sized SOEs and town and village enterprises. They have been restructured under 'the 1993 CCP decision on building the socialist market mechanism', to be sold off, contracted to individuals, transferred to employee ownership, merged with others or converted into joint-stock companies.

However, since 1997 the government has recognized the problems faced by large firms in Japan and Korea, and the advantages of the Taiwanese SME model in weathering the Asian financial crisis. Moreover, the WTO agreement and the Information Technology Agreement (ITA) minimized trade tariffs and other interventional policies for protecting domestic markets and restricting foreign investment. While China's policy after WTO accession still attempted to create large firms through state-led alliances, mergers and ownership diversification, the policy focus has since shifted towards a stronger emphasis on small firms. In 2002, the central government promulgated the SME promotion law. The policy, in the form of a legal document (the Small and Medium-Sized Firm Promotion Law of the People's Republic of China, promulgated at the Ninth Standing Committee Meeting of the National People's Congress, 29 June 2002), was aimed at improving the business environment of SMEs by offering support in a number of areas.

- *Finance*: the central and local governments established development funds for SMEs and encouraged credit lending from all kinds of financial institutions under the guidance of China's central bank. All levels of government were instructed to establish credit assessment and guarantee systems to facilitate this credit lending process. The State Council, meanwhile, issued policy guidance for industrial selection and targets for SMEs.
- *Business start-ups*: all government departments were required to support SMEs with information and consultation, and to assist disabled and unemployed people, and new graduates to set up individual businesses in order to create employment opportunities. Tax deductions and exemptions were applied to high-tech SMEs and enterprises set up by disabled people or located in the rural minority residential areas. All government agencies were required to promote foreign JVs and to introduce FDI and technologies to SMEs.
- *Technology innovation and upgrading*: the government aimed to support SMEs to innovate new products, to adopt and upgrade technologies, new production processes and equipment, and to improve product quality and technological capabilities by easing their land-use rights, protecting their ownership rights, providing financial and infrastructure support and human resource training, as well as establishing technology incubation centres that are used to provide technology transfer, services and information from R&D institutions to SMEs. All SME projects that complemented the large enterprises in developing their value chain or technology upgrading could receive reductions on bank loan interest.
- *Market expansion*: The government intended to use direct policy measures to promote cooperation between large and small and medium-sized enterprises in sharing materials, production facilities, sales networks and R&D activities, and to help SMEs to merge and acquire other enterprises in order to diversify their financial and production resources as well as their ownership. The government also decided to give its procurement priority to SMEs and provided guidance and financial support for them to engage in export and technology cooperation with foreign entities, outward foreign investment and sales exhibitions abroad.

In response to the central government's SME promotion policy, the MII relaunched Li Tieying's strategies with little modification in 2002. Chinese policymakers expected these SMEs to become 'little giants' in the world market and to play an important role in completing the domestic supply chain so as to support the large firms in targeted niche markets such as new and crucial components and optical electronics (Wu J. C. 2003). Like the overall reform style, the SME promotion strategy was a broad visionary blueprint. Unlike in Taiwan, local officials were decentralized, so that they could promote domestic small-scale firms entirely on the basis of their own judgement, preferences and plans – although this may not prevent discrimination against private enterprises, at least those without strong networks with local authorities. All in all, the whole idea of the SME strategy was to complement the big business strategy in order to create a large ICT industry within China's territory that is capable of producing and exporting large volumes of Chinese-designed and -manufactured products from upstream to downstream of the industry. Large enterprises are used to achieve scale economies while SMEs are created to complete the domestic value chain and occupy niche markets.

Drawbacks on two sides: large conglomerates versus SME strategies in developing the ICT sector

Large conglomerate strategies

The logic behind China's adoption of a big business strategy in the ICT industry at first sounds very reasonable. As historians and economists have observed, the substantial level of economic growth in the eighteenth and nineteenth centuries was largely due to technological progress, to which large industrial enterprises made a more significant contribution than small-scale firms, and large firms were therefore the major driving force behind economic development (Nolan 2001). Large firms are often the first mover in new technologies or processes and the first to commercialize them into products and services. Their strong financial position, derived from exploiting economies of scale, enables them to invest heavily in R&D and compensate for the inherent market failure issues associated with high technology and knowledge-intensive industries. Their ability to accumulate valuable human resources ensures that they have a sustainable technological capacity to maintain innovative activities (Chandler 1990). When it comes to trade, large firms can achieve superior internal economies of scale in an integrated world market compared with those in a purely domestic one. They give rise to a geographical and technological concentration of production, and their large economies of scale eventually lead to an imperfectly competitive market structure (Brander and Krugman 1983). With technological and cost advantages, they become oligopolies in the market, dominating major sectors, leading technological progress, creating spillover effects and providing job opportunities (Chandler and Hikino 1997).

These theoretical benefits can also be found in Marx's *Capital* and thus provide further political support for Chinese policymakers to pursue the big business strategy: '[T]he productiveness of social labour presupposes cooperation on a large scale [through the accumulation of capital]'. The Western capitalist model, however, enabled only a few individual producers to accumulate capital and prevented Western societies as a whole from achieving an even larger scale of production by turning into 'one immense factory' (Marx 1867).[7] The intention of the Chinese policymakers was to create a few large-scale state-owned and -controlled firms instead of allowing a few individuals to achieve 'the accumulation of capital', raising 'the social productive power of labour' and increasing production of 'surplus value and surplus product'. Unlike Lenin's fully centralized 'state syndicate' approach, adopted in China in the 1950s and 1960s, large enterprises have been given autonomy, and a small percentage under diversified ownership have been allowed to take part in the newly established market environment since the early 1990s. Moreover, the Chinese leaders learned from history that successful later-industrializing countries, from the United States in the late nineteenth century to South Korea in the late twentieth century, all have a few large companies, especially in capital- and knowledge-intensive industries. For example, in the ICT sector the United States has IBM, Intel and AMD, Japan has Toshiba and Sony, Korea has Samsung and LG, the Netherlands has Philips, Finland has Nokia and Germany has Siemens. These policy propositions, based on economic, political and historical studies, demonstrate the possible advantages to China of developing large firms in the electronics/ICT sectors.

However, the East Asian large-scale firm development model that Chinese officials are keen to follow revealed many serious issues a few decades after having been successfully implemented in the tiger countries. Since the Asian financial crisis of 1997–1998, the close relationship between state and big business as fostered by the Korean government has been criticized by neo-liberals as being inefficient (IMF 1997; Wade 2004). Promoting big businesses seems to be a good idea to improve technological capabilities in the short run, but in the long term, problems may develop. Neo-classical economists believe that when an industry is monopolized by a single large firm, product prices will rise and production quantities will decrease. The existence of large, oligopolistic firms will lead to market inefficiencies. More importantly, their powerful market position, together with their strong financial capabilities, tend to give them great influence over government decisions. Relatively perfect competition, where there are no large firms that could develop their bargaining power sufficiently to influence the market, is therefore both economically and politically desirable.

Big firms may have other disadvantages. Marshall argues that the large firm is only a temporary phenomenon, and that when it reaches a certain point it becomes less elastic and creative than it used to be. Eventually it will be broken down by competition (Marshall 1920). In Korea's case, the *chaebols* have become increasingly hierarchical and bureaucratic in structure and management styles. Their ability to adjust to today's fast-changing competitive environment in the ICT sector is relatively weak and slow. They are trapped in a cycle still focusing on catching up in hardware production with narrow product ranges and have not yet intensively moved into software sectors (Hobday *et al.* 2001).

Yet another problem is that the financial institutions required to facilitate the development of big business are generally weak in developing countries, including China. Excessive governmental financial intervention may lead to macroeconomic instabilities while the financial market is liberalized. As it was believed that *chaebols* were able to cover short-term learning costs, overcome high entry barriers and move to high value added and high profit in the long run, banks tended to provide more credit to these big firms than to SMEs. This process was reinforced by government financial intervention to support large firms (e.g. by direct credit subsidies). Although the Korean government retained control over all forms of credit so as to direct or discipline *chaebols*, after financial liberalization in the 1980s, large firms could get away from this control system and easily raise huge amounts of investment from abroad. Such rapid debt-led expansion of the *chaebols*, both encouraged by the government and spurred on by FDI after 1993, eventually caused the macroeconomic problems. Some economists argue that the crisis represented not a failure of state-directed credit, but rather one of excessive financial deregulation (Krugman 1998; Wade 1998, 2004). The late-industrializing countries still need to reform their financial institutions in order to restrain macroeconomic instability so that excess credit scenarios do not threaten the progress of individual firms, in electronics as in other sectors.

In implementing 'big business' strategies, China as a developing country may not only encounter problems similar to those faced by Korea, but also face more obstacles unique to its own position. First, China's domestic economy had difficulties in supporting large-firm strategies in the 1970s and 1980s, as its levels of income, urbanization and privatization were far below those of Korea at the time (Nolan 2001). Domestic demand was still mainly for cheap, low-quality ICT products. With the low entry barriers, geographical distance, poorly developed transportation and information systems, and strong local governmental protection, SMEs could still survive by producing relatively cheaper and lower-quality products and easily compete with them in some regional markets.

Second, there are many barriers to creating large firms through government-led mergers and alliances. Since 1993, China's industrial policies have aimed at increasing autonomy and separating the functions of enterprises and government. Firms that follow this path and diversify their ownership (e.g. through listing shares) are relatively independent and it is impossible to merge them with other firms. Moreover, 'forced marriages' or 'high-speed fattening' could cause blind expansion (Wu J. L. 2003b). Some local authorities whose definitions of large firms were unclear would merge large firms in their region that had nothing in common – and these large firms would still be small-scale by national standards. Such mergers and alliances result in an 'illusion of scale', diversifying the core business and creating problems of corporate governance in managing different firms.

Third, China's large ICT firms were formed from former large SOEs which provided for large numbers of employees. Restructuring them will lead to downsizing, putting strains on the weak Chinese welfare system and possibly causing social instabilities (Nolan and Wang 1998). Some local authorities resisted the idea of mergers and alliances because they were afraid that their local enterprises

Table 5.2 Percentages of industrial sales, output, profit, exports, value added and assets of the targeted large group companies

	Industrial sales	Industrial output	Operating profit	Exports	Value added	Assets
1997	10%	10%	7%	9%	9%	13%
2000	15%	16%	11%	14%	12%	19%
2003	14%	23%	11%	11%	11%	16%
2004	8%	8%	1%	6%	9%	12%

Source: Information Technology Yearbook, various years.

Note: the large group enterprises include the MII-controlled enterprises. In 1997 and 2003, these enterprise groups included ZhongShan Group, Panda Electronics Group, ZhongCi Devices, Changbai Computer Group, Hualu Limited Group, Shenzhen Saige Group, Rainbow TV Group, Great Wall Computer Group, Shanghai Changjing Computer Group, Zhenhua Electronics Group, China Electronics Corporation Group and Shanghai Changjing Computer Group. In 2003 and 2004 these enterprise groups included China Electronics Corporation Group, China Electronics Technology Group, China Potevio (Putian) Information Industry Group, China Great Wall Computer Group, Tianjing Electronics Group, Changbai Computer Group, Hualu Limited Group, Shanghai Guangdian Group, Shanghai (Yidian) Electronics Development Holding Group, Shanghai Aviation Group, Shanghai Changjiang Computer Group, Panda Electronics Group, Shenzhen Saige Group, Zhenhua Electronics Group and Rainbow TV Group.

would be allocated less competitive activities and suffer from downsizing or unemployment problems as a result of business expansion.

Lastly, the performance of these large group companies is not as expected (see Table 5.2). For example, in 1997 the government announced that the total industrial sales, production output, exports and value added of 12 targeted large firms accounted for roughly 10 per cent of all indicators of the total. However, in 2004, 15 targeted large firms, including the MII-controlled large group enterprises, accounted for only 8 per cent of total industrial output, 8 per cent of industrial sales, 1 per cent of total industrial profit, 6 per cent of total exports, 9 per cent of total added value and 12 per cent of the total industrial assets (Information Technology Yearbook 2004; Ning 2007). Large domestic firms have not demonstrated their significance in improving the performance of domestic ICT firms compared with foreign enterprises, which by 2005 had come to dominate and control the industry's domestic market (57 per cent of the total), trade (84 per cent of imports and 92 per cent of exports) as well as production output (75 per cent). (See also Table 5.4 on p. 100 and Chapter 6 for time series data concerning the overall performance of the domestic ICT enterprises.)

Strategies towards small and medium-sized enterprises

Chinese policymakers were keen to support small and medium-sized ICT enterprises in targeted niche markets while the statist trade and industrial policies were dismantled by 2005. Can Taiwanese-style SMEs improve China's competitiveness in the ICT sector?

According to neo-classical economic theory, increasing degrees of competition can provide firms not only with an incentive to improve their technological and managerial capabilities, but also with a selective mechanism to maintain healthy development by forcing less competitive firms to exit. Opening up to trade will engender such competition, reduce the market power of local monopolies and allow a more efficient allocation of resources. Moreover, small firms are regarded as having played an important role in long-term economic structural change where jobs move from one sector to another or new sectors after trade (Aghion and Blanchard 1993). Their flexible nature allows them to respond quickly to market changes and become more diversified so to withstand the volatilities of financial shocks (Wade 1998, 2004). They often specialize in niche markets, and by engaging in international trade they can gain from producing differentiated goods on a scale commensurate with a world market (Helpman and Krugman 1985).

This neo-classical view supports the notion that developing countries should adopt a liberalized regime, rely on the market and exploit their comparative advantages in material-based and labour-intensive sectors. Industrial policies aimed at supporting the growth of large-scale capital and technologically intensive policies and trade protection will distort international production networks and are thus not desirable (Hirst and Thompson 1995). Accordingly, there was a need for China to join the WTO and rapidly become integrated into the world economy. It should start from material-based or labour-intensive industries or segments and base its production on small and medium-scale firms in order to fully exploit and reflect these two comparative advantages.

In supporting this view, neo-classical economists have used Taiwan as an example and concluded that its success is due to its initial decision to develop labour-intensive light industries and that its small-scale industrial structure reflects the comparative advantages of local factor endowments (Lin *et al.* 1996). However, the case of Taiwan was not only about the progressing performance of small and medium-scale firms. There are disadvantages in promoting small and medium-scale firms for the Taiwanese electronic industry and for big countries such as mainland China. SMEs have limited resources and financial capabilities to invest heavily in R&D and improve their technological capabilities. Although they could specialize in certain niche markets, their ability to develop these markets further is very weak. They are often hesitant to enter new segments because of their financial condition and their relative inability to cope with market failure. In the ICT sector, where new products and technologies are introduced at an immensely fast pace, they would often find themselves technologically disadvantaged. Apart from the historical determinants, the Taiwanese government intervened intensively and protected its local markets during the catching up period. For example, in order to help firms to enter targeted markets, it gave local firms many incentives and imposed technological transfer conditions and trade restrictions on foreign firms. It also directly entered selected sectors through establishing SOEs so as to reduce learning costs and create spillover effects. Without such interventions, large foreign firms could easily have entered the market amid the fragmentation of

SMEs with low-cost products, as a result of their large-scale, efficient production techniques, advanced technologies, R&D capabilities and marketing. They could have squeezed small firms out of business in a very short period. To compete, SMEs must rely constantly on the government for financial assistance, R&D investment and new technologies.

Also, governmental spending on any one sector is limited and therefore selective. As SMEs rely heavily on government assistance, they may miss opportunities to develop some high-value-added products that are more suitable for the individual firms' conditions. Selective trade and technological policies in general may improve the internal knowledge base of particular sectors even if they lead to market failure or cause small firms to miss development opportunities. However, small firms may not use this acquired knowledge base to innovate or to enter new markets because of financial constraints, insufficient technological capabilities and unwillingness to cope with market failure. When the government cannot provide desirable technological assistance, firms are often advised to seek assistance from foreign companies. From such cooperation, they can access international markets and improve technological capabilities. Nevertheless, their buffering capabilities against heavy fluctuations in international demand are still in question. Furthermore, small firms have difficulties in achieving economies of scale in differentiated goods, as various national tastes and regulatory and safety standards present difficulties for small firms to adjust to. Because of these difficulties, exporting firms have often found that producing non-differentiated or intermediated products on a large rather than small scale enabled them to gain from trade in international markets (Perdikis and Kerr 1998). Some small firms such as Acer have eventually grown into big global companies through processing semi-finished goods and components for foreign firms. As observed by Hobday *et al.* (2001), the majority of Taiwanese SMEs have been seen as relying heavily on large Japanese and US firms to provide product design, key components and capital goods. Product ranges are narrow and firms are weak in design and brand, and highly sensitive to the US market.

Taking these disadvantages into account, there are more reasons for China not to shift towards an SME strategy. First, as the World Bank suggested, countries of the former USSR and Eastern Europe whose economic systems were similar to that of China strongly supported SMEs in their economic transitions from a centrally planned economy. Their economic performances, however, are not as good as China's (Smyth 2000). Second, as opposed to Taiwan, China has a large domestic market to satisfy and is not significantly affected by exports. The huge domestic markets are still generally poor and demand low-value, low-priced products. The abilities of SMEs to deal with fast-changing international niche markets and to satisfy huge domestic demand at the same time are in question. Third, China, like most developing countries, has a relatively undeveloped financial market. Can this poor financial system provide small firms with sufficient financial assistance for them to carry out R&D activities and cover the cost of market failure? Finally, if firms relied heavily on foreign technologies, the government would face increasing concerns in relation to national information security.

The controlling ownership of the state

The most important drawbacks that Chinese policymakers ignored when replicating Korea and Taiwan's strategies were the different nature of the enterprises and the different economic environments. As observed from above, China's policy reforms have much in common with the corresponding industrialization processes of its East Asian neighbours. They all started from labour-intensive export activities and intervene heavily in technological learning. However, China's economic, political and historical background and circumstances were fundamentally different from those found in Korea and Taiwan. Government interventions in China were much stronger than those in Korea because of the nature of China's centrally planned economic system and the fact that China's ICT industry was heavily involved in military production in the past.

Moreover, the Chinese leaders had strong political considerations, which stressed the state's primary controlling ownership in the strategic 'pillar' and high-tech industries for the purpose of consolidating the socialist system, ensuring national security, supplying public goods, adjusting economic structure and leading economic growth.[8] The 'dual use' (military and civilian) high-tech ICT industry was accordingly retained with a dominant ratio of state ownership among domestic enterprises. Chinese leaders stressed that state ownership should dominate and lead economic growth in the pillar and targeted sectors, although non-state and foreign ownership could play important parts in China's socialist market. China's large 'converted' enterprises thus in many ways had 'lineage' with SOEs, exhibiting close relations with the state at all levels. Table 5.3 shows a parallel shift of total industrial assets from traditional SOEs to JSCs. More recently available Chinese statistics, however, indicate that total assets of ICT SOE and SCEs still accounted for an average of 73 per cent of the domestic assets in the ICT industry during the period 2003–2005 (see Table 5.4).[9] The total assets of the private ICT sector never grew to more than 0.5 per cent of the industry's total and 0.8 per cent of the domestic total before 1997. Up to China's accession to the WTO in 2001, the government shifted the policy focus to promote domestic firms, as long as they are Chinese-owned, in response to progressively fierce foreign competition. Private-sector companies have since increased dramatically, accounting for 4.9 per cent of the industry's total assets and about 15 per cent of the domestic assets in 2005.[10] Unlike the routes followed by Korea and Taiwan, China's promotion strategy based on the size of firms was designed primarily for state-owned or state-invested firms, especially in pillar industries such as the ICT sector.

Together with the differences in international political and domestic economic conditions, it seems that China had to overcome many structural and historical problems to be able to replicate the East Asian-style strategy successfully. The question that remains is whether such strategies could improve the competitiveness of China's ICT firms. This leads to an examination of the overall contributions of big businesses and SMEs to the ultimate objective of China's ICT industrial strategy, export and production expansion on a world scale, in the following chapters.

Table 5.3 Number of firms and total assets (in billions of yuan) by enterprise type in China's ICT industry, 1997–2005

Year	Foreign funded		Wholly SOEs		Collective		Joint stock		Private		Industry total	
	No. of firms	Percentage of total assets	No. of firms	Percentage of total assets	No. of firms	Percentage of total assets	No. of firms	Percentage of total assets	No. of firms	Percentage of total assets	No. of firms	Total assets
1997	753	33.5%	1,225	46.4%	954	8.40%	156	10.0%	30	0.4%	2,914	3,828
1999	735	35.8%	1,001	37.4%	618	8.00%	311	15.6%	46	1.1%	2,839	5,220
2001	865	36.8%	789	30.1%	474	9.60%	689	18.9%	117	2.4%	3,062	7,813
2003	3,987	58.6%	860	12.9%	857	2.60%	1,725	21.1%	2,607	3.6%	10,596	14,342
2005	6,480	67.9%	659	7.3%	617	1.70%	2,555	17.6%	5,180	4.9%	16,007	21,305

Source: Information Technology Yearbook, 1997–2005.

Table 5.4 Percentage of state-owned and -controlled ICT enterprises in domestic-owned enterprises and in the total ICT industry, 2003–2005

	No. of firms		Sales		Assets		Profit		Value added		Industrial output		Export	
	Domestic	Total	Domestic	Total	Domestic	Total	Domestic	Total	Domestic	Total	Domestic	Total	Domestic[a]	Total
2003	23%	15%	75%	21%	79%	21%	54%	18%	76%	76%	95%	29%	111%	14%
2004	19%	11%	67%	16%	71%	16%	41%	9%	81%	81%	67%	16%	102%	15%
2005	15%	9%	66%	14%	70%	14%	19%	4%	55%	14%	66%	13%	119%	8%

Source: Information Technology Yearbook, various years.

Note: Export includes state-controlled foreign joint ventures. 'State-controlled enterprises' includes all state-promoted large group enterprises, as the ownership of the pillar industries has not been as largely diversified as others.

Conclusion

Economic liberalization has arguably been seen as a means to improve the technological capabilities of developing countries. Governments in East Asian latecomer countries disagreeing with this view implemented a set of selective industrial policies and have achieved remarkable success. China attempted to follow these countries' experiences and responded to economic liberalization by promoting big business. As the degree of liberalization becomes greater, China is also keen to promote SMEs. This chapter found that neither the Korean nor the Taiwanese firm size strategies could improve the technological capabilities of China's ICT industry.

First, China's firm size strategy primarily targets SOEs against the background of its gradual market reform of the centrally planned economy, whereas the Korean and Taiwanese strategies focused on private firms in economies that were market oriented. The mechanism of operation of both the targeted companies and the national economy is very different in China from what is found in Korea or Taiwan.

Second, it can be seen that historical elements mainly related to Japanese colonial influences and the availability of local private capital have shaped policy decisions in Korea and Taiwan. Conversely, China does not have either of these elements and would face huge social and economic costs if it adopted such policies.

The following chapters will continue to argue that competitive ICT firms in the global economy are increasingly moving from manufacturing to network-controlling activities. China's current firm size strategies still focus on the former. It would take a long time for China to catch up with the global ICT leaders competing in the same activities even though it is making a policy adjustment now (see Chapter 6). Additionally, the core path that Korean and Taiwanese strategies used in order to protect firms from fierce international competition and intervene extensively in their technological learning is now unavailable for China (that is upgrading from imitation to innovation), given the WTO and ITA agreements and the changing global political environment (see Chapter 7).

6 The 'attracting in' and 'walking out' trade and investment strategy

> Foreign-funded enterprises in China are allowed to make some money in accordance with existing laws and policies . . . the government levies taxes on those enterprises, workers get wages from them, and we learn technology and managerial skills. In addition, we can get information from them that will help us open more markets. Foreign-funded enterprises are useful supplements to the socialist economy, and in the final analysis they are good for socialism.
>
> (Deng Xiaoping, Southern Tour, 1992)

The ultimate goal of the big business and SME strategies was to achieve export competitiveness through increasing production scale and establishing a value chain from upstream to downstream of the ICT industry in China. The second role of the government described by Hu Qili was also developed according to this central objective. Hu explained that China's ICT industry needed to 'integrate its domestic market to the international one'. By developing the domestic market and improving product features and quantity, the ICT industry could not only satisfy domestic demand, but also achieve some degree of scale production. China could also utilize its own comparative cost advantages to explore foreign markets ('walking out', *zouchuqu*) and occupy a position in the international market.[1] Hu Qili also emphasized 'to stimulate the internal growth through external (exogenous) factors' ('attracting in', *yjnjinlai*). He said that China should utilize foreign investment, markets, technology, human resources and management expertise to build the foundation of China's ICT industry, and to increase scale expansion, R&D activities and levels of innovation, so as to accelerate the growth of the industry (Hu 1993).

Two decades after the strategies were launched, China seems to be making incredible progress in catching up with the world's leading ICT players. The ICT industry is now the most open to the world market of all China's industries. In 2003, having joined the WTO in 2001, it became the world's third largest ICT-producing sector, and has accounted for close to 15 per cent of the world market since. China also successfully overtook the position of Japan and the European Union in 2003 and overtook the United States in 2004 to become the biggest ICT exporter in the world (OECD 2006a). A number of large domestic ICT enterprises are approaching multinational stages, operating worldwide and acquiring firms in advanced economies. The ICT industry is now China's number one 'pillar' industry, contributing significantly to the Chinese economy (see Chapter 1). It seems that China is now making a leap from being a simple manufacturing centre to becoming an advanced technology 'superstate' (Preeg 2005). But is the growth really as impressive as it appears? Has China really become more competitive and taken a lead in the ICT industry? Is this phenomenon similar to the rise of the Japanese auto, steel and electronics industries, which surpassed their US counterparts in the 1970s? Have technologies really flowed into China and have local firms become more competitive as a result of policy reforms? On what basis did the Chinese leaders design and promote these trade and investment strategies? How did these strategies evolve towards the neo-liberal reforms that China agreed to before joining the WTO? Was China successful in fostering 'pillar' industries through simultaneously liberalizing its import regime in exchange for technologies? How did all these policies work together?

This chapter attempts to analyse how the 'walking out' and 'attracting in' policies have been applied to the ICT sector, and to determine how successful they have been in promoting this industry. The policies have close relevance to the big business SME strategy as firms' aggregated performance reflects the competitiveness of the ICT industry as a whole. In turn, the industry's overall performance can demonstrate whether the big business and SME strategies have been successfully implemented to achieve Chinese leaders' development objectives. This chapter explores the questions raised above in the context of trade and investment. It begins by identifying the unique characteristics of the 'walking out' and 'attracting in' strategies, which were crucial to understanding the state's aims and its efforts to promote the growth and global expansion of the industry. It then investigates whether the strategies have improved Chinese enterprises' competitiveness and are responsible for such vigorous growth and expansion. It then discusses the challenges the strategies faced in the emergence of the GPN.

The mechanism of China's 'attracting in' and 'walking out' strategies in the ICT industry

Chapter 4 has shown that, by the end of the 1970s, China had recovered from internal chaos and ended its confrontation with the West to look outwards. The dynamism of the newly industrialized East Asian countries (NIEs) undoubtedly made the Chinese leaders reconsider the idea of introducing a market-oriented and export-led development approach. After the 1978 Plenum, there was consensus among the Chinese leaders that international and domestic exchange through markets was necessary for economic development. They believed that China could benefit from utilizing foreign capital for production, by increasing its foreign exchange reserves and by gaining technologies and management knowledge through 'opening up' (Deng 1993). The highly self-reliant policy of the Mao era was accordingly replaced with one that emphasized economic cooperation. The earliest development of foreign investment was geographically concentrated and institutionally discrete. A dual governing system was established, separating foreign matters from the domestic economy. Foreign entry to the domestic market was highly restricted (see Chapter 4).

Jiang Zeming (the former MEI minister) recognized that this highly controlled trade and investment regime prevented the ICT industry from gaining from technology spillover effects and forming the start-up basis for production. He argued that capital- and technology-intensive industries such as the electronics industry could not be established on the basis of developing countries' own capabilities. Countries such as Brazil and India, which focused on across-the-board import substitution, experienced many difficulties in increasing their foreign reserves. Their capabilities were too weak to develop new products and they had to import costly technologies and equipment for production. Conversely, the East Asian 'tigers' had switched to an export-oriented strategy and achieved great success. Jiang argued that China's ICT industry was still an inward-oriented industry as its total exports accounted for only 10 per cent of the total industrial output. This would put China in a similar situation to Brazil and India and drain China's precious foreign reserves in acquiring imported technology and equipment (Jiang 1993). During his term of office at the Ministry of the Electronics Industry, he launched a set of more liberal trade and investment policies, namely the 'attracting in' and 'walking out' strategies, based on Deng's 'open door' policy at the national level. These strategies were in fact China's leaders' logical reactions to China's own overall economic circumstances. These strategies have worked in three unique ways, shaping the development of the ICT industry.

'Attracting in' and 'walking out' together formed the 'opening up' economic strategy to initiate the ICT industry

At the time the policy was launched, Chinese leaders explained that 'opening up' was intended to liberalize the domestic market while exploring foreign markets. Jiang Zemin, as the president in 1997, reiterated that 'attracting in' and 'walking out' were the two crucial components of the opening up policy and complements of each other (Jiang 1997). The country could not encourage foreign inputs to China's economy ('attracting in') without domestic outputs that simultaneously flowed out to the rest of the world ('walking out') (Jiang 1993). Although a small number of outward investments were made for political motives, the early implementation of the policy was largely about 'attracting in'.[2] This was mainly determined by China's economic and political circumstances at the time. In the early 1980s, China faced major crises simultaneously: energy shortages, a shortage of agricultural goods, and rising unemployment. To prevent the outbreak of crises, a structural reorientation reform policy was initiated in the hope of shifting resource allocation away from energy-intensive, heavy and military industries to labour-intensive light industries and agriculture. The reform took place at a time when market institutions were virtually absent. Macroeconomic imbalances frequently emerged and led to serious open inflation throughout the 1980s and early 1990s. Austerity policies were brought into play to restore the 'plan', cutting down the state budgetary investment as well as restraining aggregated consumption and the money supply (Naughton 1995). Given these unfavourable domestic economic conditions, state allocation of large shares of credit to the electronics industry was unfeasible even though China's leaders had a clear vision that involved promoting the industry. It thus differed from the 'picking winners' strategy of other developed countries described by Amsden (2001).

As minister of the electronics industry in the mid-1980s, Jiang argued that a relatively liberalized regime and financial incentives were necessary to 'attract in' FDI if the domestic economy was unable to provide substantial kick-start investment for the technological- and capital-intensive electronics industry. Table 6.1 shows that both the amount of capital investment and newly increased fixed capital fall significantly in the mid- to late 1980s, when austerity policies were launched to cool down the economy. Jiang reported that China's spending on basic industrial construction and R&D averaged about 1 per cent of the total value of the industrial output. He believed that the gap between China and the leading industrialized countries would become unbridgeable if the government could not keep up with the investment level that developed countries maintained, around 10 per cent of the value of their total industrial output. Jiang stressed that the selective introduction of FDI to develop this sector was particularly helpful to alter China's industrial production structure towards export-oriented labour-intensive light industries. The country could thus reveal its 'comparative advantage' in some sectors and accumulate foreign currency for technology imports. Moreover, China's trade and investment regime needed to be liberalized to enable 'learning by doing', especially when both internal technological and innovation capability, as well as resources, were absent.[3]

Based on the experience of the East Asian 'tigers', which had specialized in electronics, Jiang proposed to step into the international electronics market

Table 6.1 Completed electronics R&D projects, capital construction and newly increased fixed capital (millions of yuan) by the central government

Year	Number of completed projects	Capital construction	Newly increased fixed capital
1982	11	44.1	63.1
1983	14	35.6	36.5
1984	12	38.7	28.1
1985	7	53.3	33.4
1986	30	52.5	42.8
1987	31	54.0	33.1
1988	202	54.9	33.7
1989	0	13.1	11.0
1990	0	11.1	15.0
1991	68	18.9	11.1
1992	71	26.4	14.8
1993	17	76.3	52.3

Source: *Yearbook of the Electronics Industry*, various years.

through carrying out assembling and OEM activities for foreign firms (Jiang 1993; Li 1993). In the 1980s, the government began to introduce 'special economic zones' in order to provide market export-oriented institutions and preferential policies outside the plan system to attract and support FDI activities. After Deng had pushed forward a renewed reform agenda in 1992, special provisions and more liberal policies were made much more widely available for FDI (e.g. tax and tariff concessions, relaxation on business area and foreign exchange restriction, etc; see Appendix 2).

The main motivations of the policy were to use FDI 'to lay the foundation [of the ICT industry], bringing up the [technological, production and management] level', and to gain financing for production and marketing channels to the advanced economies (Wang 2001). China could then acquire or absorb technologies, management skills and marketing channels from developed countries, and eventually master a production capability to export its own internationally competitive electronics products in the same way as Japan caught up with the United States, and Korea and Taiwan took market share from Japan. The development logic of Chinese leaders was that a well-guided 'attracting in' strategy would stimulate the growth of indigenous production capability and in turn achieve the first step of 'walking out' for Chinese products: export growth.

The 'attracting in' and 'walking out' policies are an integral part of China's industrial strategy, intended to foster the competitiveness of Chinese multinationals

In contrast to its liberal market and trade reforms, China intended to pursue an industrial strategy similar to that of East Asian latecomers and centred on the development of high-tech industries. The ultimate goals of such a strategy were to regain China's historical status, to ensure economic and technological autonomy, and to be at the frontier of international competitiveness (see Chapters 3 and 4). The strategy has been selective, nationalistic and interventionist, and implied that the early 'attracting in' was a mixture of the import substitution and export promotion strategies. In the ICT sector, Jiang advocated strict import substitution of low- and medium-tech products such as consumer electronics during the early opening-up process. Conversely, at the high-intensive end of the industry, the government needed to introduce selectively those products which had spill-over effects and were difficult for domestic enterprises to produce. The aim was not to produce all such products initially, but to enable learning effects and build up indigenous capability (Jiang 1993). The MEI began to announce targeted areas in the ministerial 'five-year plan' (e.g. computers, integrated circuits, telecommunications equipment, software, etc.). However, China's self-financing 'dual use' science and technology programmes (e.g. the 863, 909 and 'Torch' programmes) had only limited success, neither producing substantial commercial spin-offs nor improving general capabilities to close the gap with the advanced countries in the industry (Suttmeier and Yao 2004). The Chinese leaders decided to liberalize domestic market access further in the hope of exchanging market access for newer and desirable technologies (*shichang huanjishu*).

To direct FDI into selected sectors following the national industrial planning, a regularly revised investment and trade guideline system was established in 1995. It publicized industrial investment priorities that had previously been kept internal, and thus for the first time promoted transparency. The guideline divided industries into four categories (encouraged, restricted, permitted and prohibited). It was assumed that in the 'encouraged' category joint ventures could upgrade technologies and labour-intensive industries and were therefore often given a warm reception, great freedom of control, and access to incentives. In 'restricted' sectors, foreign investors were required to demonstrate advantages that could not be perceived by Chinese officials. 'Permitted'-type sectors were those not included in the other two categories. The central authority reserved the right to reject any projects under any catalogues.

In the ICT/electronics industry, there was no prohibited sector but many restricted ones during the early stages of trade liberalization. For example, the 1995 catalogue largely reflected Jiang's mixed trade strategy, which focused on substituting low- and medium-tech consumer electronics and encouraging 'high-tech' production (see Appendix 2). A number of products, such as radios, tape recorders, video recorders and related components, television tube components, low-performance microcomputers, satellite components, etc., were restricted in order to provide shielding for domestic enterprises to expand. 'Encouraged' sectors were those that Chinese leaders felt the electronics industry had technological or financial difficulties in developing, such as semiconductors, new components, optical devices, high-performance computers, newly innovated TVs, visual devices and audio equipment, etc. *The Guideline Catalogue of Foreign Investment Industries* was revised in 1997, 2002 and 2004 according to the development priorities. Restricted and prohibited areas and trade barriers have been gradually reduced, to be consistent with the protocol of China's WTO accession.[4] After experiencing difficulties in obtaining advanced technologies in some targeted areas such as semiconductors, the government finally permitted wholly foreign-owned enterprises (WFOEs). It was hoped that new products at the high end of the industry could be manufactured in Chinese territory (see Chapter 7).

The ultimate aims of a more liberal 'attracting in' policy were still to capture a competitive cost advantage for export expansion, and, more ambitiously, to foster international competitiveness of domestic enterprises to move from the first step of 'walking out', exports, to the second step of outward investment. In the first stage, large, vertically integrated state-owned or state-controlled ICT enterprises, of the type associated with the Japanese/Korean model, were created to absorb 'attracted' technologies and to turn them swiftly over to large-scale production to achieve cost-comparative advantages over other international players (Ning 2007).[5] At the Sixteenth CCP Congress, in 2002, Jiang reiterated that China should utilize the opportunity of having joined the WTO to participate in global competition and technological cooperation so as to stimulate domestic economic growth through greater economic liberalization. To do so, China is in need of a few 'backbone' multinational enterprises (*gugan qiye*) with an international comparative advantage to 'walk out' of the country in terms of both export and outward investment, and to achieve a leap forward from the foreign-invested simple OEM activities to Chinese-sourced, -funded and -produced complex, technology-intensive ODM activities. Simultaneously, the government should attract and guide FDI to infrastructure, technology and capital-intensive as well as some service industries by removing restrictions on China's huge and tempting domestic market and by improving the legal and investment environment for foreign investors (Jiang 2002). Also, in the absence of large-scale privatization, 'attracting in' was used to foster a greater degree of competition than would have otherwise existed to improve the efficiency of domestic enterprises.

In the second stage, Chinese leaders began to encourage these large, 'capable' indigenous enterprises to engage in outward investment. Again at the Sixteenth CCP Congress in 2002, Jiang reiterated the importance of combining state-led outward investment with a trade expansion strategy to achieve national competitiveness (Jiang 2002). On the one hand, China's motivations were to access more directly technologies that foreign investors were reluctant to bring to China's territories, explore human and financial resources, and to obtain the material and energy resources that China is lacking from other developing countries. On the other, the second step of the 'walking out' of indigenous enterprises was thought to be for them to improve their exporting capabilities exports by enlarging their foreign markets to achieve greater scale economies, quickly improving exporting of the technological contents and building up their brand image and their overseas distributing, services and marketing channels.

To encourage firms to go abroad to set up R&D centres and JVs, or to merge with or acquire foreign firms, the government has relaxed its controls on restricted sectors: it has simplified approval procedures, provided free information services, abolished the foreign exchange requirement and backed Chinese firms with easily obtained bank loans. After seeing the limitations of the Japanese/Korean conglomerate models during the East Asian financial crisis, the government also decided to place some emphasis on small enterprises. It is expected that a group of ICT 'little giants' (*xiaojuren*) will grow in targeted niche markets to reduce the structural problems and to complete the domestic supply chain in order to support existing large enterprises (Wu 2003a). Small and private firms were not discouraged from 'walking out' but as yet have not been intensively promoted and heavily backed with easily obtainable bank loans by the state.

The 'attracting in' and 'walking out' strategies have remained focused on state ownership, owing to the transitional nature of the Chinese economy

The path of China's reform has featured gradual and partial changes, dualistic systems and decentralization (Naughton 1995). This reform affected the types of enterprises that participated in 'attracting in' and 'walking out'. In the early 1980s, state-owned enterprises (SOEs) were given sufficient autonomy to expand production above the plan. A 'dual' ownership structure was created to allow non-state enterprises to exist as buyers in support of the outside plan market channel for SOEs and as sellers to bring competition. They were permitted to expand but kept to a small scale to take over labour-intensive low-tech activities and to absorb surplus urban labour. Although China has not gone through a large-scale privatization of state assets, most traditional command-oriented wholly owned SOEs are being nibbled away at. In the late 1990s, large SOEs were gradually converted into 'modern market-oriented firms' (e.g. joint-stock companies and limited liability companies) with diversified financial resources and an 'autonomous' Western style of management (Wang 2001).

As is discussed on pages 99 and 106, China's leaders had to give strong political consideration towards the dual use and pillar high-tech industries, such as the ICT sector. A large percentage of state ownership was maintained in order to retain primary controlling shares in the industry. Many converted 'modern' enterprises in many ways have links with SOEs and strong ties with central and regional authorities. As Chapter 5 shows, totally state-controlled ICT enterprises accounted for an average of 73 per cent of the domestic assets, while private firms increased as a proportion of the total from 5 per cent to 15 per cent in the period 2003–2005. Considered together with small-scale industrial output, export as well as technological capability and political support for private enterprises, the 'walking out' strategy was primarily designed for SOEs and SCEs. The motivations for these Chinese 'pillar' enterprises might appear very similar to what is suggested in the theoretical models of firms' internationalization in terms of cutting down transaction costs, expanding markets, accessing new technologies and market channels, but their initiative of inward or outward investment has remained highly state-oriented (rather than enterprise-oriented, as was the case in Korea) throughout the whole 'walking out' process.[6]

On the whole, all China's strategies are about achieving international competitiveness through large, vertically integrated, state-controlled ICT 'backbone' enterprises that are capable of operating worldwide with cutting-edge technologies and dominating the world market from the upstream to downstream of the ICT value chain. Yet the question is, has this highly state-led approach 'attracted' desirable technologies to improve the technological capability of domestic enterprises, and assisted Chinese enterprises to 'walk out' of the country with true competitiveness, as China's leaders expected?

The outcome of 'attracting in' and 'walking out' in the ICT sector

Regardless of whether these two strategies have achieved technological upgrading and improved China's international competitiveness, they do appear to have been very successful in quantitative terms. This section documents the tremendous growth of China's ICT industry.

The dramatic growth of 'attracted' capital resources

The implementation of a more liberal 'attracting in' policy led to a sharp rise in FDI, which has become the industry's main investment source and reduced pressure on the tight state budget since the mid-1990s.[7] Chinese statistics demonstrate that, similar to the overall growing trend of FDI inflow, the actually utilized FDI in ICT soared to US$345 million in 1995 and US$931 million in 1997. Although exhibiting a decline during the Asian financial crisis, the figure remained high, reaching US$1.44 billion when China joined the WTO in 2000, and a record US$8.6 billion in 2004 (see Table 6.2). Chinese officials estimated that the total value of FDI was more than twice that of government investment in the industry, 180 billion yuan, in the period 1990–2002. By 2005, the accumulated value of FDI had reached more than US$100 billion, and 90 per cent of the top 500 IT enterprises listed on *Fortune* have invested in China (Information Technology Yearbook 2005). Measured by total assets, FIE took a 33.5 per cent share of the industry in 1997 and a 67.9 per cent share in 2005. The total number of firms also increased by nearly nine times, from 753 in 1997 to 6,480 in 2005 (see Table 5.3). The dramatic growth appear to have been the result of the ongoing international outsourcing movement and China's 'attracting in' strategy, which facilitated the relocation of foreign business from other East Asian countries. China's openness in the electronics industry was much higher than Japan's and Korea's had been during their development in the 1980s and 1990s.

China's emergence in the world ICT industry: export 'walking out'

Along with the massive inflow of 'attracted' FDI has come the incredible growth in industrial output and the success of the first step in Chinese manufactured exports' 'walking out'. During 2003–2005, China remained the world's third largest ICT producer, with an increase in industrial output from US$14.7 billion to US$20.1 billion. These figures represent 13.1 per cent and 15.1 per cent respectively of the

Table 6.2 China's actually utilized ICT foreign investment, 1995–2004

Year	Actually utilized FDI (millions of US$)
1995	345
1996	–
1997	931
1998	836
1999	447
2000	1,437
2001	1,343
2002	–
2003[a]	4,000
2004[a]	8,637

Sources: Information Technology Yearbook and Yearbook of the Electronics Industry, 1986–2006

Note: Exact figures may vary from time to time due to frequent changes in the statistical methods used by the Ministry of the Information Industry. Consistent official data have never been published. The figures are in millions of US dollars at an exchange rate of 8.2 yuan to the dollar. [a]From available figures announced by ministerial officials in the yearbook. Figures before 2000 may include only the electronics manufacturing industry.

world's total ICT output. China has been closing the gap between its world output share and that of Japan, the world's second largest ICT producer, from 2.1 per cent to 0.6 per cent and the gap with that of the United States, the largest, from 12.4 per cent to 5.5 per cent (see Figure 6.1). In terms of exports, China overtook Japan and the European Union (15 countries) in 2003 to become the world's second-largest ICT-exporting country (see Figure 6.2). In 2004, China's ICT exports soared to US$180 billion and it took the lead over the United States (US$149 billion) to become the biggest global ICT exporter. China's total share in international ICT trade (exports and imports) has increased rapidly from less than US$35 billion in 1996 to US$329 billion in 2004. The slowdown in China's export growth from 44 per cent to 18 per cent after the dotcom bubble in 2000 and the 9/11 attacks in the United States seemed to be temporary. Chinese ICT exports grew by 55 per cent from 2002 to 2003 and by 46 per cent from 2003 to 2004, at an overall annual growth rate of 38 per cent since 1996. Despite a short period of trade deficit of around US$3 billion from 1999 to 2001, China's exports exceeded its imports by about US$3 billion in 2002, and in 2004 China ran a trade surplus more than 10 times greater than that of 2002 (US$32 billion).

Looking at the extent of China's penetration into regional markets also shows the startling export growth of the Chinese ICT industry. In 2000, China's ICT exports (of office and telecom equipment) represented 38.5 per cent of the total market share in North America, 29.5 per cent in the Asian countries and 23.7 per cent in Europe. Affected by the economic downturn of the United States and other East Asian countries as well as by international pressures to revalue the yuan, China's market share in these two regions shrank slightly in 2004, but is still growing at a fast pace. China's annual growth rate was almost 10 times more than the world's average, at 38 per cent, 39 per cent, 43 per cent and 53 per cent in each principal market in the period 2000–2004. Fastest was the growth of China's ICT export in the European market, reaching 86 per cent in 2003 and 53 per cent in 2004 (Table 6.3). Taking a specific country as an example, China accounted for only 9.7 per cent of US imports, while Japan had a share of 18.7 per cent, Mexico

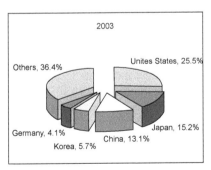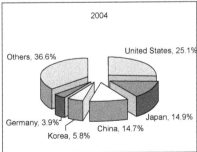

Figure 6.1 Share of ICT output of the top five world economies: comparison of 2003 with 2004.

Source: Yearbook of the Electronics Industry 2005.

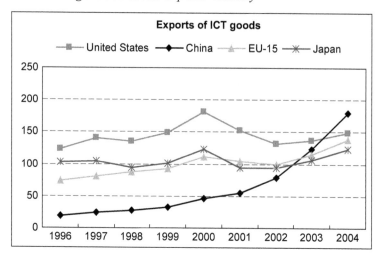

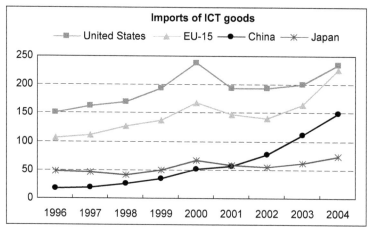

Figure 6.2 Imports and exports of ICT products by major countries, 1996–2004.

Source: OECD 2006, ITS database.

Note: Data for the European Union exclude intra-EU trade. (billions of US dollars)

11.7 per cent, Malaysia 9.4 per cent, Taiwan 9.0 per cent and Korea 8.7 per cent in 1999. Since 2002, China has steadily increased its share, reaching 18.1 per cent to become the largest ICT exporter to the United States. Conversely, the shares of all other countries have declined.[8]

Improved production and increased technological sophistication of exports

The qualitative restructuring of Chinese exports equally demonstrates China's growing competitiveness in the ICT sector. The more liberal 'attracting in' strategy

Table 6.3 Exports of office and telecom equipment by principal region and economy, 2004

	Value (billion dollars)	Share (%)						
		Region's exports		World exports		Annual percentage change		
	2004	2000	2004	2000	2004	2000–04	2003	2004
World Total	1,133.8	–	–	–	–	4%	12%	19%
China to								
World	171.8	–	–	4.5%	15.2%	41%	56%	46%
North America	61.1	38.5%	35.6%	1.7%	5.4%	38%	57%	54%
Asia	47.3	29.5%	27.6%	1.3%	4.2%	39%	42%	43%
Europe	43.2	23.7%	25.2%	1.1%	3.8%	43%	86%	53%
All other regions	20.1	8.3%	11.7%	0.4%	1.8%	53%	43%	18%

Source: WTO statistics 2005.

Note: Office and telecom equipment includes electronics data processing and office equipment, telecommunication equipment, and integrated circuits.

has been rewarded with an increase in access to foreign technologies. Many global leading MNEs have been encouraged to set up R&D centres or labs in China. Chinese statistics show that there were over 750 foreign-funded R&D centres by 2006, the majority of which are in the ICT industry (MOC 2006).[9] Reliable data on R&D-related FDI ICT activities in China are not readily available, but Chinese press reports have estimated the number of ICT R&D centres at between 120 and 400 (Walsh 2005). Research conducted by Tsinghua University on 466 foreign R&D centres based in China shows that by 2004, 52 per cent were ICT related (Zedtwitz 2007).

The composition of China's ICT industrial output and export has consequently shifted from basic low-value-added simple consumer electronics to complicated high-end production (see Table 6.4). Computers and related sectors has remained the largest output share since 2002, accounting for more than 30 per cent of the industry's total. In parallel, the shares of televisions, telecommunications equipment

Table 6.4 Composition of China's ICT production (major sectors, selected years)

	2004	2003	2002	1999	1998	1996	1995
Telecommunications equipment	18.1%	19.4%	21.0%	23%	23%	18%	28%
Radar equipment	0.4%	0.4%	0.5%	4%	7%	7%	6%
Broadcast television equipment	0.3%	0.3%	0.3%	23%	25%	26%	28%
Computer equipment and related	32.5%	31.0%	23.7%	15%	14%	12%	8%
Consumer audio/video equipment	13.8%	15.7%	13.6%	–	–	–	–
Electronic devices	11.6%	10.2%	0.3%	13%	13%	14%	16%
Electronic components	13.1%	13.2%	22.8%	13%	13%	17%	18%
Electronic instrument and meters	0.6%	0.5%	0.3%	–	–	–	–

Source: Information Technology Yearbook, various years.

and components have shrunk, except for audio and video consumer goods. Correspondingly, China's export structure has become increasingly sophisticated. Computers and related equipment constituted the majority of the ICT exports, rising sharply from 29 per cent in 1996 to 46 per cent in 2004. Of the computers sold in the world, 23.6 per cent are now made in China. The country also exported 27.5 million laptops (60.9 per cent of China's total computer export) in 2004, surpassing Taiwan as the world's largest laptop producer. Similarly, it has captured the largest share of the global TV market, representing 55 per cent of the world total and growing by 22 per cent annually. China also produced 35.1 per cent of the world's mobile phones and was the largest producing and sales country in the world in 2004 (Information Technology Yearbook 2005).

The rise of Chinese ICT multinationals: enterprises 'walking out'

Finally, a few Chinese multinationals seem to be rising in the world market and 'walking out' of the country to set up business abroad. China's outward FDI has dramatically increased. China's total outward flow in 2004 almost doubled the amount in 2003, reaching US$5.50 billion, and the cumulative figure by the end of 2004 was US$44.78 billion. The Ministry of Commerce predicts that China's outward investment will continue to grow at an annual rate of more than 22 per cent in the next five years and exceed US$60 billion by 2010 (Xinhua News Agency 2005). The pattern of the outward investment simultaneously shifted from acquisitions in the energy sector to manufacturing, commercial services (including R&D services) and the wholesaling and retailing sectors. In 2005, these three sectors took the majority share of the total outward investment activities, accounting for 40.3 per cent, 22.8 per cent and 22.6 per cent respectively, while the energy sector has declined from 32.7 per cent, the largest, to 16.8 per cent, the fourth most important (China Statistical Yearbook 2003–2005).

Breakdowns of the composition by industrial sectors are not available, but the Ministry of Commerce (MOC) confirms that most of the manufacturing activities are related to the ICT industry, and an OECD report shows that US$1.1 billion was spent on acquisition in the ICT services sector (MOC 2006; OECD 2006b). The MII announced that a quarter of China's top 100 ICT firms had already set up foreign subsidiaries by 2004. The total number of Chinese-invested R&D centres in advanced countries reached 20.[10] In order to access foreign markets and technologies swiftly and directly, many Chinese enterprises were encouraged by the state to follow the global trend of cross-border M&A activities to take over foreign firms. For example, China's premier PC company, Lenovo, acquired IBM's PC business for US$1.75 billion by 2005. China's TCL TV giant purchased the German-based Schneider Electronics in 2002, and then merged with the French-based Thomson to take over its TV business. In 2004, it joined with Alcatel to take over its mobile phone manufacturing business. BOE spent US$380 million acquiring Hyundai's TFT-LCD in 2003, hoping to reach global markets though Korea's network and to gain advanced LCD technologies.

All these impressive achievements seem to imply that the 'attracting in' strategy has successfully introduced much sought-after foreign capital, and, as Chinese officials expected, has laid a 'foundation' for the global expansion of the industry. Given the assumption that China has taken over some consumer electronics markets, ministerial officials have become more convinced that the Japanese/Korean-style industrial policies will enable the industry to leapfrog to a 'higher stage of development' and achieve the global technological leadership position before 2020.[11] China's products will soon replace those of Western MNEs, and Chinese technological standards will be used all over the world. But has China really become a technological and export powerhouse? A close inspection of China's ICT production, export and technological activities reveals a very different picture.

The illusion of China's ICT 'walking out'

Trade structure of the 'walking out'

China's ICT trade and production structure includes a large proportion of industrial growth that was not generated by Chinese enterprises but overwhelmingly by foreign-invested enterprises (FIEs). At the beginning of China's renewed reform movement, FIEs contributed 38 per cent of China's total ICT exports, while Chinese domestic enterprises still played an importing role, representing 62 per cent of the total in 1993. As Figure 6.3 indicates, since 1994 FIEs have surpassed all domestic enterprises in terms of exports. After China's WTO accession, FIEs' share of exports soared to 89 per cent and accounted for 92 per cent of the total in 2004. Looking more closely at the long-term trend of share changes by ownership, WFOEs instead of joint ventures (JVs) became the main drivers of China's ICT exports, especially after China's WTO entry (Figure 6.4). WFOEs were responsible for nearly 66.8 per cent of the total exports in 2004.

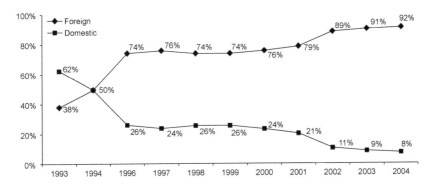

Figure 6.3 Percentage of China's ICT exports by foreign and domestic enterprises.

Sources: Information Technology Yearbook and *Yearbook of the Electronics Industry*, various years.

Note: data for comparative analysis in 1995 is unavailable.

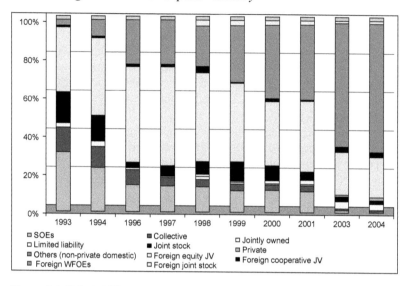

Figure 6.4 China's ICT export by type of enterprise, 1993–2004.

Source: Information Technology Yearbook, 1993–2005.

Note: Data for comparative analysis in 1995 and 2002 are unavailable. The figure covers only those enterprises whose output share makes up more than 1 per cent of the total output for the year.

In contrast, the share of domestic-funded firms shrank dramatically from 21 per cent in 2001 to 14 per cent of the industry's total in 2004. In the same period, SOEs' share of exports declined from 10.9 per cent to only 0.7 per cent. Although increasing sharply in export value from 85 million yuan in 1996 to 19.7 billion yuan in 2004, private enterprises never accounted for more than 1.4 per cent of the total. These figures show the dominant position of enterprises under full foreign control in both China's ICT trade and and its ICT production. As WFOEs have strong incentives to protect their technologies, this trend also implies that there is a decreasing diffusion of technological spillover to domestic firms. Moreover, FIEs were also big importers, representing 72 per cent of the total imports in 2002 and 82 per cent in 2004. FIEs' net exports reached US$29.6 billion, in 2004 and only 16.7 per cent of their exports' total value. By contrast, domestic firms ran a trade deficit. They contributed 16 per cent in 2003 and 14 per cent of the total exports in 2004 while importing 23 per cent and 18 per cent of the total imports respectively in those years (Table 6.5).

Production structure of the 'walking out'

Through lack of technological and managerial capabilities, Chinese domestic firms are far behind FIEs not only in exports, but also in industrial output. FIEs produced the largest share of industrial output in the 1990s (see Figure 6.5).

Table 6.5 Accumulated exports and imports of ICT products by type of enterprise, 2002–2004

Exports	Value ($ billion)			Share of the total (%)			Percentage increase[a]		Imports	Value ($ billion)			Share of the total (%)			Percentage increase		Net exports		
	2002	2003	2004	2002	2003	2004	2003	2004		2002	2003	2004	2002	2003	2004	2003	2004	2002	2003	2004
Foreign-funded enterprises																				
WFOEs	48.60	84.50	131.00	53%	59%	63%	74%	55%	WFOEs	40.70	75.80	112.00	48%	57%	62%	86%	48%	7.90	8.63	18.80
Equity JVs	21.90	31.00	42.90	24%	22%	21%	41%	39%	Equity JVs	18.10	23.90	33.30	21%	18%	18%	32%	40%	3.84	7.12	9.60
Cooperative JVs	2.98	3.51	4.09	3%	2%	2%	18%	17%	Cooperative JVs	2.11	2.68	2.91	2%	2%	2%	27%	9%	0.87	0.83	1.18
Sub-total	73.50	119.00	178.00	80%	84%	86%	62%	50%	Sub-total	60.90	102.00	148.00	72%	77%	82%	68%	45%	12.61	16.60	29.60
Domestic-funded enterprises																				
State-owned enterprises	15.40	16.50	19.50	17%	12%	9%	7%	18%	State-owned enterprises	21.10	23.00	23.50	25%	17%	13%	9%	2%	–5.72	–6.53	–4.09
Collectives	1.97	2.82	3.59	2%	2%	2%	43%	27%	Collectives	0	1.85	2.00	0%	1%	1%	–	8%	1.97	0.97	1.59
Private enterprises	0	3.83	6.45	0%	3%	3%	246%	68%	Private enterprises	1.66	4.89	6.89	2%	4%	4%	195%	41%	–1.66	–1.06	–0.44
Others	1.11	0	0	1%	0%	0%	0%	0%	Others	1.41	0.06	1.00	2%	0%	1%	–96%	1,567%	–0.30	–0.06	–1.00
Sub-total	18.50	23.10	29.50	20%	16%	14%	0%	27%	Sub-total	24.20	29.80	33.40	28%	23%	18%	23%	12%	–5.71	–6.68	–3.94

Source: Information Technology Yearbook 2003–2005.

Notes: [a]average increase for total imports/exports. The percentages of exports shown here may be different from those in Figure 6.4 because of different statistical methods used by the MII.

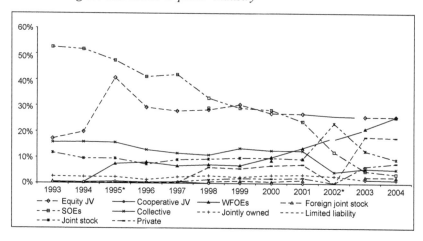

Figure 6.5 Share of output by type of ICT enterprise, 1993–2005.

Source: Calculated from the Information Technology Yearbook 1993–2005.

Note: *data for comparative analysis in 1995 and 2002 is unavailable.

Total output share by FIEs soared to 44 per cent in 1996. They surpassed the total of all domestic firms in 2001 and generated 75 per cent of China's total ICT output. This figure shows that China's whole ICT 'walking out' strategy has relied heavily on FIEs to produce exports.[12] Conversely, SOEs' share shrank steadily from 49 per cent in 1993 to 1.2 per cent in 2005 as a result of the

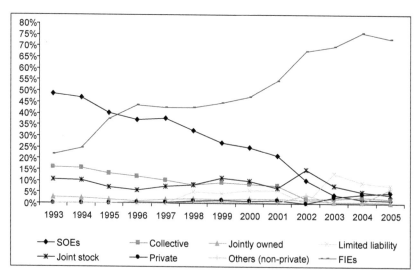

Figure 6.6 Percentage of domestic market share by type of enterprise, 1993–2004.

Source: Calculated from the Information Technology Yearbook, various years.

'modern enterprise conversion'. Although they rose significantly, private firms' share of output never reached more than 1 per cent before 2000 and accounted for 4.9 per cent in 2005.

With superior technological and management capabilities, FIEs have undoubtedly put more intensive pressure on China's domestic firms than policymakers intended. This also shows that China's big business strategy was unable to improve the international competitiveness of domestic firms or to help them move towards the same competitive activities as those engaged in by the global leaders. Neither could domestic enterprises control the greater part of China's domestic market. FIEs have already become more dominant in the domestic market (see Figure 6.6). The conversion of traditional SOEs has led to a steady increase in the domestic market shares of JSCs, LLCs and private enterprises from less than 20 per cent in 1993 to 34 per cent in 2004. Private firms rose dramatically from almost no share in the early 1990s to 7.5 per cent in 2004, although still remaining small compared with all other domestic firms. However, during the same period FIEs increased their share from less than 20 per cent in the early 'attracting in' stages to 53 per cent in 2003, and made up 57 per cent of the total domestic industrial ICT sales in 2004. As Table 6.6 indicates, the profit to sales ratio of the industry as a whole was as low as 4.7 per cent on average. The lower profit to sales ratio and larger percentage of exports of FIEs implies that their foreign trade activities are taking place mainly within the MNEs themselves.

Technological structure of the 'walking out'

Both trade and production statistics indicate that China's 'walking out' phenomenon has relied heavily on FIEs. The 'attracting in' and big business strategies are failing to achieve the goal of China's industrial policy to improve the competitiveness of domestic firms. Virtually no domestic enterprise is capable of controlling China's own export and production networks, or developing competitive technological sources. China may benefit from FIEs in terms of acquiring basic technologies rapidly to improve the make-up of exports and generate positive upgrading impacts through the training of workforces in the long term. However, it does not mean that they could help China quickly achieve a position of technological leadership. A closer look at China's ICT technological trade structure indicates that ICT exports still encompass a large share of labour-intensive manufacturing activities. Throughout the period 1997–2004, China's exports comprised about 70 per cent FDI-led import processing activities, except in 2001, which was affected by the world ICT industrial downturn (see Table 6.7). These figures suggest that local value added in relation to the export process is in fact very low. Chinese statistical data show that average added value of the sales value in the industry has remained around 21.5 per cent (see Table 6.8). These figures suggest that about 80 per cent of the value added content of China's ICT products for export is created elsewhere in the world.

Table 6.6 Percentage of profit over sales by type of enterprise, 1993–2004

Year	Foreign-funded					Domestic-funded								Total for the industry
	Equity JVs	Cooperative JVs	WFOEs	Joint-stock	Sub-total	SOEs	Collective	Jointly owned	Limited liability	Joint-stock	Private (non-private)	Others	Sub-total	
1993	6.0%	8.0%	3.8%	–	5.9%	2.5%	2.2%	2.4%	3.6%	8.0%	23.7%	14.4%	3.3%	3.9%
1994	5.9%	4.1%	3.9%	–	5.7%	2.4%	1.6%	0.9%	2.1%	8.2%	5.4%	6.6%	3.0%	3.7%
1995	–	–	–	–	–	–	–	–	–	–	–	–	–	–
1996	5.0%	3.8%	11.8%	–	6.7%	2.7%	2.6%	4.6%	–	5.4%	5.1%	-2.6%	3.0%	4.8%
1997	4.2%	2.2%	9.8%	–	5.5%	2.3%	4.0%	5.0%	–	5.4%	9.0%	19.2%	3.2%	4.3%
1998	–	–	–	–	–	–	–	–	–	–	–	–	–	–
1999	5.7%	5.2%	8.0%	7.3%	6.4%	2.8%	7.1%	5.7%	5.2%	7.3%	7.0%	2.4%	4.9%	5.6%
2000	7.3%	3.7%	6.1%	6.9%	6.8%	4.1%	8.3%	5.4%	7.1%	7.6%	9.0%	14.4%	6.0%	6.4%
2001	4.8%	10.0%	6.3%	7.3%	5.5%	3.7%	7.8%	6.1%	4.7%	5.5%	7.7%	3.3%	5.2%	5.4%
2002	–	–	–	–	–	2.3%	4.5%	5.1%	–	5.7%	–	6.4%	4.8%	4.3%
2003	4.8%	2.6%	3.2%	8.7%	3.9%	3.1%	4.0%	8.6%	4.7%	5.3%	5.7%	1.4%	4.8%	4.1%
2004	4.2%	1.4%	4.1%	13.1%	4.3%	3.5%	3.2%	8.4%	3.2%	4.5%	4.9%	2.2%	3.9%	4.2%

Source: Information Technology Yearbook, various years.

Table 6.7 China's ICT exporting activities, 1997–2004 (%)

	1997	1998	1999	2000	2001	2002	2003	2004
Processing imports[a]	70.0	66.9	66.0	70.0	43.5	72.6	74.7	74.2
Processing materials[b]	20.0	22.7	23.0	20.0	11.5	17.2	15.0	14.8
Ordinary trade[c]	8.0	7.6	9.2	8.3	34.5	7.7	7.6	7.7
Others	2.0	2.9	1.8	1.9	10.6	2.5	2.8	3.3

Source: Information Technology Yearbook 1998–2005.

Notes: [a]processing with imported materials; [b]processing with customer's materials; [c]exports made by enterprises with foreign trading rights.

Looking at trade structure by specific products leads to the same conclusion. The industry relied heavily on foreign imports of key components and advanced equipment for production. Component imports have noticeably increased from less than 50 per cent before 2000 to 65 per cent of the total ICT imports in 2004. Apart from meeting domestic demand, many of these high value added parts went essentially to those sectors in which China took leads in, in terms of export and production. For example, China ran trade deficits of US$50 billion in integrated circuits, US$7 billion in semiconductors for producing mobiles and computers, as well as the small number of tubes for television production. In short, while China become the world's largest ICT-exporting country (US$180 billion), China's imports contained overwhelmingly parts and components for producing its exports (US$149 billion). Net exports were only US$31 billion in 2004 (Figure 6.7). Principal export products are either mature, standardized, non-differentiated and price-sensitive products (e.g. DVD players, laser printers, LCDs and digital cameras) or parts and peripherals for finished ICT products (see Table 6.9). Firms producing these goods are competing on a very low margin where costs of production, especially labour costs, are crucial.

All these figures imply that China's ICT 'walking out' is of a low-tech nature; domestic enterprises are far from being the leaders in innovation and still rely heavily on foreign supply of core technologies and components for production. China's ICT industrial growth should thus be seen as China seizing opportunities in the global value chain where labour costs matter most, rather than as head-to-head competition with leading MNEs.

'Walking out' at the firm level

The illusory nature of 'walking out' is further confirmed by firm-level data. China's MNEs remain small, although they have established subsidiaries abroad and taken over some foreign businesses. The OECD ICT report shows that none of China's MNEs has so far been listed in the top 250 companies in the world (OECD 2006b).[13] China's largest PC maker, Lenovo, quadrupled its turnover to US$13 billion in 2006 after taking over IBM's PC business. However, in terms of

Table 6.8 Percentage of value added over sales by type of enterprise, 1993–2004

Year	Foreign-funded					Domestic-funded								Average for the Industry
	Equity JVs	Cooperative JVs	WFOEs	Joint-stock	Foreign average	SOEs	Collective	Jointly owned	Limited liability	Joint-stock	Private	Others (non-private)	Domestic average	
1993	24.4%	23.2%	38.7%	–	25.1%	26.0%	29.6%	27.5%	35.2%	23.0%	37.0%	33.2%	26.3%	26.0%
1994	19.8%	25.3%	25.1%	–	20.2%	19.6%	25.1%	17.3%	19.9%	26.0%	30.9%	31.2%	21.5%	21.2%
1995	19.7%	22.7%	40.7%	–	23.0%	21.8%	23.2%	28.0%	–	25.4%	43.4%	25.5%	22.8%	22.9%
1996	20.7%	20.7%	33.5%	–	24.0%	23.6%	23.7%	26.4%	–	24.9%	44.0%	15.2%	23.9%	24.0%
1997	23.1%	31.3%	20.4%	–	22.5%	23.0%	24.4%	15.8%	–	27.3%	30.7%	33.3%	23.7%	23.1%
1998	21.5%	13.8%	35.1%	13.5%	24.2%	23.3%	26.2%	22.8%	25.6%	19.4%	40.1%	22.1%	23.6%	23.9%
1999	21.8%	24.3%	24.2%	5.6%	22.0%	22.3%	25.1%	33.6%	25.3%	24.5%	30.1%	39.5%	24.3%	23.2%
2000	20.9%	13.3%	19.3%	7.4%	19.8%	21.0%	25.7%	25.6%	26.9%	20.2%	35.7%	0.9%	23.0%	21.4%
2001	19.5%	28.1%	22.6%	9.8%	20.5%	20.2%	21.7%	30.2%	26.9%	21.7%	29.0%	31.6%	22.4%	21.4%
2002														10.3%
2003	20.4%	19.6%	20.8%	19.9%	20.6%	19.6%	19.0%	19.0%	20.3%	18.6%	19.0%	18.9%	19.4%	20.3%
2004	20.1%	26.3%	21.4%	20.8%	21.2%	24.1%	17.8%	29.0%	22.7%	23.5%	25.5%	–	18.2%	20.4%
Means	17.3%	18.8%	21.9%	6.4%	18.2%	18.2%	19.3%	20.6%	14.0%	19.3%	27.4%	18.2%	18.6%	19.3%

Source: Calculated from the Information Technology Yearbook, various years.

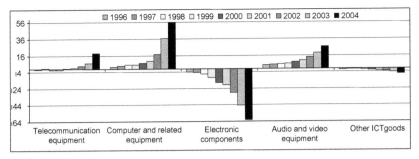

Figure 6.7 China's trade balance by ICT goods categories, 1996–2004.

Source: the Information Technology Yearbook, various years.

turnover it was still one-ninth the size of IBM (US$91 billion) and one-fifth the size of Dell (US$55 billion) in 2006. Haier had a turnover of only US$0.7 billion and Huawei of US$3.8 billion in 2004. Furthermore, contrary to the intended outcome of the 'walking out' strategy, China's top ICT exporters are not these Chinese MNEs at all (see Table 6.10). In 2005, Hongfujin Precision, a wholly owned subsidiary of Taiwanese Foxconn, was China's largest ICT exporter and the second largest exporter across all industries for the third successive year. It had exports of US$14.5 billion, seven times more than Huawai (US$2.0 billion). The second was Fengda Shanghai Computer, a wholly owned subsidiary of Taiwanese Quanta, which had exports of US$11.5 billion, ten times more than Lenovo (Lenovo IPC US$1.3 billion and Lenovo group US$0.1 billion). Coming in third was ASUSTeK Computer, wholly owned by ASUS Taiwan, with exports of US$6.2 billion. This is followed by Motorola with US$6.4 billion and Samsung with US$3.5 billion in 2005.[14]

Taking into consideration trade, technological capacity and total sales of domestic and foreign-funded firms, the Chinese government's attempt to build globally competitive large ICT firms through reforming SOEs is falling short of its goal. Currently, China is still competing on the lower-end value chain where labour costs are vital and domestic firms are suffering from a lack of technological capabilities.

Challenges for 'attracting in' and 'walking out' in taking a lead in the world ICT industry

The dramatic rise of the East Asian tigers has shown that there were great possibilities for fast-developing countries to establish their own high-tech industries in the second half of the twentieth century. China's 'attracting in' and 'walking out' strategies, which built on the experiences of the newly industrialized East Asian economies, have not substantially improved China's competitiveness in the ICT industry, nor put it in a position to catch up with the leading countries. Even so, following the path of the East Asian tigers, China has been able to produce and export large volumes inexpensively during its early development stages.[15] It might be

Table 6.9 Top ten Chinese ICT import and export items by four-digit HS code, 2004 (in units of US$10,000)

Main exports		Main imports	
8471 Automatic data processing machines, magnetic readers, etc; computer hardware	59.9	8542 Integrated circuits	61.7
8473 Parts etc. for typewriters and other office machines; computer accessories	24.0	8471 Automatic data processing machines, magnetic readers, etc; computer hardware	14.5
8525 Transmission apparatus for radio telephony/telegraphy/broadcasting, television	21.8	8473 Parts etc. for typewriters and other office machines; computer accessories	14.4
8529 Parts for television, radio and radar apparatus	2.0	8529 Parts for television, radio and radar apparatus	12.4
8542 Integrated circuits	11.2	8541 Semiconductor devices	9.8
8517 Electrical apparatus for line telephony or telegraphy telephone sets, teleprinters, modems, facsimile machines	7.7	8534 Printed circuits	5.1
8521 Video recording or reproducing apparatus	7.4	8525 Transmission apparatus for radio telephony/telegraphy/broadcasting, television	4.0
8528 Television receivers video monitors, video projection television receivers	5.5	8532 Electrical capacitors, fixed, variable or adjustable: parts thereof	3.8
8522 Parts and accessories for sound/video recording or reproducing equipment of 8519–8521	4.2	8517 Electrical apparatus for line telephony or telegraphy telephone sets, teleprinters, modems, facsimile machines	3.5
8534 Printed circuits	3.8	8522 Parts and accessories for sound/video recording or reproducing equipment of 8519–8521	3.0

Source: OECD (2006b).

Table 6.10 China's top ICT exporting firms, 2005

Rank in the ICT industry	Rank in all Industries	Enterprises	Exports (US$10,000)	Imports (US$10,000)	Net (US$10,000)	Type of enterprise	Country
1	2	Hongfujin Precision Shenzhen Ltd	1,447,417	1,269,280	178,137	WFOS	Taiwan
2	3	Fengda Shanghai Computer Ltd	1,145,468	531,221	614,247	WFOS	Taiwan
3	6	ASUSTeK Computer (Suzhou) Ltd	621,127	479,597	141,530	WFOE	Taiwan
4	7	Motorola China Ltd	645,099	235,764	409,335	WFOE	US
5	8	Sumsang (Suzhou) Semiconductor Ltd	353,789	432,019	−78,230	WFOE	Korea
6	9	China Potevio (Putian) Information Industry Group Company	434,974	274,792	160,182	Large group	China
7	10	Yingshunda (Subsidiary of Inventec Groups) Technology Ltd	419,928	234,318	185,610	WFOE	Taiwan
8	12	Youda AUO Suzhou Photoelectric Ltd	183,075	345,274	−162,199	WFOE	Taiwan
9	13	Nokia China Investment Ltd	355,625	167,487	188,138	WFOE	Finland
10	14	Intel (Shanghai) Ltd	249,013	240,318	8,695	WFOE	US
a	49	China Electronics Import and Export Group Company	123,955	99,411	24,544	Large group	China
a	51	Haier Group Company	128,593	88,775	39,818	Large group	China
a	63	TCL Group Stock Ltd	101,286	78,872	22,414	Large group	China
a	99	Lenovo International IT Shenzhen Ltd	136,050	18	136,032	Large group	China

Source: MOC 2006.

Notes: WFOE, wholly foreign-owned enterprise; WFOS, wholly foreign-owned subsidiaries. [a]Selected Chinese large ICT firms.

assumed that Chinese domestic enterprises will soon progress to dominate global markets, accumulate technological and operation experiences and eventually leapfrog global leading firms. One might think that Chinese officials were right in anticipating that wholly Chinese-innovated, -sourced and -produced branded products will soon 'walk out' of the country and dominate the global market as industrial leaders. Yet the global ICT industry itself has evolved significantly. China's industrial policy may well be said to provide the necessary conditions for the start-up of the ICT industry, but the strategy has turned out to be very inflexible in responding to changing international competition. China now faces a very different global environment and set of opportunities in today's competitive ICT industry compared with those experienced by NIEs.

'Network controlling capability': the new meaning of ICT competition in the era of the global business revolution

When the East Asian ICT latecomers competed in the international market, their foreign incumbents were relatively stable and focusing on manufacturing activities. NIE companies could target the same activities and gain market share by providing lower-cost substitutes in the price-sensitive lower ends of the markets. Import substitution and subsidies were at that time a positive-sum game for maturing industries that faced technological constriction and market saturation in the developed world. Moreover, it was in the US interest to strengthen these countries' economies by easing US market and technology access and tolerating their trade and industrial interventional strategies. This occurred throughout their early development stages as a result of their 'front-line' positions against Soviet expansion during the Cold War and the Vietnam War (Ning 2007). In the 1980s, the early electronics technologies became more mature and reached the stage of seeking market expansion and increasing economies of scale. Cost-driven manufacturing 'redeployment' from advanced countries to NIEs generated huge outsourcing demand and provided financial resources for constructing local infrastructure, as well as creating a learning environment for local enterprises. Most importantly, global production networks were built up and led to a significantly rising outflow of exports of final products back to the advanced countries from NIEs. It seemed that an economic 'miracle' had suddenly emerged in East Asia (Mehdi 2005).

Unlike what happened in these countries, China's entry to the world ICT industry occurred while a transformation of modern capitalism or, let us say, a new wave of global business revolution, was taking place, which altered substantially the core meaning of industrial competition. In the 1980s, the world economic and political environment experienced profound changes: the collapse of communism in the USSR and Eastern Europe marked the end of the Cold War. Many developing countries abandoned inward-looking development strategies and Soviet-style central planning. The international political relaxation and opening up of developing countries under the neo-liberal development framework engendered a massive trend towards liberalization of international trade and capital markets, together with widespread privatization and deregulation. Since the 1990s, the world economy has entered a 'globalization' era that features more integrated national economies, a rapid outward shift of technological frontiers, an enhanced global production network (GPN) and an explosion of global M&A. The 'global business revolution' has taken shape, demonstrating a shifting pattern of competition from domestic oligopolies to a few MNEs in the global market. It has also heralded an increasingly complicated organization of economic production, with the adoption of the managerial innovations of system integration, and the nature of the modern capitalist corporation has changed to become progressively larger in size and dominant in 'strategic' segments of the value chain (Nolan 2001; Nolan *et al.* 2007a, b; and see also Chapter 2). China thus faces profound changes in the global economic environment, a situation that differs greatly from that faced by the NIEs during the heyday of their catching up.

In respect of the organization of economic production (the concern of this book), information technologies have enabled firms to codify and modularize highly sophisticated production, splitting it into a few steps and then transferring production to lower-cost plants all over the world to enjoy cost advantages – although this process is not yet complete. Manufacturing activities based on these mature, standardized technologies are often at the end part of the GPN. They generally have a shorter life cycle, facing stagnating markets with less potential for improvement, and are considered to generate less value added, be less profitable and show low productivity. By the mid-1990s, increasing shares of the total production of firms based in developed countries had been significantly allocated abroad (Dicken 2003; Gangnes and Assche 2004; Nolan 2001; UNCTAD 2001).[16]

In the ICT industry, most production has become increasingly modularized and requires not proprietary and integral parts, but open and standardized resources that could easily be sourced from elsewhere (Sturgeon 2004). As both production efficiency and firms' capacity have increased as a result of their use of the new technology and a global production process, products once aimed at a few high-income countries have become affordable commodities and are now sold in mass international markets. China took the opportunities of production relocation accelerated by MNEs' 'modularity' manufacturing innovation and integrated itself within GPNs (Naughton and Ernst 2005). With a great cost-comparative advantage, a large number of Chinese firms can relatively easily become entrants to most manufacturing sectors today. By comparison, during the catching-up decades faced by the NIEs, neither standardization nor GPNs were readily available. Some scholars have argued that China's integration into the ICT GPN came about through a larger volume of FDI than Japan and Korea ever received. The Chinese ICT industry will, they think, eventually develop its own successful and sustainable technological and management development models (Naughton and Ernst 2005).

However, with a 'global business revolution' taking place, the world's industrial leaders have simultaneously begun to streamline and consolidate their own operations through massive mergers, acquisitions and divestment to strengthen their leadership position in the world market. They will retain in-house only those operations that confer strategic advantages (their 'core business'), while outsourcing all the rest to 'external firms' (Nolan 2001; Nolan *et al.* 2007a, b). This enables the leading international firms to engage in a transformation into 'global flagships' so as to concentrate on a few core-function 'network-controlling' tasks at a global scale (Ernst 2003).[17] These controlling tasks include:

- ensuring stable connectivity, coordination and support of geographically and organizationally dispersed networks and standardized activities;
- managing international supply chains as well as information- and knowledge-sharing systems with global subsidiaries and affiliated firms;
- focusing on R&D in order to enhance the firms' positions as original leading innovators;
- battling to set the dominant product design, definition and industrial standards;
- providing products and services with high value added;
- strengthening global marketing communication, brand development and sales networks.

By concentrating on these activities, global flagships can raise a 'static' network controlling power through their capacity for system integration. They can reap profits more rapidly from innovations to increase their financial competence and offload the fixed costs and risks involved in establishing and supporting global vertically integrated company structures through outsourcing to the supplier level (also known as the result of the 'deverticalization' or 'disintegration' process; Dicken 2003; Ernst 2004, Hobday *et al.* 2005; Lakenan *et al.* 2001; Pavitt 2005; Sturgeon 2004). This is particularly important in the world ICT industry, where international demand fluctuates greatly and the market often exhibits periodical regression.

Moreover, as evidenced by their geographical arrangement, global leaders are often based in industrialized countries with a good skill base and scientific and technological infrastructure (UNCTAD 2001). In these countries, they can again achieve self-reinforcing dynamic competitive advantages by constantly modernizing and rejuvenating existing technologies and processes, and by frequently creating new products or services, improving their system integration capabilities and strengthening their marketing, design and service to provide competitive, high-quality products or services to global customers. Global competition is thus no longer a relatively stationary phenomenon that focuses primarily on manufacturing activities, as in the decades when the NIEs were catching up. It has become a fairly dynamic one, with constant changes resulting from rapid technological advances and managerial innovation. The reality of global competition today is thus a moving targeting for latecomers (Perez 2000).

Given this new meaning of ICT competition, industrial policies in most advanced countries have become more focused on creating an innovation and investment environment as well as a set of foreign policies to ensure the stability of their MNEs' overseas operations. However, China's strategy is not related to keeping up with the new direction of competition. The argument here is not that China's strategies based on the NIE supplier-oriented upgrading approach have failed to enable domestic firms to master more complex production technologies and processes, or that Chinese firms are performing poorly in the manufacturing and selling of high-tech products.[18] Rather, the point is that catching up is a dynamic and unending process. China's industrial policy has not been able to promote today's dynamic competitive activities and assist domestic ICT enterprises to take a lead in the world. It now faces many emerging challenges.

Technological upgrading and learning

Unlike the East Asian tigers, China was long viewed as a 'strategic competitor' by the United States and constrained from acquiring technologies in the same way as they were able to. Additionally, China's WTO accession and the Information Technology Agreement have swept away most conventional protection and conditions regarding FDI, which were extensively used by the NIEs to foster technology learning and imitation (Ning 2007; and see Chapter 8). Simple, aggressive policies to promote alliances with global industrial leaders may generate a larger volume of exports. However, there is no guarantee that such policies will improve international competitiveness or indigenous technological capabilities (Chandra and Kolavalli 2006); they would not help firms to cope with the highly dynamic nature of the industry. However, there is no guarantee of improving.

'Attracting in' largely enabled China to integrate into the GPN as a newly emerged lower-tier supplier and to become the most popular site for modularized innovation offshoring of leading MNEs. However, the benefits China can gain from these activities are very small, as high-volume standardized outsourcing production does not allow many changes in design (Sturgeon and Lester 2004). While conditions placed on FDI were phased out, increasing quantities of components and materials continued to be imported. Even when global leaders did come to China, they tended to choose the WFOE entry model to eliminate the risk of technology exposure to potential competitors, to ensure standard quality and to ensure that production procedures were carried out as designed. Moreover, MNEs often retain most newly innovated products at their early product cycle prior to modularization and high-valued-added activities in their home countries. For example, Toshiba shifted the entire Japanese production of standard television sets to Dalian, a city in the Liaoning province of northern China, in April 2001. The old domestic Toshiba television plant was converted to make liquid crystal projectors and digital televisions (People's Daily 2001). Toshiba also moved its entire notebook production to Huangzhou Zhejiang Province in China in 2005. Its Tokyo plant now focuses on R&D and the production of prototype models (Forbes 2004). Similarly, Intel expanded its chip assembly plants from Shanghai to Sichuan (Lemon 2003). Texas Instruments, Acer Taiwan and Samsung Korea are also moving production to China.

Similarly, China's first step in 'walking out' as a result of the 'attracting in' is full of modularized activities and primarily generated and managed by MNEs. They not only dominate controls over resources allocation, decision making and knowledge diffusion, but also determine the pace of technological progress and rule the supply, production, export and sales chain. No matter how much progress Chinese firms like Lenovo can make in expanding their product ranges vertically, they still have to incorporate the core components of the leaders into their products (e.g. 'Intel inside', 'Designed for Microsoft Windows') to comply with the new industrial standards set by the leaders, and purchase their newly available modularized activities in order to stay in the industry. When new innovations such as pocket PCs become available, Chinese firms have to pay heftily again to take over these newer standardized manufacturing activities shed by the leaders.

China's strategies have apparently not been able to move domestic firms' activities away from non-differentiated commodity production towards the centre of today's competition, helping them to generate branded and higher value added products, to control the global production and sales network, and to harness the potential of GPN and FDI by building up indigenous technological capability. As has been shown in previous sections, China's processing activity share of total exports has not declined – on the contrary, it has increased to more than 90 per cent – but added value remains only 20 per cent. In the absence of a set of dynamic policies to keep up with the global competition trend, FDI-led exports could cause a country to remain permanently stagnant, technologically, and leave it unable to make real progress beyond the assembly of imported components and the establishment of low-cost manufacturing sites in the GPN (Yusuf 2004; Yusuf *et al.* 2004). Different political economic situations together with new global industrial structures faced by NIEs have shut Chinese firms out of developing competitive activities and forced them to remain in cut-throat cost competition, further eroding their profit margins and inhibiting efforts to upgrade and innovate.

Keeping up with dynamic competition

Instead of concentrating on their own areas and becoming dominant through technological progress, Chinese firms tend to stay away from risky and costly investment in R&D and skills, and instead to diversify by entering into other low-barrier sectors so as to continuously exploit low-cost scale economies. For example, Haier expanded from manufacturing home appliances to mobile phones, TCL and Panda from televisions to mobile phones and personal computers, Lenovo from computers to printers and digital video/audio devices. This problem in fact has its roots in the characteristics of China's nationalist, rather than dynamic, industrial policies.

As we have seen, China's 'pillar' industrial strategies, largely influenced by political self-sufficient ideas, were designed on the assumption that a country can still create a particular industry from upstream to downstream and the whole supply chain within its territory. These strategies artificially forced the local vertical integration of industries, and pushed activities, regardless of their technological connectivity, under the roofs of a few large national group enterprises. The SME strategy was similarly launched in the hope of reducing dependence on foreign imports of key components and to support the 'backbone' large enterprises by serving as their domestic supply chain (Ning 2007).

The state administratively intervened in the market to ensure the success of national industries without having a clear picture of the dynamic development of the global ICT industry (Naughton and Segal 2003; Steinfeld 2004). Globalization associated with GPN has led to a blurring of the national geographic boundaries of industries. Product design could be carried out in the United States and Europe, and components could be manufactured all over the world. Competitive suppliers today require global outsourcing capabilities to search worldwide for low-cost, high-quality parts and raw materials (Sturgeon and Lester 2004). Given the new meaning of ICT competition today, it is difficult to see how China's strategy can be effective in assisting domestic enterprises to move towards the core competitive activities and truly benefit from the state-led 'walking out' strategy.

Chinese enterprises have increasingly become experts in lower-cost manufacturing and high-volume production, perhaps also because China's ICT strategy devoted too much attention to manufacturing technologies, tangible assets and production and export volume. A hugely oversupplied and low-skilled labour force was another factor that put fierce pressure on Chinese leaders to concentrate on physical manufacturing activities in order to create employment opportunities (Gilboy 2003). The inferior size of the Chinese industry put it at a disadvantage when engaging in head-to-head competition with global leaders. That fact, together with the lower-end market segments in which it is competing, often mean that Chinese enterprises are facing low profit margins and have less funding to reinvest in risky and ground-breaking R&D. China's technological capabilities are still far behind those of the advanced ICT countries it has 'caught up' with. For example, in 2003 China's R&D expenditure on added value for both electronic telecommunication (5.4 per cent) and computer office equipment (2.5 per cent) was much lower than in other leading ICT countries, for which the figure was in excess of 30 per cent in 2001 (Table 6.11). China still has a considerably smaller share of ICT expenditure in terms of GDP (0.13 per cent in 2002, including the R&D spending of wholly owned and JV FDI firms) than other leading countries (Figure 6.8). Although OECD data show that China has a relatively larger pool of low-cost scientists and engineers, the world's fifth largest, ahead of Germany but behind France, Korea, Japan and the United States, this could only be said to have great technical potential (Figure 6.9). Much of China's R&D activity seems to be directed towards technological learning and imitation; very little of it could lead to truly competitive innovative products (Zedtwitz 2005, 2007).

Table 6.11 Ratio of R&D expenditure to value added for the ICT industry in selected countries

	Electronic and telecommunications equipment (%)	Manufacture of computers and office equipment (%)
China (2003)	5.4	2.5
United States (2001)	37.2	36.7
Japan (2002)	20.4	90.4
Germany (2001)	44.1	19.8
France (2002)	57.2	15.8
United Kingdom (2002)	23.4	5.9
Korea (2003)	23.4	4.4

Source: Yearbook of China's High Tech Industries 2005.

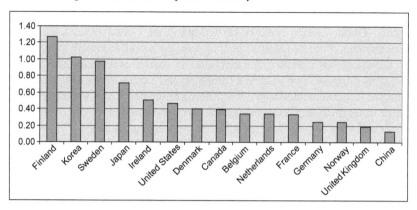

Figure 6.8 ICT R&D spending percentage share of GDP in selected countries, 2002.

Sources: OECD 2006b; the Information Technology Yearbook 2003.

The growing number of 'attracted' foreign-funded R&D centres can hardly be the main source for China to build up competitiveness, either. These research centres are owned, controlled and directed by MNEs primarily to localize or adjust existing technologies and have recently expanded to develop new products and manufacturing processes for the Asian markets (Armbrecht 2003). They may generate some spillover effects to China's domestic firms, but these are limited to regional markets and may not be the core competitive or desirable technologies that the local industry needs for its long-term development. Moreover, given the size of China's ICT industry, these effects are fairly small. Additionally, there is not enough time for less experienced Chinese firms to innovate, as the pace of

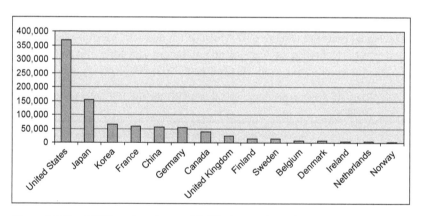

Figure 6.9 Total ICT engineering and R&D the number of personnel, 2002, for China compared with major ICT leading countries.

Sources: China's Statistics Yearbook of High-Tech Industries, 2005; OECD 2006b.

Note: All personnel are full-time equivalents.

technological progress is very rapid. Purchasing foreign technologies has become the only time-saving and cost-effective option to enable domestic firms to start production sooner. This allows them to concentrate on cost reduction through efficiency innovation and scale economies. As a result, even though Chinese firms have 'walked out' to set up a few R&D units overseas, these are generally small and mainly used to search for suitable technologies that can be transferred back to China. This trend has been seen by some as a reversed global outsourcing model, focusing on technology outsourcing (Liu 2005). Chinese firms have become a platform for turning foreign technologies into production for export or to serve its own fast-growing market (Zedtwitz 2005). This general trend shows that Chinese firms still lack the capability to engage in either product innovation or industrial product definition, although the government has begun to use China's market size to promote its own international industrial standards (Linden 2004).

Emerging Chinese firms could capture manufacturing activities, but the former leading manufacturers have cut off such business, even whole chunks of their overseas production networks. Chinese firms' 'walking out' acquisition of other global leaders' mobile phone or LCD television businesses are all in manufacturing-intensive segments of particular value chains. The problem is that Chinese firms are still competing on these modularized activities through low costs. They often face very low profit margins and suffer from a lack of network-controlling capabilities. For example, prior to 2000, IBM's hardware business had the largest share of revenue, but this had dramatically declined to 34 per cent by 2002 and was replaced by IBM's service division at 45 per cent and software at 16 per cent. In the period 1992–2004, service revenues increased at 17 per cent a year and software revenues rose from 30 per cent to over 50 per cent of IBM's total income. Other leading global firms also demonstrated significant service activities. Services consisted of 44 per cent of Fujitsu's and 18 per cent of Hewlett-Packard's turnover in 2002 (OECD 2004a, 2006b).

It is thus easy to understand that IBM's sale of its PC unit to Lenovo of China had as its main purpose the cutting down of low-margin activities. IBM could then concentrate on its highly profitable and rapidly growing technology, 'post-architectural' design and business service activities. Similarly, Lenovo's closest US counterpart, Dell, had a very small proportion of manufacturing and assembly activities but intensively focused on distribution network building. The rise or the global expansion of Chinese ICT firms is thus better understood as China's response to the GPN, which is complementary to leading firms' specialization in higher-valued sectors. It would be inappropriate to view China's whole 'walking out' situation as head-to-head competition with the leaders.

The drive of domestic conditions

Last but not least, Chinese enterprises do not have the experience or incentives necessary to fully commit to the state-led 'walking out'. An increasing number of overseas returnees may play an important role in improving China's corporate internationalization, as they can transfer knowledge gained during their employment at leading MNEs. However, this effect will take time to build up and Chinese firms are relying heavily on leading global firms to develop management capabilities for China's rapid expansion, both domestic and international. For example, Huawei is very dependent on IBM's consulting arm, Germany's Fraunhofer Gesellschaft, to develop its sophisticated integrated product development techniques and its supply chain, and to improve its R&D management efficiency and the quality of customer service (Naughton and Ernst 2005). Moreover, Chinese multinationals require additional operation experience to handle rising political opposition abroad due to their state-owned or related transitional characteristics. For instance, the US government withdrew its purchase order from IBM Lenovo in consideration of national security issues raised by uncertainty about the Chinese government's involvement in Lenovo.[19] Similarly, Huawei faces US criticism over national security issues raised by its acquisition of the Massachusetts-based 3Com network equipment manufacturer, because of its past link with the Chinese military and business deals in the Middle East (Gertz 2007).

Furthermore, while China's ICT exports grew at a rapid rate, the Chinese domestic market has expanded immensely, given the dramatic increase in GDP, business and home use of ICT products, and increasing spending on ICT-related infrastructure. China is now the world's sixth largest ICT market, with sales of US$118 billion in 2005, after the United States, Japan, Germany, the United Kingdom and France (OECD 2006b). It is also the world's largest mobile phone market, the second largest PC market and the third largest semiconductor market. Such fast-growing markets attract a large number of global firms to take shares and accelerate their operational expansion. Chinese firms are very busy fighting in domestic markets, as FIEs have taken more than half of the domestic market share (see Figure 6.5). They have very little incentive to leave such a strongly growing market to 'walk out' and conquer the markets of developing countries, which are slow-growing and require product adaptation, and those of advanced countries, where there are only a few niche markets available, and entering them would involve high costs of market penetration and would face huge competition from established global leaders. Together with their size disadvantages and weaker network controlling capability, it was very unlikely that Chinese firms would respond fully to the 'walking out' strategies and move towards today's competitive activities, apart from engaging in large-scale manufacturing activities controlled and managed by foreign enterprises.

Conclusion

This chapter argues that 'attracting in' has successfully created favourable conditions for the ICT industry to grow out of China's transitional economic and political system. Similarly, the 'walking out' strategy has enabled China to emerge as the world's largest ICT exporter in 2004. These successes were inseparable from the state effort in market reform and trade liberalization. As Deng and many other Chinese leaders had expected, the industry gained some technologies, skills, foreign markets and employment opportunities from FDI. The development of

China's ICT industry was impressive in its early stages. However, the achievement in the late stages, from 2000 on, is in many respects more illusory and limited than it initially appears. The mechanisms of the 'attracting in' and 'walking out' strategies remain static, inflexible and nationalistic. The strategies still attempt to follow the older NIE development model to create a relatively independent national ICT 'pillar' industry with its entire value chain and a number of indigenous multinational enterprises to challenge MNEs and industries based in advanced countries.

There is, however, great uncertainty as to how to adjust the industrial strategy of the East Asian catching up era to meet the challenges raised by the dynamism of global competition today. Compared with the export-led success of those other latecomers, China's experience has been very different. China has encouraged large inflows of FDI but is able neither to restrict them for the purpose of technology transfer and learning, nor to protect indigenous firms from fierce competition in the domestic market. China has also relied heavily on FIEs rather than domestic firms for manufacturing and exporting; virtually no Chinese firm has the capability to control or establish export networks. State ownership remains dominant in the industry, and will continue to be in order to meet the political sentiment of rising nationalism.

Most importantly, China's catching up attempt in the ICT industry was made at the time of the greatest deregulation and integration of the global economy that has ever been witnessed. During the process of globalization, the production and information network underwent considerable change internationally; political and trade barriers fell and logistics improved. These developments together triggered the giant global business revolution and redefined the whole meaning of global competition after the emergence of the East Asian economies. Not only are the activities of global businesses no longer the same as in the 1980s, when Korea and Taiwan caught up, but also the architecture of global production has been altered and product and technology cycles have been accelerated and shortened.

The real result of these strategies, behind the industry's phenomenal growth and global expansion, was obviously not what Chinese policymakers had intended. Instead of large indigenous enterprises, it is primarily FIEs that have led the first step of 'walking out', dominating trade and production as well as controlling China's export networks. During further economic liberalization, Chinese enterprises have gained some technologies from foreign incumbent firms, but their technological capability is still far behind the world's competitive frontier. The conventional NIE policies to improve such capability have also been abandoned during this liberalization process. A new, dynamic strategy is yet to be formulated. Chinese firms are locked into modularized activities at the lower end of the value chain, where labour costs are vital. This has also led to the second step of 'walking out', either in the form of M&A or overseas R&D seeking activities to focus on manufacturing-intensive segments of the value chain. Rather than representing head-to-head competition, China's rise in the world ICT industry complements leading MNEs' specialization in the new competitive activities.

While the process of catching up is faced with a moving target, industrial policies that can deal with this dynamic development have become those that seek to create particular communities or 'clusters' of the Silicon Valley type, to foster firms' innovation capabilities and enable them to develop network control systems that can set up industrial rules and coordinate between upstream and downstream activities in an integral process on a worldwide scale. What are not appropriate are policies that emphasize, superficially, the size of, and the self-contained nature of, national champion producers without considering how to encourage sustainable technological development. China's ambitious nationalistic strategy has fast become irrelevant in this respect. Rather than representing head-to-head competition, the growth and expansion of the Chinese ICT industry has turned out to be a complement to leading MNEs' specialization in network control and innovation.

This is not to say, however, that China's strategies have totally failed in today's era of the rise of the GPN. They may not help domestic enterprises to be as innovative and powerful as leading MNEs, but do allow them to leverage great cost advantages and thereby to remain competitive, more so than other developing countries. How did China comprehend the changing meaning of global ICT competition? How should China respond in order to keep pace with the dynamic nature of today's global production? The next chapter attempts to answer this question by looking at the third role of the state described by Hu Qili.

7   The 'breaking through' strategy of China's ICT industry

Dynamic technological catching up and challenges in developing the semiconductor sector

> We must seek outside help on the basis of self-reliance, depending mainly on our own hard work.
>
> (Deng Xiaoping 1982)

> Real high technologies, others [foreign countries] will not sell to us. We must depend on our own strength, adhere largely to self-reliance and technology import shall be complementary.
>
> (Jiang Zeming 1993)

While China has gained some technological and manufacturing capabilities and achieved enormous success in exporting, the core of global competition, as we have seen in the previous chapters, has changed from manufacturing to network-controlling activities. This change will eventually make China's cost-comparative advantage irrelevant in international competition. When designing industrial policies, Chinese leaders did, in fact, give consideration to incorporating some dynamic components into their development strategies. As early as in 1986, Deng Xiaoping pointed out the urgent need to 'trace the development of the world strategic high technologies and develop China's own high technologies'.

Similar to Deng's policy proposition, Jiang Zemin in the same year called attention to the need trace the international technological evolution and to develop China's new electronics products accordingly. The succeeding minister, Li Tieying, then embarked on the development of the chosen key sectors and vital technologies, while expanding the consumer electronics sectors. The third role of the state in Hu Qili's development strategy was thus inevitably about strengthening China's technological capability by making a breakthrough in strategic sectors, namely the semiconductor industry:

> The electronics foundation products are the footstone for the development of the electronics industry. Their speed of development affects the overall development pace of the industry. Especially, [we must] notice that semiconductor and integrated circuits were the core and key sectors for the

whole electronics industry. China could not have its own electronics industry without these two sectors. Foreign countries often prevent us from having basic and key products and technologies. We therefore must, by all means available, improve the development of key and foundation products, increase investment and selectively give policy support.

> (Hu Qili 1993, p.15; speech at the Establishment
> Meeting of the Electronics Industry)

Chinese leaders believed that the semiconductor sector was the most strategic area of the whole ICT industry. They also noticed during their overseas visits that all China's East Asian neighbours, from which China learned industrial strategies, had attempted to gain a position in the global semiconductor industry, which China's leaders believed to be at the heart of international competition. Moreover, Hu Qilin noted in his memoir that the applications of the semiconductor industry could relieve China's energy problems. Semiconductor technology could improve the efficiency of electronic machinery and save at least 36 per cent of the country's electricity every year. The sector had also became increasingly important in the ICT industry, accounting for 70 per cent of the total cost for electronics and automobile equipment, 22 per cent for military warship, 24 per cent for military transport, 33 per cent for aircraft, 45 per cent for missiles and 66 per cent for space shuttles (Hu 2006).

However, the higher up the value chain in the ICT industry, the more dynamic the sector is and the closer it is to the core areas of international competition. The targeted sector not only needs constantly updating and redefining, but also a fairly well-developed capital and R&D environment to support it. Most importantly, international politics came to play a vital part in the process of moving from labour- to capital- and knowledge-intensive sectors. Following in the steps of other East Asian countries, China made significant expansion in the industry during the early development stages. Nevertheless, when attempting to expand even just the manufacturing side of the core competitive sectors, China faced many challenges and obstacles. It is indeed not surprising that China should encounter such difficulties despite its weak economic and technological conditions. East Asian policy innovators, who benefited from their political alliance with Western countries, had long experienced many kinds of economic and political conflicts during their catching up in the core competitive sectors. Tensions over trade and technology issues eventually exploded into fierce policy conflicts. This chapter confines its attention to the state's role in the semiconductor sector, in which the Chinese government desperately wanted to build up indigenous production and innovation capability over the course of its evolution.

Reviewing the full range of evidence on the East Asian countries' industrial development in semiconductors and their disputes with the United States would be a massive undertaking. Instead, this chapter sketches out the core industrial and technological development strategies that Japan, Korea and Taiwan undertook, and compares them with the strategies China learned from them during the process of creating its own industry. After pulling together the threads, this chapter examines the nature of their semiconductor trade disputes with the United States and thereby hopes to tackle the issues surrounding conflicts between Western economic orthodoxy and East Asian development policies, which were eventually revealed as inherited pitfalls in China's following of the East Asian strategies. This chapter begins with an analysis of the national semiconductor development pathway of the four countries and notes the importance of government institutions during the whole process. It then compares and contrasts the nature of and solutions to the US–East Asia semiconductor disputes. The following section outlines key questions addressed in this introductory section and analyses the factors that hampered, and continue to hinder, China's progress in this industry.

A cross-country comparison of industrial and technological development strategies in the East Asian semiconductor industry

The origins of the world semiconductor industry date from 1947 at Bell Laboratories. Today, semiconductors have evolved into more complicated forms of memory and logic chips, and are the critical components of consumer electronics, telecommunication, computers and industrial equipment as well as modern military systems. Because of its external spillover effects for other industries and its vital importance for national security, many governments have considered the semiconductor industry to be a strategic sector and have played an active role in promoting its growth. Table 7.1 summarizes the main findings and illustrates the strategies of four countries before their trade disputes. For historical and cultural reasons, Korea linked to Japan while Taiwan bonded with the US market and China connected to the USSR. The variations between countries' catching up strategies, industrial structures and ownership patterns were mainly caused by their differing development visions and political choices, and differing US attitudes towards their industrial growth. FDI was treated as the main means for technological leveraging; policies focused on selectively introducing FDI and then excluding it when domestic firms started rising, except in China's case, where such policies have become difficult to pursue, given the WTO rules.

Japan, the leading goose, 1950s–1986

Japan's strategy towards the semiconductor industry has been characterized by active government involvement in industrial and technological upgrading. The first step in the development of the sector was taken by state laboratories (e.g. NTT and laboratories owned by the Ministry of International Trade and Industry, MITI) in the early 1950s. In 1951, the Bell Laboratories' discovery was successfully duplicated. In 1953, only a year after the PN junction transistor became available in the United States, three large privately owned electronics *keiretsu* (conglomerates), Hitachi, Toshiba and NEC, had mastered the technology (Yoshitaka 2000). Japan's

Table 7.1 National pathways of industrial and technological development in semiconductors before disputes with the United States

	Japan (1948–1986)	South Korea (1965–1992)	Taiwan (1966–1998)	China (1956–2003)
Initiation of the industry	Imitating US technologies, engineers' frequent US visits enabled information inflow. Mass production was delayed until 1956 owing to the weak infrastructure, relatively low domestic demand and an initial investment in vacuum tubes.	Labour-intensive assembly and test operation established by US and Japanese firms; technological information inflow through overseas-educated engineers during the development stages.	Labour-intensive assembly and testing production for US and Japanese producers; early technological information inflow through overseas-educated engineers.	Manufacturing for military defence applications until opening up in 1979. Overseas-educated engineers and foreign aid enabled information inflows but these were interrupted during the Cold War and the political split with the USSR.
Direct policy intervention at the firm level	A state-led industry with strong intervention and institutional centralization and autonomy in the 1950s but declined in the late 1970s under US trade pressure. For example, strong trade and credit interventions, tax incentives, and selective export targeting and promotion.	An FDI-initiated chaebol-led industry with limited state vision and intervention until the early1970s, when an increasing governmental role appeared with the promotion of the electronics industry. In the early-1980 financial crisis, the state's role declined and was restricted by international parties and the growing chaebols.	An FDI-initiated state-led industry with a firm state vision and role in providing supporting infrastructure (e.g. Hsinchu science parks and export processing zones) and intensive subsidization of capital, R&D support and export incentives for many small- and medium-sized firms, low interventions at the firm level and reduced interventional roles in technological upgrading after the rise of private firms in 1970s. The state's role has declined since the late 1980s.	Industry initiated by an extremely statist government. The government adopted a command economy and decided all aspects of the sectors' development and firms' decisions and resource allocation until 1979. The state's role was shifting towards neo-liberalism only very slowly. During WTO accession, the government abolished most statist approaches but the state's influence remained in policy designs.
FDI strategies and relations	Heavily restricted wholly foreign-owned structure, selectively promoted JVs and	Large presence of foreign investment throughout the 1960s. From the mid-1970s to the 1980s,	Large presence of foreign investment but entry of WFOEs was discouraged. The state	Heavily restricted FDI entry, gradually opened up in the form of JVs during the 1980s

Table 7.1 Continued

with MNE subsidies	licensing for technology access	FDI was regulated to access domestic market. JVs and licensing, but WFOEs were selectively encouraged, to secure access to technology.	encouraged local firms to ally with global players such as Phillips, Toshiba and RCA.	and extended to WFOEs after WTO accession.
Promotion of domestic enterprises and ownership patterns	Large *private* firms (*keiretsu*)	Large *private* firms (*chaebols*)	*Private* small and medium firms and SOEs (TSMC, UMC) for technological spinning off to private firms.	Large *SOEs* only in the early stages, shifting to promote companies of all sizes, with diversified domestic ownerships.
Institutional structures and roles of public research institutions	Established governmental agencies to design and coordinate policies and promoted the industry through legislation. Cooperative pre-competitive R&D and production consortia involved private firms and played strong roles in spinning off technologies.	Various institutes were established mirroring Japanese strategies, however, the political divergence on economic liberalization caused poor coordination of policies and weakened the proposed strong scientific and technological support for firms.	Emulated Korean and Japanese strategies for building centralized and autonomous governmental agencies and large-scale research consortia (ITRI, ERSO), which contributed significantly to the sector.	Moving away from the USSR-style centrally planned methods, attempted to incorporate Western market-oriented policy designs into its reforming systems. Large-scale research projects and high-tech park strategies showed less contribution in improving SOEs' performance.
US policy and attitudes towards the semiconductor industry	Positive; provided relatively accessible information (a Wassenaar member).	Strategic alliance; provided incentives for importing products manufactured abroad by US firms (a Wassenaar member).	Positive and considered politically important; provided incentives for importing products manufactured abroad by US firms.	Highly restricted during the Cold War period; still under export control and Wassenaar agreement for importing advanced manufacturing equipment.

Notes: TSMC, Taiwan Semiconductor Manufacturing Company; UMC, United Microelectronics Corporation; ITRI, Industrial Technology Research Institute; ERSO, Electronics Research & Services Organization.

rapid technological progress was eased by its alliance with the United States, which brought economic cooperation and access to technological information. Engineers were permitted relatively free access to US technologies through frequent conference attendances and company visits during the 1950s and 1960s (Flamm 1996). By concentrating on acquiring US licences and patents, Japanese firms soon were able to start low-cost mass production by the late 1950s. By 1959, Japan had overtaken the United States in output volume to become the world's largest transistor producer. However, the nature of the rapid rate of technological advance in the semiconductor sector ensured that Japan's low-cost 'copycat' strategy soon became irrelevant, as American firms altered competition entirely by introducing more sophisticated integrated circuit (IC)-based products in 1959.

It was against this background that Japan's 'catch-up' and 'take lead' strategies emerged in the mid-1960s. The renewal of the 1951 Electronics Promotion Law in 1964 marked the shift of policy focus from consumer and general electronics to computers and semiconductors. With the passage of successor laws in 1971 and 1978, Japan's strategy was easily identified as deviating from the neo-liberal policy prescription. These strategies included:

- policymaking coordination through an Electronics Industry Council to form close government–industry–academia collaboration;
- the targeting of markets and technologies by MITI;
- financial subsidies and incentives for selected research projects and production activities, for example low-interest loans from the state-owned banks, tax benefits, and production procurement on preferential terms;
- technology transfer through selection of domestic firms to enter into foreign JVs, rejection of wholly foreign-owned subsidiaries (WFOSs), and local content requirements;
- collective technological upgrading, diffusion and commercialization through the creation of large-scale production and research consortia;[1]
- heavy investment in training and education;
- shielding of the emerging domestic markets through high trade barriers.

Boosted by the increasing end-use demand for consumer electronics and computer industries, the Japanese semiconductor industry had grown substantially by the late 1960s. At the same time, intense foreign political pressure had mounted on Japan to liberalize its trade and investment regime. Although most trade and investment restrictions were removed in the late 1970s, market opening was rather selective. Heavy state intervention (mostly in the form of financial incentives and aid) was put in place to prevent domestic producers from the shock of market liberalization and to continue assisting R&D. By the mid-1980s, Japanese firms had clearly succeeded in semiconductor manufacture and arrived at the technological frontier in key industrial products (see Figure 7.1). Governmental intervention was believed by many to have strengthened MITI's ability to act on collective industrial interests in response to threats from foreign producers and to

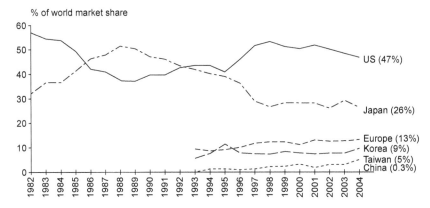

% of world market share

Figure 7.1 Worldwide semiconductor market share, 1982 to 2004.

Source: Calculated from SIA trade statistics (2004).

Note: China's world market share as claimed by China's Ministry of the Information Industry were 3.64 per cent in 2001, 4.98 per cent in 2003 and 5.64 per cent in 2004.

have enhanced the technological learning and R&D activities of Japanese domestic firms (Dahlman 1990; Fong 1998; Langlois and Steinmueller 1999).

Korea's taking off, 1965–1992

For historical and cultural reasons, Korea's broad economic development strategy was greatly influenced by its Japanese colonial culture and export-oriented growth strategy. Various Japanese interventionist policies and its *keiretsu* corporate structure were closely mirrored in promoting industrial development during the 1960s (Ning 2007). Yet technology-intensive sectors such as semiconductors were left rather untouched and less protected. As Table 7.1 indicates, Korea's semiconductor industry was initiated by US investments and thus differed from Japan's, which primarily relied on domestic enterprises. In 1965, a small US company named Komi was permitted to establish a JV with a 25 per cent share to operate Korea's first transistor assembly line. This was followed in 1966 by substantial investment from Fairchild in setting up a WFOS.[2] Korea attracted these US investments for a number of reasons. First, experiencing stiff competitive pressure from Japan, US semiconductor firms were looking for low-cost plants abroad. The rising wage levels in pioneering Hong Kong plants forced them to turn to lower-cost countries such as Korea and Taiwan. Second, the Korean government immediately eased its control over FDI when perceiving this opportunity. Third, in consideration of Korea's military assistance during the Cold War, the US government provided exceptions for the US-invested firms to import goods assembled abroad under section 806.30/807.00 of the tariff schedule (Mathews and Cho 2000).[3]

Unlike in Japan, *chaebols* undertook to develop semiconductors independently. Although early attempts, such as that made by Goldstar in 1972, failed, Samsung formed a successful JV with NEC in 1974. The substantial growth of *chaebols'* semiconductor business happened in the mid-1980s. The *chaebols* took advantage of demand-pull effects generated by the electronics industry, which was booming as a result of the state promotion plan and the semiconductor market shortage after the US–Japanese trade disputes. This phenomenon made it clear to the Korean government that its development strategy should cover semiconductors and be directed towards changing the status of its FDI-driven cheap chip assembly plants (Kim 1996).

The policy's implementation was hindered, however, by four main factors. First, to obtain help from the IMF and World Bank in order to handle the 1980 Korean financial crisis, the government was forced to abolish expansionary policies and liberalize its markets. Second, developed countries, led by the United States, threatened to impose trade restrictions on Korean products if the government failed to comply with these terms. Third, the state control authority was significantly weakened by the growing political and economic power of the *chaebols*. Fourth, political divergence over whether to follow the Japanese model had led to redistribution of central state power to many ministries and departments (Cherry 2003). Nevertheless, Korean officials pushed forward many favourable policies through which *chaebols* could foster indigenous technological capabilities. For example, the government provided general R&D subsidies, tax incentives and technological support from state-run research institutions, and also 'persuaded' foreign firms to form JVs with *chaebols* to enable technological spillover (Mathews and Cho 2000; Sung 1997).

In response to the state efforts, the *chaebols* went further to overcome their dependency on Japanese and US licensing and OEM by increasing their own R&D spending and acquiring foreign firms and laboratories, such as in Silicon Valley in the 1980s. Korea's semiconductor industry finally achieved world-class status around 1992, but structural problems, both technological and financial, remained, preventing the industry from sustaining its success. The industry continued to focus on low-cost, scale-intensive and high-quality production technologies and markets. This approach was originally designed to take market share from Japan rather than the United States. Taiwan, by contrast, moved towards upper-stream activities (Keller and Pauly 2000).

Taiwan: from OEM to fabless (1966–1998)

As in Japan, Taiwan's state institutions took the initial development step. Basic IC technology was first developed from a project funded by the National Science Council at Chiao-Tung University. The process of expanding the sector was similar to that which occurred in Korea. Not only did it start in the same period, but it benefited from similarly favourable international factors. In the 1960s, both Taiwan and Korea were considered to be alternative low-cost countries by many US firms. Perceiving this opportunity, Taiwan immediately established the world's first 'export processing zone' (EPZ) in 1965 to welcome FDI. A lead was taken by General Instruments in 1966 and soon many others followed suit, including Philips, Texas Instruments, RCA and Mitsubishi. As in Korea, Taiwan's semiconductor development process was eased by its political proximity to the United States and its front-line position during the Cold War.

The problems of EPZs were that they often encouraged FDI to bring labour-intensive activities while isolating them from the rest of the economy. Taiwanese officials felt that FDI's potential for industrial development and technological spillover was rather insignificant. Furthermore, Taiwan's governing ideologies had ensured that the industrial structure consisted of small- and medium-sized private enterprises (Ning 2007).[4] Firms were less likely to risk carrying out large-scale capital-intensive R&D or to obtain expensive foreign technology licences. During the global economic recession of the early 1970s, the government found that the national economy was seriously affected, as it relied heavily on the export of primary goods (Sung 1997). Finally, intensive state-led development policies were launched for upgrading the industrial structure and promoting strategic sectors, beginning in 1973 (see Table 7.1).

Those strategies directly related to the semiconductor industry included:

- creating an industrial technology research institution, closely modelling Korean and Japanese agencies to promote technological activities;
- setting up a committee to include overseas Taiwanese engineers for advice; using SOEs for foreign technology absorption experiments and demonstrations;
- spinning off SOEs into many private–state JVs at no or low cost to private firms, e.g. United Microelectronics Corporation (UMC) and Taiwan Semiconductor Manufacturing Company (TSMC);
- building the Hsinchu science park to attract foreign firms and to encourage overseas-educated Taiwanese engineers to return.

Compared with Korea, Taiwan showed clear state planning and intervention roles in technology learning and diffusion. Unlike Japan and Korea, it does not have subsidized firms with huge amounts of direct credit for business operation, nor has it intervened much in trade and investment. An exception was made to discourage WFOEs in order to ensure technology spillover to Taiwanese firms. Domestic firms finally began entering the sector driven by the rapid expansion in demand from the booming local PC manufacturing industry. As opposed to the situation in Korea and Japan, Taiwanese firms mostly chose to forge strategic alliances with multinational corporations for technologies and investment. This led to a large presence of foreign firms.[5] With the growth of free trade bodies and pressures from foreign parties, the Taiwanese state's role declined in the early 1990s. Driven by FDI, the local industry had grown substantially in size (see Figure 7.1). In the late 1990s, the industry began to shift towards more valued added design activities and engage in outsourcing investment (labour-intensive assembly activities) in mainland China (Chang and Tsai 2000; Tung 2001). Taiwan's case shows that the state's efforts to foster indigenous technological capabilities, rather than market forces or the involvement in

MNEs' global production and sourcing networks, have played an important role in leading the successful creation of the domestic semiconductor sector.

China's catching up, 1956–2003

China's semiconductor industry has been through a fundamentally different path from that of others. The industry received a high development priority from the government because of its military defence implications. Continuously threatened and strategically isolated by both the West and the USSR, the appeal of 'self-reliance' and 'self-sufficiency' dominated policy decision making. The common economic system adapted in the 1950s significantly aided the government in allocating huge amounts of human and financial resources to build inland industrial bases to prepare for war (MII 1999). To enable IC production, China for the first time imported semiconductor manufacturing equipment from Japan in 1965. However, the development of the sector was halted during the Cultural Revolution. In 1976, the government made a second development attempt by importing production lines, again from Japan, but the project failed to lead to massive production because of China's lack of technology knowledge and supporting production techniques. The third attempt was made in the late 1970s when the government, under Deng's leadership, launched a gradual reorientation reform, shifting towards a market-oriented economy and the growth of civilian and export goods.

As China normalized its foreign relations in the late 1970s, the industry was immediately able to import a small amount of production equipment. Again, domestic enterprises with weak technological capabilities could not simply move to massive production. Although the science and technology (S&T) system received heavy investment and was reformed to provide 'dual use' potential (e.g. the Torch, 863 and 908 plans), much spending went on large-scale defence-related projects, which had few substantial commercial spin-offs. Because of the industry's military implications, semiconductor enterprises were also kept wholly state owned. Until the late 1980s, the Chinese leaders felt it impossible to build a 'self-sufficient' S&T system (Cai 1998). The government made a fourth attempt by relaxing its stance towards foreign ownership in the late 1980s in the hope of broadening technology transfer. The formation of 50:50 JVs was initially encouraged between foreign parties and selected SOEs. A lead was provided by Shanghai Belling Microelectronics, in which Belgium's Alcatel was allowed to acquire a 40 per cent stake in 1988.

Even so, the Chinese leaders still found it hard to attract a large number of foreign investors, given the US technology embargo and China's weak supporting infrastructure (Hu 2006). They became more anxious that failure to master semiconductor production capability would lead to technological dependence and create serious threats to national autonomy. In 1996, a large-scale IC technology promotion project, '909', was launched. To commercialize technological outcomes derived from this project, the big business strategy was applied in the creation of Shanghai Huahong Microelectronics. Chinese leaders also realized that the government could not build up such a highly dynamic and market-oriented industry in the same way as the atomic bomb was developed, in which no cost, investment and consumer demand needed to be taken into consideration (Cao 1994). After reviewing the experience of NIEs, Hu Qili, minister of the electronics industry, was convinced that China needed to 'sail out with borrowed boats' (*jiechuan chuhai*).

Central officials gave the introduction of FDI a decisive push. From the prime minister to local officials, the Chinese government had frequently contacted the Japanese CEO of NEC in 1996 to 'encourage' the company to expand from Shougang NEC to Huanghong Group Company. To ensure NEC's commitment to technology transfer, the government permitted the company to have a lower cash investment of around 25–30 per cent of the total JV and to appoint a Japanese CEO with full management rights for five operational years. Furthermore, the Chinese officials successfully reached an agreement with the Japanese government to allow Huahong NEC to import equipment and components from Japan. Chinese leaders thought that this approach could avoid US intervention and eventually allow Chinese enterprises to export assembled IC products through NEC's sales network. Most importantly, the government had undergone a significant shift to a set of more liberalized polices towards FDI, minimizing bureaucratic interference and providing many tax incentives. This reached a peak when China joined the WTO in 2001 and ITA in 2003, under which China agreed to dismantle the licensing and quota system and to minimize governmental intervention. WFOEs were permitted in the sector. In general, the role of direct government intervention has declined, but the NIE-style interventional industrial strategy remains an important part of China's policy in fostering domestic technological and production capability (Ning 2007).[6]

The US–East Asia semiconductor trade disputes and their aftermath

The comparative review of each individual East Asian country's strategies in the previous section demonstrates a common pathway in developing the indigenous semiconductor industry which differed from the neo-liberal policy prescription: all these states took a bigger and deeper role in managing their economic, technological and international political affairs to their advantage, thus increasing the inflow of external knowledge and resources, and increasing access to export markets of leading countries. This section takes a look at how the US government and businesses have reacted to the growth and development strategies of the East Asian semiconductor industry.

The 1986 US–Japan semiconductor trade dispute

Japan was the first developing country to successfully climb the semiconductor technology ladder by following a statist, indigenous capability-building approach. In the 1970s, the growing *keiretsu* began aggressively investing in production facilities with the objective of producing better and cheaper chips than their

American counterparts. Backed by the state financial institutions, they were not afraid to increase capital spending even if faced with an adverse cash-flow situation or an industrial downturn. When formal trade and investment restrictions were liberalized in 1975, the MITI introduced informal non-tariff countermeasures to discourage local firms from using foreign chips; for example, denying import licences (Flamm 1996). Japan's import share of semiconductors continued to fall from 12.3 per cent in 1982 to 9.8 per cent in 1986, while its global market share began to soar, jumping from about 15 per cent in the 1970s to 46 per cent by 1986. Conversely, the US share had fallen dramatically: from 60 per cent in the world market, 95 per cent in the domestic market and 25 per cent in the Japanese market at the end of the 1970s, to 42.4 per cent, 82.8 per cent and 8.6 per cent, respectively, in 1986 (Irwin 1994).

In response to Japan's challenge, US firms first banded together to form the Semiconductor Industry Association (SIA) as their lobbying arm at Congress in 1977. The SIA has since been used to complain about Japanese industrial policies on market protection and subsidies, which allowed Japanese firms to engage in below-cost dumping. Mounting pressure from chip producers succeeded in getting the US government to become involved in semiconductor trade issues. Considering that use of extensive protectionist measures against Japanese chip imports could generate negative impacts on the international economic system, the United States initially suspended the domestic producers' petition. Instead, it sought to form a bilateral agreement with Japan. In 1982, a High Technology Working Group was established by both governments to encourage freer semiconductor trade, protect intellectual property rights (IPRs), remove informal non-tariff barriers for US firms, and open up Japan's investment market to allow foreign-owned subsidies. In addition, the US government passed the Semiconductor Chip Protection Act in 1984 in order to create an entry barrier for imitation products and to ban infringing chips from abroad.

On Japan's side, the government was concerned about a negative impact on its relationship with the United States with regard to both national security and exports. Concessions were made mainly in two ways. First, the state ended its role in promoting national R&D projects. For example, the very large-scale integrated circuit project was immediately closed down in 1980. Second, it provided 'guidance' to encourage the *keiretsu* to purchase American chips and reduce production volumes (Flamm 1996). Unfortunately, neither method worked. The state's role had become insignificant as the industry was already on a self-sustaining development trajectory. Unlike their strong collaborative capability in promoting the sector, state agencies' ability to regulate firms was weak. The MITI was not a statutory authority and hence had insufficient power to force any private firms to reduce production or purchase US chips. Firms could easily evade the loosely enforced MITI measures. Additionally, it was difficult for the MITI to persuade firms to adopt new measures when facing strong opposition from the Electronic Industry Association of Japan, which rejected the US accusations.

During the 1985 cyclical industrial downturn, large US firms such as Intel, National Semiconductor and Mostek announced that they would exit from dynamic random access memory (DRAM) production. On the other hand, they filed two anti-dumping petitions under the Tariff Act of 1930 against Japanese manufacturers to urge the government to take action immediately.[7] Economic conflicts over semiconductor trade, investment and technology turned into severe political confrontation. In 1986, the US government reacted by putting in place protectionist measures to force the Japanese government to agree to end semiconductor 'dumping' in the US markets, set a price floor monitored by the United States and secure 20 per cent of the Japanese domestic market for foreign producers within five years (GAO 1987).[8]

Neo-liberal ideas did not significantly shape the US–Japan agreement but were instead utilized by the United States to foster a government-managed and -enforced international cartel that restricted trade and production and fixed prices. The 1986 agreement was renewed with minor changes in 1991 and evolved into two joint statements in 1996 and 1999. With the increasing degree of global economic liberalization and the creation of the World Semiconductor Council (WSC), the international cartel eventually faded away. Japanese-style state-led development policies as well as similar efforts by the United States to promote Sematech (Semiconductor Manufacturing Technology), its own consortium, were limited under the WTO and International Technology Agreement (ITA) framework. The dispute solution thus reveals that under foreign political pressure, Japan's strategies have been pushed from the statist to the neo-liberal side (see Figure 7.2). Nevertheless, Japan's technological and production capabilities have both been clearly established, and in some areas Japan even pulled ahead of the United States before the dispute.

The 1992 and 2003 US–Korea semiconductor dispute

Korea has had two trade disputes with the United States. They were different in nature and led to considerably different solutions. As we have seen, in the post-1980 period the Korean government was constrained from fully implementing Japanese-style development strategies by both internal and external factors. The United States learned from its painful experience when allowing Japan to pursue statist policies. In the 1980s, the US government began to push Korea to adopt IPR-related laws and threatened it with protectionist measures (Super 301 rules or anti-dumping measures). However, unlike in Japan's case, Korea's semiconductor growth was led not by the state but by *chaebols* in the 1980s (see Figure 7.2). The initial lawsuits brought by US chip producers against *chaebols* focused on the 'reverse engineering' method that Japanese and Korean firms used for technology learning (Sung 1997). Later, US firms attempted to restrain Korea's rapid increase in production scale, which it achieved through rapid debt expansion. In 1992, Micron filed an anti-dumping petition alleging that 1 million DRAMs imported from Korea were being sold in the United States at less than fair market value. Only modest dumping duties, which were calculated especially for Korea's major semiconductor players, were imposed by the Department of Commerce: 0.82 per cent for Samsung, 11.45 per cent for Hyundai, 4.97 per cent for Goldstar

(LG), and 3.89 per cent for all the others.[9] The most effective factor was, perhaps, as in Japan's case, the price monitoring of export chips that constrained Korean producers in the 1993 US–Korea bilateral semiconductor trade agreement. Both the Korean industry and the Korean government voluntarily agreed to increase sales of US chips and equipment 'demonstrably and measurably' and to eliminate Korean tariffs in exchange for a suspension of the anti-dumping case.

Although the first trade dispute was at the firm level, the s econd dispute was directly against the Korean government. Since the mid-1980s the state had sought to end the *chaebols'* growing economic and political powers, which they saw as an unhealthy link between politics and business. *Chaebols* could often illegally conduct internal transactions, circular investments and tax evasion (Business Korea 1999). With increasing economic liberalization, deregulation and social democratization in the 1980s, the state could no longer rely on authoritarian and financial measures to control *chaebols*. Large firms could easily raise huge amounts of investment from abroad or domestic non-bank financial institutions. Such rapid debt-led expansion of *chaebols* after 1993 spurred by FDI and favourable government policies eventually contributed to the financial crisis in 1997. The IMF offered financial assistance to rescue Korea but on condition that the government would carry out a corporate restructuring programme, the so-called Big Deal. The programme involved the strengthening of *chaebols'* core business through merging or swapping their business operations, but its implementation required heavy state intervention. Foreign parties questioned the rising interventionist role of the state and President Kim's commitment to create a free market economy.

Against this background, it was in July 2002 that the European Commission (EC) first launched a countervailing investigation, initiated by the German firm Infineon Technologies. Infineon alleged that Korean producers had received illegal state subsidies regarding debt-for-equity swaps, debt forgiveness and R&D. In November, Micron Technology filed a similar complaint with the US Department of Commerce (DOC) and the International Trade Commission (ITC), accusing the Korean government of providing subsidies to domestic firms (e.g. Hynix) as part of a government-supported bailout. Consequently, in 2003 the DOC and EC announced 44.71 per cent and 33 per cent import duties respectively against Korean DRAMs.[10] Should the Korean government withdraw its assistance from *chaebols*? The Hynix bailout case showed that *chaebols'* support was still crucial in assisting the government to achieve its political goals (e.g. in the event of securing a North–South Korean summit) and in ensuring sustained economic recovery, because of the *chaebols'* size in the national economy (Cherry 2003). The Korean government had little choice but to help them survive even under great foreign pressure.

The 1998 US–Taiwan semiconductor dispute

The US–Taiwan dispute was less fierce than those with Korea and Japan. Its cause reflects the different roles of the state in the development of the sector. Taiwan's dispute with the United States originated from the anti-dumping petition filed by Micron Technology against the import of static random access memory semiconductors (SRAMs) from both Korea and Taiwan in 1997. In 1998, relatively heavy dumping duties were placed on Taiwanese SRAMs: for Advanced Microelectronics the rate was 113.85 per cent, for Alliance 50.58 per cent, for Best Integrated Technology 113.85 per cent, for Integrated Silicon Solution Inc. 7.59 per cent, for TI-Acer 113.85 per cent, for UMC 93.87 per cent, for Winbond 102.88 per cent, and for all others 41.98 per cent. Dumping duties on Taiwanese DRAMs were imposed in 1999: Etron Technology 69.00 per cent, Mosel-Vitelic 35.58 per cent, Nan Ya Technology Corporation 14.18 per cent, Vanguard International 8.21 per cent, and all others 21.35 per cent.[11] Charges on SRAMs were revoked in January 2002, while those on DRAMs were still under review.

A number of factors contributed to the fact that the case was resolved quickly. Unlike in the cases of Japan and Korea, Taiwan's semiconductor industry has advanced mostly by developing a strong technological base. Its domestic trade and investment market are kept relatively open, with a large presence of foreign invested firms. The main instruments the government used were to spin off state-owned research institutes and manufacturing complexes into private–state JVs. Although manufacturers' ownership was not the basis for the US duty imposition, a large presence of foreign investment to some extent eased the revocation of the order. The SRAM case shows that a majority of the firms subject to specific dumping margin calculation are US-invested or -owned, whereas in the DRAM case all the firms are either Taiwanese private or spin-off state–private JVs that focus on foundry activities. These spin-offs could have been the source of great international conflict, but what distinguishes the Taiwanese case from the earlier ones is that the most successful spin-off, TSMC, was complementary to US fabless companies rather than competitive with them.

Furthermore, as was discussed earlier, the role of the Taiwanese government has declined since the early 1990s in both providing pilot plants for technology adoption and financial assistance for launching new ventures (see Figure 7.2). The private sectors at this time had grown strong enough to take initiatives for technological and market expansion. Unlike Korea, which continues to exploit low-cost fabrication sectors, the Taiwanese industry had shifted towards the upstream activities of chip design in the early 2000s (Brown and Linden 2005; Keller and Pauly 2000). The next logical step, taken by Taiwanese firms around 2002, was to push the government to relax its restrictions on technology and investment in mainland China to enable them to expand fabless business models. As neither the Super 301 rule nor the Dumping Act recognized the increasing globalization of semiconductor production, the US actions were limited to being against imports of the country that actually manufactures and exports the chips. The offshoring movement perhaps greatly reduced Taiwan's direct semiconductor trade conflicts with the United States, but on the other hand it became a factor that accelerated possible tension between the United States and the country to which Taiwan has migrated its fabrication plants – China (PWC 2004).

The 2004 US–China semiconductor dispute

Compared with the other disputes, that between the United States and China would seem to have been the simplest, with the quickest resolution. The case was not initiated by a particular American company, nor were specific dumping charges laid against the Chinese semiconductor industry or any particular firms. In 2003, the SIA started a discussion with Chinese officials regarding the preferential tax treatment of ICs produced in China. Under the 2000 State Council Circular 18, China subjected all semiconductors sold to 17 per cent value added tax (VAT), but firms with local production capacity were eligible to receive an 11 per cent tax rebate rising to 14 per cent if their production was based on local designs. After a few interactions, the SIA felt that Chinese officials were prevaricating about its request to remove such measures. It then began to lobby the US Congress for political support. Members of Congress and the Senate wrote to the US trade representative (USTR) requesting that action be taken. Similar political recognition came from the WSC, which in May issued a joint statement critical of China's VAT rebate programme. Under mounting pressure from domestic firms and the 'election syndrome', on 18 March 2004 the Bush administration authorized the USTR to file the first WTO complaint against China in the form of bilateral consultation.

Counter-claims were launched by Chinese officials. They asserted that the government always maintains fair market access for all foreign firms. In 2003, more than 80 per cent of the domestic market was met by imports. The promotion policies such as the VAT rebate have not been of substantial benefit to Chinese semiconductor firms. Additionally, qualifying foreign chip producers are equally eligible for the tax rebate. China was not in breach of the WTO national treatment and Most Favoured Nation rules, nor had foreign exporters been materially affected. Chinese officials also argued that foreign chip manufacturers often receive VAT refunds on their capital equipment at home, whereas Chinese firms were subjected to VAT on domestically produced equipment. The VAT rebate programme is required in order to 'equalize' domestic enterprises (Howell *et al.* 2003).

The US side responded that China's tax rebate policy not only discriminated against foreign imports, but also distorted international investment in the semiconductor sector. The Chinese preferential tax treatment applied only to ICs produced in China. It discriminated between domestic and foreign products and violated the WTO Most Favoured Nation and National Treatment principles (GATT Article III). Furthermore, China's IC market became the world's third largest in 2003 and is expanding rapidly. The estimated cost to US firms of the VAT rebate policy was considerable, approximately US$344 million, 16.8 per cent of the total US IC exports (US$2.02 billion) to China (USTR 2004). The US side also pointed out that China's rebate tax policy or other tax-based incentives were not market-based factors, but state interventions used to encourage or discourage investment in certain production activities or locations. These policies encouraged inward FDI to increase China's production capability and thus discouraged imports. With regard to China's VAT 'equalization' assertion, the SIA replied that China is not able to produce equipment for making advanced

Table 7.2 World market shares and growth rates of major countries in 2003 and 2004

	2003 ($ million)	2004 ($ million)	Growth	Share of world market
US companies	87,733	105,206	20%	46.70%
Japanese companies	46,291	53,841	16%	25.60%
EMEA companies	21,461	27,298	27%	12%
S. Korean companies	14,007	21,988	57%	10%
Taiwanese companies	8,362	10,820	29%	5%
Chinese companies	388	727	87%	0.30%
Total	178,242	219,880	23%	–

Source: Calculated from SIA (2004) and Gartner (2005).

Note: EMEA, Europe, the Middle East and Africa.

semiconductors on the basis of its current technological capabilities. Nearly all the leading Chinese firms have relied on imported duty-free, rather than domestically produced, equipment for production. IC design firms that generally spent less on capital goods are eligible for the VAT rebate given the current policy coverage. There is no preferential tax policy in the United States to refund the VAT to chip export firms (Howell *et al.* 2003).

On 14 July 2004, just four months after the case was filed, China and the United States signed the official memorandum of understanding to settle the dispute. Although the resolution ensured that the VAT rebate was to be fully eliminated on 1 April 2005, concerns about China's industrial policies and compliance with its WTO commitment remain. The United States was concerned that China would not give up the industrial policies that had been pursued by the East Asian latecomers for technological learning, even though the Chinese semiconductor industry was still in its infancy. In the world market, China's share remains small and has increased from 0 per cent in 1999 to only 0.3 per cent in 2004, although in that year domestic firms' growth rate was 87 per cent, the highest among the countries shown in Table 7.2.[12] Technologically, the world leaders in the field of semiconductors are now able to produce 12-inch wafer and 0.11-micron circuitry, whereas most Chinese firms are still relying on 8-inch wafers and ICs at 0.25 microns or above.[13]

Kicking away the conventional technological upgrading ladders: lessons from China's disputes

After putting together the big picture of four East Asian countries' developmental pathways and trade conflicts with the United States in the semiconductor industry, this section, at the risk of oversimplification, sketches tentative answers to the causes of the trade disputes from the view of policy design for industrial and technological development. It discusses some key policy issues for China, the newcomer to the industry, and reveals the inherited challenges China faces in seeking to continue implementing the East Asian-style strategies. It suggests that the conventional technological upgrading ladders were kicked away in the WTO era. The state intervention in coping with the dynamic nature of some high-tech and fierce global competitive ICT sectors will incur a huge political cost.

Why are there frequently disputes within the semiconductor industry during globalization?

The semiconductor industry has historically been at the forefront of trade frictions in East Asia. This is due to the nature of the industry, which means it has had a high degree of state involvement. The semiconductor industry embodies all the key features of a high-tech industry. It is not only capital- and R&D-, but also scale-intensive. Competition among producers is typically marked by rapid technological progress and sustained product innovation, which consequently leads to very short product life cycles. Firms have only a relatively short space of time to earn sufficient profit not only to offset the huge upfront R&D and capital expenditure costs associated with each new product life cycle, but also to finance themselves for future cycles. However, the large fixed investment, which can rise to billions of dollars, causes the minimum efficient scale of production to be quite large, and the scale effect is amplified by a learning effect that drives down marginal costs as a function of cumulative total output. As the industry is very dynamic, with the technological frontier moving rapidly forwards and products quickly reaching the end of their life cycle, the most economically logical way for firms to proceed was perhaps to quickly achieve economies of scale in production before the end of each product life cycle. Driven by constant competitive pressure, firms thus always have to be on the lookout for the largest market possible, the international market, to achieve scale economies and maximize their profits in order to enable high levels of R&D and capital spending for future competition rounds. The drive to sell in the world market has inevitably led to a situation where during cyclical industrial downturns, firms (e.g. the US firm Micron) lobby the government to attack foreign imports at home or undercut prices of international rivals ('dumping') in order to maximize the return on their fixed R&D and capital investment. These distinctive characteristics of the semiconductor industry made market entry expensive and difficult.

The East Asian latecomers often found both technological acquisition and upfront investment in R&D too expensive. Even though these countries had allocated huge investment to technological learning, the Western monopoly on science and innovation made it impossible for them to keep up with the technological changes in the industry. To increase their chances of survival in such a dynamic industry, latecomer firms often chose to use 'unfair' techniques, such as piracy of IPRs, 'reverse engineering' and close imitation. However, what firms desired most was government support to give them the advantage of being able to quickly achieve scale economies in each new product life cycle. Bureaucrats in latecomer countries often believe that this sector can serve 'strategic' purposes for their countries, especially when their electronics industries have generated huge end-use demand for semiconductors. The government are thus more willing to intervene in the name of the collective interest. The common approach found in the experiences of four East Asian countries was, while shielding the domestic market, to assist firms to enter the industry and learn new technologies by providing subsidies, direct credits, loans and incentives, and selectively introducing FDI.

With state assistance, latecomer firms built enormous capacity in the quest for sales growth even without regard to profit, and so their volume helped them to go beyond the capacity level that Western incumbent firms assumed that they could not breach. This short-term strategy made learning economies unimportant and captured the profits from incumbent firms for themselves to prepare for the future rounds of competition. Inevitably, latecomer firms together with their governments entered into a battle on the international market, initially with leading firms and later their governments, when both wanted to achieve scale economies to maximize their returns on their large fixed R&D and production equipment investment. This battle happened during each frequent product cycle. It can be seen as a challenge to the trade and governance system at the global level, which is set up on the basis of neo-liberal rules and supported by developed countries – a challenge caused by the 'developmental state' approach, which focuses on technological and institutional capability at the national level. Thus, the latecomers' approach has politically tested the limits and tolerance of the foreign policies of the leading country, the United States.

How were the different disputes resolved? How did disputes affect latecomers upgrading technological structures?

The solutions to the US–East Asian semiconductor trade disputes were to push the role of each government away from the statist end of the spectrum, which emphasized state intervention, towards the neo-liberal side, which claims that competitive market forces should determine economic outcomes. This was achieved through bilateral trade agreements, under which countries that failed to comply would face serious US protectionist measures against their exports. Given the increasingly export-dependent nature of these economies, governments have to consider the huge political cost of their interventions to facilitate firms to achieve scale economies or technological learning.

From the results of the comparative study conducted in earlier sections of this chapter, changes in policy direction for each country following their disputes are plotted in Figure 7.2. Each country demonstrated a different path, because of their differences in both internal and external factors. In the case of Japan, state intervention was not reduced, but altered from supporting to controlling firms, so as to cut back production or investment. In short, a state-led cartel was created to meet the US-regulated price floor and the quantitative target for market access, until the mid-1990s, when the multilateral World Semiconductor Council was established. Nevertheless, Japan had successfully broken through the Western monopoly on semiconductor technology and innovation. The

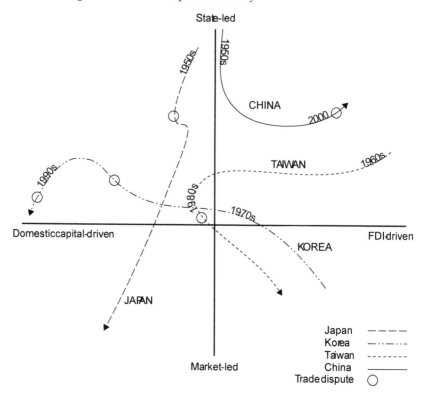

Figure 7.2 The roles of the state, foreign direct investment and domestic capital in the development of the East Asian semiconductor industry.

industry was clearly established and subsequently followed a self-sustaining development trajectory.

Although it was copying Japanese industrial strategies, the Korean government fell short on its vision and was constrained by internal and external political factors from supporting semiconductor firms intensively in technological learning and upgrading. Firms' strategies were initially focused on achieving high volume production to take market share from Japan rather than from the United States. Fuelled by financial resources easily gathered from abroad during financial liberation, large Korean firms aggressively expanded their investment. Threatened with protectionist policies by the United States, the Korean government concluded a bilateral agreement that contained a price floor control mechanism monitored by the United States to regulate *chaebols'* 'dumping'. Because of the limits on the state's capability to collaborate and promote technological learning, *chaebols* continued to focus on rapid debt expansion in production scale. Deep structural problems were inevitably exposed during the Asian financial crisis. When the state intervened to rescue them, trade disputes arose again.

The situation in Taiwan was the opposite of that in Korea. Right from the beginning, the state had a very clear vision of how it wished to develop the semiconductor industry. Leaving aside sensitive areas associated with market access and production scale, the government concentrated on launching repeated rounds of technological upgrading. It followed an institutional structure, starting from public sectors and then rapidly privatizing acquired technologies through SOE spin-offs to its small and medium-sized firms. When a state-led phase had decisively given way to a firm-led phase, Taiwanese firms embarked on moving to upstream activities such as chip design. This industrial policy perhaps significantly released Taiwan's trade tension with the United States, as the US anti-dumping and countervailing laws only addressed activities that directly affected a country's final manufacturing volume. The most important factor was that Taiwanese firms chose to be complementary to US companies rather than competitive.

Figure 7.2 shows that China's semiconductor industry was primarily FDI-led, but the state intervention remains. Although the China–US dispute was about the WTO, and China agreed to remove its tax rebate policies, the issues were rather more complicated than just the confrontation of statist and neo-liberal industrial development strategies. In the case of Japan, Korea and Taiwan (anti-dumping and intellectual property cases), most of the US actions were caused by pressure from US firms. In the Chinese case, there were both military and commercial reasons. The following question particularly addresses China's issues.

What are the challenges for China in seeking to pursue indigenous technology building policies under the WTO rules?

Although these countries' industrial strategies and structures have differed, the common element of the rapid development in the four East Asian countries mentioned has been the state's role in securing their knowledge and market access from developed countries while providing an institutional framework to intensively assist domestic firms to acquire and upgrade their technological competencies in semiconductor production or design. The roles that these states played owed nothing to neo-liberal notions of free market and trade. After Japan first introduced the 'catching up' strategies, many other countries followed suit in close proximity. While these policies were successful, they were very costly politically. This means that neither Japan nor its followers' approaches were suitable for others to pursue in an identical fashion, especially today, when the rules of competition have been set under the WTO/GATT regime and the United States maintains unilateral powers against those not complying. The 'technology leverage' or 'reciprocal control mechanism' that made NIEs' transition from low- to high-technology industries is no longer universally viable. The areas addressed in the US–East Asian semiconductor trade dispute demonstrate that many key elements are not feasible for latecomers to use as a 'ladder' to climb to the top of the value chain.

Many examples can be easily identified from China's bilateral agreement, by which the United States maintains the ability to use anti-dumping methodology for 15 years if China pursues any of the core strategies used by other NIEs (SIA 2004; White House 1999; WTO 2004).[14] These include the following.

1   Tariffs and quotas. Protection of the domestic market through tariff and non-tariff barriers, and trading and distribution restrictions. While phasing in the WTO agreement, China's industrial tariffs have fallen to 9.4 per cent by 2005, and tariffs for ICT products, as agreed in the ITA, have been reduced to zero. China also committed itself to abolishing all quotas and licensing or other quantitative restrictions by 2005. In principle, China can no longer create a protected domestic market for local firms as Korea and Taiwan did in their early development stages. Additionally, China can no longer manage foreign imports or use its large market size to exercise significant influence over the technology transfer decisions of multinational corporations.

2   Trading and distribution. China has agreed to extend the provision of trading and distribution rights to foreign enterprises. Under the agreement, trading rights were progressively phased in over three years. Distribution rights are provided even for China's most restricted distribution sectors, such as wholesale, transportation, maintenance and repair. In principle, China could not use this measure to prevent foreign firms from reaching the corners of its domestic market.

3   Conditions on foreign investments. China has agreed to implement the Trade Related Investment Measures Agreement upon accession, eliminating local content requirements where governments require foreign enterprises to use or purchase domestic products; trade balancing measures, where governments impose restrictions on imports of an enterprise or link the amount of imports to the level of its exports; and foreign exchange balancing requirements, where an enterprise has the level of imports linked to the value of its exports in order to maintain net foreign exchange earnings. China no longer attaches conditions to the right of foreign firms to import or invest, which thus dismantles the main areas of the selective trade and industrial policies of Korea and Taiwan. In terms of technological learning, foreign firms may not generate spillover or demand effects to local supply industries as they are now free to make a purchase decision from local suppliers or abroad. China also agreed not to make the approval of imports conditional on technology transfer requirements or to 'persuade' foreign firms to form JVs with selected local firms. It was required to join the Agreement on Trade-Related Aspects of Intellectual Property Rights with no transition period. In principle, it could no longer 'abuse' foreign technologies in order to reduce the technological entry requirement of the industry during its nascent stages.

4   Technology transfer requirements. China has agreed not to make the approval of imports conditional on technology transfer requirements. It will also impose or enforce provisions relating to the transfer of technology only if they are in accordance with the WTO agreements on protection of intellectual property and patent rights and other trade-related investment

measures. Although foreign companies might transfer some technologies for their own advantage, China cannot use this requirement to select its most desirable technologies to guide the direction of the development of its ICT sector.

5   State-owned and state-invested enterprises. Purchases of goods or services by state-owned and state-invested enterprises do not constitute 'government procurement' and are thus subject to WTO rules. Foreign firms have been given equal rights to sell products to SOEs. China has agreed to ensure that state-owned and state-invested enterprises will make purchases and sales based solely on commercial considerations and that it will not influence these commercial decisions (either directly or indirectly) except in a WTO-consistent manner. China has agreed that the United States can monitor whether SOEs have been given soft loans and equity injections as government subsidies. There is limited scope for governmental support for SOEs, which China uses to create large companies. For example, the SIA questioned China's electronic identity card programme, which would be used to subsidize selected SOE/SIEs (State Invested Enterprises).

6   Subsidies for technological learning. Korean- and Taiwanese-style policies supporting firm learning are now explicitly limited, and will prove challenging for China to implement. Under the agreement, assistance for R&D activities conducted by firms or by research establishments is limited to 75 per cent of the costs of industrial research or 50 per cent of the costs of pre-competitive development activity. Subsidies are limited to the costs of personnel, instruments, equipment, consultancy, and permanent land and buildings for the research activity only; assistance to promote adaptation of existing facilities and processes to new environmental requirements for firms with financial difficulties is limited to one-off payments of 20 per cent of the cost and do not cover replacement.

7   Financial subsidies and incentives. This point covers financial subsidies and incentives for technological learning through the purchase of production inputs on preferential terms, tax relief, preferential loans from the state-owned banks, and facilitated listing on equity markets. China is now required by the US government to notify it of existing subsidy programmes or related resource allocations and to explain their purpose. For example, China's policy on paying interest on bank loans for a number of years for SOEs across industries purchasing certain facilities for upgrading is believed to constitute unfair practice, and further explanation is required by the United States. The WTO rules also call into question provincial governmental assistance to local enterprises, such as the fact that Semiconductor Manufacturing International Corporation and the Chengdu government jointly invested US$175 million in a semiconductor assembly and testing plant in 2004. The local government as the majority shareholder played the key role in purchasing the land and production inputs on preferential terms and providing guarantees for borrowing bank loans. Tax incentives such as VAT rebates were abandoned as a means of industrial promotion. Other export-based tax incentives adopted from the NIE

models, such as tax-preferential measures maintained in the special economic and technological zones, are also under question (SIA 2004; WTO 2004).

(Source: Ning 2007)

Challenges beyond the WTO rules for China's industrial promotion strategy

Last but not least, the experiences of Japan, South Korea, Taiwan and China in the development and dispute over semiconductors reinforce another lesson: there are specific factors – not just economic but political ones – that created difficulties for technological learning and could potentially trigger trade disputes.

One of the crucial NIE technology leverage/learning approaches in the early development stages was to attach themselves to a given technological trajectory. That means latecomers need continuously to import foreign technologies at the start in order to enter new sectors rapidly. As we have seen, the NIEs have benefited substantially from the external political environment in securing their knowledge source. During the Cold War, their front-line positions against Soviet expansion in Asia brought them economic and political support from the United States. Not only were they able to secure knowledge and financial resources from the developed countries, but also their maintenance of various intervention and protectionist measures during their early stages of semiconductor development were tolerated.

Conversely, in the Cold War period China had an economic and technological blockade imposed on it by the United States and other Western countries. When joining the WTO, China hoped that by giving up some interventionist policies it could increase the inflow of foreign technological and financial resources in the semiconductor sector. However, China's acquisition of advanced semiconductor technological and manufacturing capabilities is viewed, even today, by many US policymakers as a significant security threat to the United States and Asia Pacific regions because of the dual-use nature of the industry. Although Washington worries that US firms may lose opportunities to benefit from China's large and fast-growing market, while their international counterparts are taking advantage of low costs and expanding their market share or foundry plants in China, political and security concerns take precedence.[15]

The current US strategy focuses on a broad 'two generations behind' policy as a regulatory benchmark to impede China's rapid growth in semiconductors (GAO 2002). Tight controls remain on exporting semiconductor equipment and technologies to China. All US domestic licence applications are subject to a case-by-case assessment by the Departments of Commerce and Defense. Sanctions are rigidly imposed for export control compliance. For example, in 2004, the Department of Commerce charged Lattice Semiconductor Corporation a $560,000 civil penalty for exporting temperature-range programmable logic devices to China and for releasing related technical data and offering training to Chinese nationals without the required export licences (BIS 2004). At international level, the United States tried to deny China access to leading-edge semiconductor technology through a strengthening of the 1996 Wassenaar Arrangement, the multilateral export control system among major producer states. Although the absolute effectiveness of the agreement was questionable, the situation implies that China could not obtain relatively advanced technologies as easily as NIEs in their early development stages.[16]

International political factors continue to constrain China from securing technological sources. This gives fuel to China's historically rooted concerns for national security and technological autonomy in addition to the simple economic consideration of employment. Because of deep suspicion of US pressure directed against China, for example over Taiwanese issues, China's leaders continuously emphasize the strategic importance of developing independent and proprietary high technologies as a crucial means of building a modern, economically and militarily powerful state. The Chinese government has little choice but to bear the cost of pursuing any industrial policies possible that can assist in obtaining foreign technologies and to foster indigenous technological capabilities for both commercial industries and the defence industry.

With increasing economic liberalization and integration into the global economy, China's leaders have found that central planning, support for SOEs, and now, after the WTO rules, the East Asian interventionist policies for technological learning must gradually be abandoned. Yet they will try all possible means to obtain or develop core or critical technologies and make them indigenous, especially manufacturing technology. For example, the tax rebate policy was one of the East Asian-style strategies that China thought it could follow to promote the sector after WTO accession. What matters to the government is no longer state ownership or the size of the firm but the ability to secure foreign sources of knowledge and to develop native R&D competence. China's strategies, which had successfully promoted plant migration and outflow of human resources from Taiwan, have raised US concerns about future economic well-being and national security (Juster 2003).

Moreover, economically, China's ICT industry, which has an even greater coverage of dual-use goods than semiconductors, has grown rapidly. In 2004, it successfully overtook the United States to become the world's largest ICT export sector. The sector generated huge end-use demand for semiconductors, the third largest IC consumer market, of which China's current capability can meet only about 30 per cent (see Table 7.3). How could China possibly further develop its ICT industry without having its own robust semiconductor industry? Tempted by economic – and, perhaps more decisively, by political – factors, the government sees little choice but to be deeply involved in national investment or promotion in the semiconductor industry. The US–China dispute was thus inevitable, and reveals fundamentally different political and economic tensions over semiconductor exports, investment, technologies and learning issues from those that occurred in relation to the NIEs. Tensions have become more obvious during political and economic fluctuations. The 2004 US–China dispute happened alongside the 'election syndrome' and the US–China bilateral trade deficit, which reached $124 billion in 2003, the highest ever.

Table 7.3 Percentage of domestic demand for integrated circuits met by local
production in China

Year	IC demand	Domestic output	Percentage of demand met by domestic production
2001	24.5	6.36	26%
2002	36.0	9.63	27%
2003	48.7	12.40	25%
2004	65.7	21.25	32%
2005	79.0	29.60	37%
2006	95.0	38.50	41%
2007	110.0	48.10	44%
2008	125.0	57.70	46%
2009	138.0	69.30	50%
2010	150.0	83.10	55%

Source: Calculated from Semiconductor Industry Report 2005, China Semiconductor
Industry Association, CCID 2005.

Note: Figures for 2005 onwards are predictions.

Conclusion

The role of the government in economic development and the East Asian economic 'miracle' has long been the subject of debate. Moving from labour- to some capital- and knowledge-intensive ICT sectors such as semiconductors, the inherent 'institutional logic' of development in East Asian countries was very different from the neo-liberal 'prescription'. These states took a very active role, focusing on fostering indigenous technological and production capability to create the semiconductor industry during a time of economic globalization and liberalization. None of these NIEs could simply 'borrow' or 'get' technologies from the West. Latecomers often started by buying foreign technologies (often those in stages of decline) and invested in skills and infrastructure to adapt them. With limited capital resources, the latecomer states have to make decisions 'strategically' on the priority of their purchases during the early development stages. Moreover, the costs of both technological acquisition and upfront investment in R&D were high; the latest technologies, which are US incumbent firms' core competitive advantage, are hard or impossible to obtain.

Facing fierce competition in semiconductors, latecomers chose more cost-saving but politically risky methods. One was to imitate new chip designs by 'reverse engineering'; the other was to increase firms' production scale to improve the profit potential from the huge capital spending costs associated with R&D for new complex semiconductors and constructing high-volume production facilities. The former caused all these countries to be subject to bilateral US IPR protection charges, and the latter led to anti-dumping charges directly against any government attempts to facilitate (or rescue in Korea's case) firms to increase investment scale. The result of acquiring technologies from MNEs in various industries was mixed: development planners often found that the labour-intensive sector prospered but little was achieved in terms of expanding, diversifying and upgrading exports in favour of the high-valued-added sectors. In order to gain from knowledge sources, these countries developed an institutional 'control mechanism' that selectively disciplined or encouraged certain economic behaviours by all the parties involved (Amsden 2001). Some countries have found that learning from MNEs is expedited by requiring them to form JVs with local firms and using domestic market access to trade for newer technologies. The growth of NIEs in the semiconductor high-tech sectors eventually challenged the US leadership and the WTO-supported neo-liberal development 'wisdom'.

Tensions between these countries' national capacity-building practices and the neo-liberal competition rules backed by the unilateral protectionist measures of developed countries inevitably exploded into fierce economic and political conflicts. Recuperating the capacity of the state apparatus in development becomes not only an economic but a political problem during globalization. In the WTO era, there is therefore great uncertainty about the possibility of pursuing or adapting the industrial strategy of the East Asian countries' catching up era. Policies are likely to shift between statist and neo-liberal approaches and eventually lead to trade disputes in which domestic firms or nationalistic politicians lobby the state to protect the local market and provide subsidies on domestic security grounds, while, under the WTO rules, developed nations put political pressure on latecomer governments to liberalize their markets, to dispense with ambitious independent development strategies, to readjust their economic structures and to minimize intervention.

China followed the East Asian industrial strategies to build indigenous semiconductor industries, and has encountered similar obstacles and challenges, especially given the pervasive neo-liberal WTO rules. In order to widen technological access from developed countries, the government has made compromises by giving up some East Asian interventionist policies. Nevertheless, unlike all other East Asian countries, China is still viewed as a security and economic threat to the United States. International political factors continue to constrain China from securing technological sources, because of the dual use nature of the semiconductor and ICT industry. This gives fuel to China's historically rooted concerns for national security and technological autonomy in 'strategic' sectors, in addition to the simple economic consideration of employment. Chinese leaders have little choice but to pursue any industrial policies possible that can assist Chinese enterprises in obtaining knowledge from the leading countries and to foster indigenous technological capabilities through all possible subsidies for both commercial and defence industries. On the basis of an international comparative study of one of the most dynamic ICT sectors, this chapter argues that China's 'breaking through' strategy could not enable the ICT industry to dynamically catch up with leading countries, and that it exhibits the economic and political pitfalls inherited from its East Asian neighbours. The Chinese government has to bear a huge political and economic cost to climb the technology ladders in order to reach a self-sustaining dynamic innovation trajectory. China's strategy thus needs to be constantly adjusted according to dynamic changes caused by both industrial/technological and international political factors.

Part IV

Rethinking the notion of state intervention

Lessons from and limitations of the Chinese experience

> The world is developing; in particular, high technology is advancing at a tremendous pace. China must not be content to remain backward. It should participate in the development of high technology from the very beginning . . . although China is poor, it has no choice but to undertake them. If we don't, the gap between China and other countries will grow wider.
>
> (Deng 1988)

> We must follow our own road in economic development as we did in revolution.
>
> (Deng 1984)

The main contribution of this book has been to interpret the role of the state in the emergence of China's ICT industry, and it has thus provided the first comprehensive account of China's ICT development model with specific reference to those of other East Asian countries. So far, previous chapters have documented and appraised China's key strategies in establishing this industry. This final part of the book pulls all the threads together, sketching out the Chinese ICT 'development model' and drawing implications for theory and policy. China's experience has important implications for economic development theories and popular debate concerning the causes of China's economic miracle. By comparing China's policy with that of the other East Asian latecomers, the second half of Chapter 8 is able to synthesize and conclude the core strengths and limitations or potential pitfalls of the model. In addition to illuminating the path of China's latecomer experience, Chapter 9 looks back to the theoretical argument presented in Chapter 2 and discusses the role the state played behind the myth of the Chinese ICT 'miracle'. The objective is not to promote a one-size-fits-all development model, but to ask what general lessons other developing countries can possibly learn from China's experience.

8 The development model for the Chinese ICT industry

Pre-reform conditions of the industry

What can explain the path China has taken to develop the world's largest ICT industry? This book shows that the development of the industry has been a unique process, although it shares some superficial resemblance with the East Asian model and has exhibited similar rapid export and production growth after opening up. The most controversial aspect of China's rise in the global ICT industry, as with all other East Asian countries, is the role that the state has played. Chapter 3 showed a type of extreme 'developmental state' under the central command regime in the early development period. Market mechanism and private ownership were completely replaced by state planning and ownership. As the country faced trade embargoes and military threats from Western countries and the USSR, the Chinese communist government naturally responded by building an independent and integrated industrial system, which, it was hoped, would allow the country to develop heavy industries quickly and so strengthen the military sectors. Centralized state control was essential for Chinese leaders to allocate resources to 'strategic' sectors.

Moreover, the market development approach was politically unfavoured, as it was associated with Western imperialism, colonialism and capitalism. The Soviet model at the time seemed to be the best feasible alternative for China to catch up with advanced countries. Consequently, the government placed development priority on the military use of the electronics industry for national defence. It owned and planned all aspects of the development of the industry. These are the crucial preconditions that one should bear in mind when discussing the developmental role of the Chinese government under the general theoretical framework presented in Chapter 2. They are clearly different from those faced by East Asian latecomers and Western economies, even though some of the policies might appear similar. As China adopted a gradualist reform approach, these pre-reform conditions continuously played a part, reflecting either in the nationalist industrial strategy or trade and technology conflicts.

The market-plan dual-track 'socialist' state approach

Chapter 4 describes phase II of the development of the electronics/ICT industry during the great opening up and economic reorientation period. As neo-liberal theorists argued that it would, opening up has increased trade and has provided access to newer technologies and knowledge of other countries' development experiences. In fact, a long period of economic and political turmoil left China with several serious economic crises in the late 1970s: agricultural goods and energy resources were in short supply, and unemployment was rising. Perceiving the end of both international and domestic political conflicts, the Chinese leaders were eager to find a pragmatic way to solve these problems in the short term and to improve the Chinese people's living standards in the longer term.

The impressive industrial growth of East Asian latecomers encouraged leaders to consider a capitalist model – more precisely an 'administration-guided' market approach. Unlike Amsden's East Asian 'getting the price wrong' model (2001), this chapter argues that neither 'market' nor 'price' existed in China at the time. The government had first to create a 'market' before it could turn the full range of the command plan apparatus into a set of selective interventionist policies. A gradualist and dualistic market-oriented economic system was cautiously built to allow a market channel to coexist with the command plan system and to separate the foreign and domestic economies, reducing political obstacles and avoiding disturbances of foreign investment in the domestic economy. State promotion in the electronics industry was therefore a natural and logical response to both internal and external changes. Part II of this book showed that the state made several important administrative and economic liberalization efforts in restructuring and reforming the electronics industry. As this chapter shows, in many ways these efforts appear similar to the East Asian interventionist approach.

China's early development model for the ICT industry, 1979–1993

Macroeconomic and administrative policies

As in all the other NIEs, the Chinese government emphasized macroeconomic stability by dealing with inflation, securing the financial systems, managing the exchange rate, and so on. The government created an experimental market-oriented environment within the command economy in order to prepare for further opening up and domestic reform.

The key features of the approach were as follows:

- macroeconomic reform, industrial restructuring and market creation;
- centralized state strategic planning and coordination;
- re-establishment of a domestic production network across geographic and administrative regions;
- military defence technology and production conversion for domestic civilian electronics consumption and export;

- reorganization of military and civil administration of the electronics industry;
- redirection of state investment and credit allocation towards consumer production.

Policies at the firm level

Firm-level reform (enterprise reform) was associated with the general market creation reform. The government attempted to increase enterprises' autonomy by withdrawing its role from their daily operation in order to make them respond to the newly created buyer market.

The key features of the policies adopted were as follows:

- decentralized enterprise autonomy on above-plan profit retention (financial and tax incentives); relatively independent financial and management decisions with contract responsibility;
- enterprise relocation and cluster creation to coastal areas and big cities;
- dominance of state ownership in the domestic economy and the electronics industry;
- experimental promotion of large state-owned electronics enterprises;
- policy relaxation on small individual private ownership to create competition;
- government procurement guarantees.

Trade and foreign investment

While the state was unable to provide and allocate domestic resources to the electronics industry effectively, foreign investment was perceived to be an appealing alternative. Openness was restricted to selected areas, outside the domestic economy and under the direct control of the state.

The key features of the approach to foreign investment were as follows:

- creation of special zones with physical and institutional supporting infrastructure to attract and accommodate FDI;
- mixed import substitution and export promotion strategies;
- state-organized foreign joint venture, licensing and other OEM activities;
- dismantling of the state monopoly on foreign trade and investment;
- direct foreign investment control.

Technology upgrading and learning

Openness was perceived as a means to obtain foreign technologies when domestic research institutions were failing to keep up with the development pace of the world ICT industry. Intensive selective and functional mixed interventions were used in the technological development of the ICT industry. It was hoped that this would strengthen national security and fulfil the political desire to attain the frontier of international competitiveness. The state guided

FDI activities towards selected coastal regions in the hope of maximizing spillover effects.

The key features of the approach were as follows:

- decentralized importation of foreign technology and R&D development at a local level;
- domestic market access in exchange for technologies from foreign investors;
- indigenous technology and innovation promotion through adapting the US state-coordinated 'research institute–university–enterprise' spin-off model (the Silicon Valley approach) and the 'dual use' technology development approach (combining military and civilian functions);
- functional targeting of R&D and human resource development in high-tech industries within selected regions;
- specific targeting of state-financed large R&D projects.

Shortcomings of the early model

The Chinese reform process has been gradual and piecemeal. The 'blueprint'-style reform has been experimental, informal and decentralized (see Chapter 4). Part II argued that the transitional nature of the Chinese economy together with the pre-reform historical conditions made it difficult for the government to carry out a state-guided industrial strategy in the ICT industry. First, unlike the 'big bang' reform in Eastern Europe, China's early reforms focused primarily on improving enterprise efficiency rather than establishing a Western-style market system. It is not surprising that uneven and partial development of market institutions eventually caused frequent short-term macroeconomic instability, which affected the growth of the ICT industry. The later reform, which attempted to develop the financial system so as to transfer urban saving into productive uses, also exhibited the undermined capability of the state to achieve a broader balance of resource allocation across regions and sectors. Autonomous enterprises continued to make investment decisions according to state-distorted prices. Fuelled by financial decentralization and 'instructions' from local governments, a flood of credit poured into SOEs and heavy industries. Rapid but imbalanced structural change eventually led to accumulated inflationary pressures that erupted repeatedly during the late 1980s.

Second, the state-controlled pricing system across sectors artificially ensured the high profitability of manufacturing sectors. It stimulated the entry of once restricted non-state sectors and generated large urban household savings, which again accelerated the growth of non-state sectors. New entrants eroded the revenues of SOEs and so reduced the traditional income of the government. The rapid growth of urban income soon exceeded the expanding production of consumer goods and consequently caused open inflation as well as an increasing demand for material and agricultural imports. The plan apparatus was brought back to cut down investment spending and slow down the growth of household incomes. Thus, China differed from the other East Asian latecomers, where the home country's demand was essential to promote the ICT industry. Given the central austerity policy launched in this period, industrial production was primarily directed towards exports. Domestic investment in the ICT industry was dramatically reduced.

Third, compared with the route followed by Japan and Korea, the Chinese industrial strategy was implemented in a less coherent and unified manner. This was particularly evident in the ICT industry. The central visionary plan turned out to signal that all local governments should concentrate their resources on the same or similar activities in the ICT industry. Duplication of technology imports and construction took place in virtually every province. Contrary to the intention of policymakers, the domestic upstream and downstream production networks as well as the supply chain were left unconstructed.

Fourth, the dualistic trade and investment regime limited the spillover effects of foreign investment, although it provided protection for domestic firms and reduced political disturbance. Although the S&T system received a higher level of investment, the projects primarily focused on 'dual' use electronics and provided very few commercial spin-offs.

The 'pillar' industry catching up model, 1993–2005

Under Deng's renewed 'socialist' market reform agenda of 1992, the Chinese government continued its overall gradualist reform, though many of the earlier structural problems remained unsettled. China has since travelled a long way towards an open trade and market regime. Market forces and institutions started building up; to improve enterprise autonomy and efficiency, many large SOEs were corporatized and converted into 'modern market-oriented' joint-stock companies with diversified ownership; small SOEs were either merged with larger ones or privatized (a strategy termed 'grasping the large and releasing the small'); the trade and investment regime became more integrated and liberalized. Meanwhile, a new set of industrial strategies was launched to promote strategically important 'pillar' industries such as the ICT/electronics industry in order to upgrade infrastructure and the overall industrial and economic structure, and improve China's international competitiveness.

The government pursued a neo-liberal market-based reform and followed the Heckscher–Ohlin comparative advantage approach. Chinese leaders assumed that openness would allow China to utilize its abundant labour to produce labour-intensive exports and to move to capital- and technology-intensive production once massive inflows of capital and technology began. This approach would quickly enable the country to achieve industrialization and gain international competitiveness. China's macroeconomic imbalance and factor prices would in due course equalize as long as domestic and international markets remained liberalized. Accordingly, China was willing to comply with neo-liberal rules, and joined the WTO in 2001. On the other hand, the state brought its industrial strategy for developing the ICT industry much closer to the East Asian statist approach. In practice, the government attempted to turn the planning command apparatus into slightly modified selective intervention strategies; it was hoped that these strategies could promote some 'strategic' industries and 'backbone' large state-owned or state-controlled firms (national champions) to meet the challenges of increasing global competition that accompanied market and trade liberalization. This nationalist approach not only won political support, but also put on hold current economic and social problems, providing some kind of political and social stability and fostering the domestic business environment, especially in the capital and technological sectors.

In the early 1990s, the Chinese leaders had a much clearer vision for developing the ICT/electronics industry than at the early reform stage because they recognized the industry's special economic benefits, and linkage to other sectors, and they learned from the experiences of other countries. Central administrative power was strengthened through the creation of a unified coordinative ministry, the Ministry of the Electronics Industry, in 1993, which later merged with the Ministry of Post and Telecommunications to form the Ministry of the Information Industry in 1998. Part III, Chapters 5–7 therefore explored the ICT catching-up strategies in more detail. It was argued that there are pitfalls embedded in these East Asian-style strategies, and the historical preconditions required for the industry to achieve global and sustainable competitiveness while WTO-mandated liberalization in trade takes place. It found that there are three main strategies followed by the government, based on the East Asian policies to extend the early development model. These are considered, in turn, below.

China's ICT pillar industry catching up model (extending that from the 1980s)

The big business and small business strategy (at the firm level)

The key features of the model at the firm level were as follows:

- dominant state-owned or state-controlled ownership in the ICT industry to achieve scale economies in production, technological progress and monopolistic market positions;
- state-mediated integration of existing state firms via alliances and mergers to create larger enterprises and clusters in selected markets and regions;
- building of the domestic demand pull and supply chain through government procurement;
- intensive use of financial subsidies and incentives after the early 1990s in selected sub-sectors (e.g. the purchase of production inputs on preferential terms, tax relief, preferential loans from the state-owned banks, and facilitation of listing on equity markets);
- promotion of small- and medium-sized firms after joining the WTO, for long-term structural adjustment, fostering the initial development of new

technologies and new niche markets, as well as supporting existing large firms by filling in the gaps in the domestic supply chain.

The 'attracting in' and 'walking out' strategy (trade- and investment-related)

The key features of the 'attracting in' and 'walking out' strategy were as follows:

- relaxation of FDI controls but extensive guidance and regulation to promote export and technological learning prior to WTO accession;
- preferential tax policies, extended business areas, relaxed trade-related rights and minimized bureaucratic procedures for promoting inflow of FDI;
- allowing domestic market access in return for transfer of desirable technologies, and selected market protection (lowering of tariff and non-tariff barriers in general, and more intensively in selected sectors or on imports of desirable production equipment);
- state-guided export market targeting (Western and developing countries' markets).
- relaxing of bureaucratic control and simplification of approval procedures for domestic ICT enterprises to engage in outward investment;
- provision of a free information service and abolition of the foreign exchange self-sufficiency requirement;
- financial assistance for state-selected large ICT enterprises to set up research centres and manufacturing sites abroad, as well as to merge with and acquire foreign enterprises.

The 'breaking through' strategy (dynamic technology/innovation catch-up)

The key features of the 'breaking through' strategy were as follows:

- direction into high-value-added and strategically important ICT sub-sectors;
- direct technology importation for SOEs/SCEs;
- aggressive approaches to MNEs through both informal contacts and diplomatic channels to enter into joint venture agreements with selected domestic enterprises and locations (combined with the 'attracting in' strategy);
- relaxation of wholly owned state ownership restrictions in the early 1990s, and the permitting of wholly foreign-owned firms after WTO accession;
- large R&D projects combined with big business strategies to create new SOE/SCEs in order to commercialize technological outcomes;
- intensive local content requirements and production, and market and trade protection in selected sectors prior to WTO entry;
- constant state demand pull and infrastructure building by involving domestic enterprises.

Performance and limitations of the catch-up pillar model

China's new strategic model, extended from the earlier one, led to a dramatic growth of the industry. The ICT industry clearly 'took off' after the mid-1990s and attained a phenomenal growth of output and international trade. Both production and exports are now the largest in the world. This development has been largely linked with China's broader integration into the global economy and production network. Liberalization of trade and investment brought to China a massive inflow of FDI as start-up production capital, which the government could not provide given the macroeconomic readjustment. When the internal marketization reform encountered difficulties, the introduction of large amounts of FDI to the domestic economy played a catalytic role. It immediately brought in competition and allowed the Chinese leaders to postpone many hard choices (such as rapid across-the-board privatization to create market competition). China also gained increasing access to foreign technologies and job-creation opportunities through promoting the entry of FDI. Exports appear to be becoming progressively 'high-tech' and expanding aggressively in several segments of the international ICT market.

Nevertheless, this book suggests that no matter how similar this strategy might seem to the neo-liberal market approach, the ultimate goal of China's industrial strategies remains to create a few self-reliant, vertically integrated, globally competitive pillar industries for national security and to fulfil nationalist political ambitions. The statist East Asian development model enjoyed considerable political appeal and was deeply embedded in China's new ICT model. Chinese officials' so-called market-oriented comparative advantage approach therefore in practice implies heavy state intervention. The market is primarily used as an incentive mechanism to improve the efficiency of existing SOE/SCEs rather than as an apparatus for Schumpeterian 'creative destruction' or 'natural selection'.

Yet the question remains as to whether this approach really enabled China's ICT industry to catch up with advanced countries and become the most competitive industry in today's world. Part III argued that China's experience was very different from the success of the statist East Asian latecomers. Different historical and economic conditions, and the international political situation, as well as the level of state capability, all restrained the industry from achieving real success and competitiveness. China's attempts to create an ICT organizational structure, associated earlier with the Japanese and Korean models and later combined with the Taiwanese model, were mainly for SOE or SCEs against the backdrop of its gradual market reform of the centrally planned economy. This institutional character marks the most fundamental difference between China's model and that of the East Asian latecomers, which focused at least ultimately on the development of private firms under market conditions with temporary state intervention. The East Asian model also shows more logical and natural reactions to historical and local economic conditions in forming the East Asian latecomers' strategies, whereas the Chinese model is more artificial and superficial.

Given the decentralized and informal style of reform, the Chinese government has still not developed a capacity to carry out industrial strategies in a unified and coordinated manner, as other NIEs have done. As in the early development period, duplicated and dispersed industrial and enterprise structural problems become unavoidable at the local level. Moreover, although China is able to encourage a large inflow of FDI, it seems that the government has insufficient capacity either to control or selectively protect certain sectors, especially after binding itself to the WTO accession protocols. China's strategies are again restrained by its market creation reform, which is based on the assumption that domestic firms could improve their efficiency if they were exposed to international competition. Unlike the NIEs, the Chinese ICT industry demonstrates heavy reliance on FIEs to carry out original equipment manufacturing production and export activities. Virtually no domestic firms can significantly control their own export and production networks or have competitive technological sources. Together with the absence of adequate management skills, weaker commercial technology capabilities and huge domestic demand, a large number of domestic firms may not be able to take advantage of the 'walking out' outward investment strategy and will have to retain a high degree of localization.

Most importantly, compared with the past experience of the NIEs, China's ICT industry strategy was very static. The state had exhibited an inflexible role in leading domestic firms to catch up and achieve real competitiveness within the dynamic development of the world economy. Compared to conditions during the NIE 'catching up' era, contemporary capitalism has undergone a profound transformation. A 'global business revolution' has taken place as a result of expansion of economic liberalization since the 1980s. Global competition is no longer relatively stationary, focusing primarily on manufacturing activities. It has become very dynamic, constantly changing with the rapid advances of ICT technologies and managerial innovation. Real catching up is now aiming at a moving target. Modern enterprises need to develop comprehensive 'network-controlling' capabilities to cope with the global scope and scale of their businesses and to manage their complicated global inter- and intra-firm relations (see also Chapter 6). This new wave of development makes China's imitated strategies irrelevant.

China's ICT industry policy was still following the traditional follower strategy, focusing on expansion of manufacturing output and export, competence in complex manufacturing processes, and the speed of launching possible lower-cost substitutes and other cost-reduction competition, rather than the fostering of network-controlling and innovation capabilities. Manufacturing activities have been standardized or modularized and transferred through MNE-controlled global production networks all over the world (MNEs' offshoring and outsourcing). These manufacturing activities are generally less profitable, of low productivity and at the end of the value chain spectrum, with little potential for improvement, and they often face stagnating markets. China's splendid ICT 'miracle' has thus turned out to be a static comparison to the industry's poor manufacturing performance of the past. Many key components, but also technologies as well as production and sales networks, remain in the hands of the global leaders. China's overtaking of advanced countries is therefore illusory: it is not in head-to-head competition with global leaders, but rather is complementary to their global restructuring.

In addition, the comparative analysis presented in Chapter 7 suggests that China faces huge challenges in dealing with the dynamic development of the industry. After failing to build a 'self-reliant' or 'self-sufficient' technological and innovation system, the Chinese leaders chose proactively to secure knowledge transfer through the opening up of privileged market access and providing preferential treatment to FDI. Following the statist premise, the government attempted to make a 'breakthrough' in certain strategic sectors such as semiconductors by providing subsidies (combined with the big business strategy) as well as creating a favourable supporting environment for domestic enterprises. China has indeed achieved significant growth in the semiconductor sector, as discussed in Chapter 7. However, not only are China's statist policies restricted by the neo-liberal WTO rules from supporting nationally controlled 'strategic' industries over foreign-owned ones, but China also faces far greater political pressures than any of the other NIE latecomers ever experienced. The NIE technological upgrading 'ladder' is no longer available for China to move from imitation and OEM to innovation. The challenges that the 'breaking through' strategy faces have extended beyond the economic into the political because of the dual-use nature of the industry. The international political environment influenced by Cold War thinking has constrained the possibilities for China to acquire or update technologies in a manner similar to that previously pursued by East Asian latecomers. This political obstacle continues to fuel China's historical concerns for national security and technological autonomy. If the government insists on climbing the technology ladders via the conventional NIE model, it may have to bear significant political costs today.

9 Theory and policy lessons

Rethinking China's ICT
development experience

This book has been constructed around some aspects of popular debate over the role of the state in economic development. Its aim has been to provide some new evidence to extend the debate by including the case of China's ICT industry. Before finally drawing some policy lessons, this part first summarizes the broader theoretical debate presented in Chapter 2.

Theoretical views of the world's development experiences

As presented in Chapter 2, there are two broad approaches to explaining the differences between the industrial and trade performance of different countries.

Rooted in neo-classical economic thinking, neo-liberals argue that the critical 'role' for all states, if there is any, is to shrink their size, liberalize trade and capital markets, provide a stable macroeconomic environment, improve the legal enforcement of market rules and the protection of private property, and invest in both infrastructure and education. In doing so, nations will not only be able to enjoy welfare gains from trade as a result of realizing their 'comparative advantages', economies of scale and efficient allocation of resources, but will also be able to access the latest knowledge and higher technologies, enlarge human capital and create spillover effects. Market liberalization is particularly supportive for developing nations to gain the economic and technological potential to catch up, through offshoring and outsourcing by developed countries.

Neo-liberals viewed the success of East Asian industries as being the result of continuously borrowing technologies from the West, largely though licensing and by taking advantage of their low labour costs with fewer price distortions. This method was believed to have enabled Japan in the 1960s and 1970s to maximize its current and future income. Korea and Taiwan then replicated Japan's achievement (Ozawa 1974; Smith 2000). All these countries began to improve their technological capabilities only when there was a need for high-tech sectors to provide higher-income jobs to meet rising wage levels (McKinsey 1998). None of these countries was at the international technology frontier. Poor latecomer countries would be worse off building up high-tech industries, neo-liberals would contend. Their principal goal of technological development should be geared towards rapidly adapting technology created elsewhere (at great cost in time and money) for the advancement of low-tech commercial applications that can provide vast employment. Given ongoing globalization and economic liberalization, there is no need to ensure the use of indigenous technologies, as MNEs enter their economies and will provide these.

Alternatively, there is the 'developmental state' school of thought as a counter-weight to the prevailing neo-liberal-style economic globalization. Scholars argue that the active involvement of the states is crucial in the indigenous industrial success of East Asian latecomers. They contend that market mechanisms are not perfect, although they remain a powerful force; all successful East Asian latecomers had been very selectively interventionist in international trade, technology transfer, domestic resource allocation and foreign investment. Neo-liberals cannot deny that the guiding hand of strong developmental states is vital to improve market outcomes, assisting local firms to discover and adapt appropriate new activities or technologies when entrepreneurship is absent and information imperfect.

This guiding hand of the state has become even more crucial as economic development has become transformed, now relying on knowledge-based rather than production-based assets (Amsden 2001). Unlike the neo-liberal premise, actual knowledge flow does not happen by itself or freely across borders. None of the NIEs could simply acquire foreign technologies for all their needs just by opening up. The state not only has to play a key role in making institutional and social arrangements to build up technological learning and absorption capability, but also has to leverage technologies from FDI and provide domestic firms with a focus point through which to catch up and to enter into the international market. The developmental state should therefore strategically intervene in the market by introducing 'reciprocal control mechanisms' based on a feedback of information that has been assessed to help firms discover the right activities, overcome learning costs and coordination problems, and build up necessary institutional capabilities beyond the pressing neo-liberal development agenda, which relies heavily on market rules and the private sector.

China's ICT development experience and policy implications

If all the competing paradigms reviewed in Chapter 2 were largely drawn from other countries' development experiences before the twenty-first century, China's emergence in the world economy continues to extend the development literature, offering many new perspectives. An important point to consider is that China's development experience and ideas have formed a new, pragmatic path as an alternative to the neo-liberal 'Washington consensus'. It is a path that enables other countries to rethink the way they develop and integrate into the global economy and society. In terms of the industrial and trade strategies this book discusses, the development experience of China's ICT industry shows that neither an extreme neo-liberal strategy nor an extreme statist one is suitable for developing countries' economic development. This book has narrowed the debate down to one concerning China's most 'successful' industry (in a static sense), the ICT industry, and has identified a few general lessons, as follows.

Market versus state in the development of high-tech industries

Like that of the NIEs, China's experience shows how both market and state have their own roles to play in the process of development and industrialization. Unlike the neo-liberal criticism discussed in Chapter 2, real developmental statists, even Frederick List himself, have never repudiated free trade and a free market as an ultimate goal for nations to achieve. That is also what China's whole economic reform is believed to be aiming for. Indeed, the market mechanism can provide many development opportunities, deal with gradual and marginal changes, and reduce rent seeking and technological sloth. In the ICT industry, market and trade liberalization enabled China successfully to 'attract in' technologies, access and expand in foreign markets, and create learning and job opportunities. Most importantly, it allowed start-up capital resources to flow into the sector when the government was unable to provide them, and thus enabled the country to carry out industrial structural adjustment.

However, developing nations, having accepted 'universal' free trade and a free market, often face more setbacks than promised benefits, because the world in reality differs so much from the neo-liberal ideal. The international market itself is imperfect, and a few large MNEs and the developed countries in which they are based have already achieved both internal and external economies of scale. Moreover, the market and the social supporting framework, 'non-price' factors, are either absent or underdeveloped in developing countries, thus restricting them from embarking on production adjustments according to the increasing variety of inputs after opening up.

The neo-liberal propositions are thus able neither to improve the efficiency of industries in developing nations through market allocation, nor to help them to gain competitiveness by breaking existing monopolistic barriers raised by leading firms and countries. Instead, following universal 'comparative advantages', they are locked into undesirable patterns of specialization during globalization. The illusion of China's rapid export and investment phenomena ('walking out') in the ICT industry after WTO and ITA accession has clearly demonstrated this point. China was still competing on the basis of cost reduction and unable to improve its real competitiveness. Although 'shock therapy' and the 'big push' strategy may establish market institutions overnight, firms' ability to respond to price signals and enter markets is still weak, and restricted by imperfect information and a poor supporting environment (coordination, infrastructure, weak capital markets, absent suppliers, etc.). What sudden changes in price structure often bring to developing countries is great social and economic uncertainty. The development of China's ICT industry was greatly affected by such changes in the 1980s (see Chapter 4).

The most difficult part of economic development for neo-liberals to explain lies in their treatment of a dynamic factor: technology. There are additional costs, time, experience, externalities, market failure and constraints involved in using newer technologies and innovation. Also, the whole technological advance is not an automatic and free process that one can simply obtain through FDI. Leaving capability building to free market forces and trade is rarely sufficient. Technological development can be slow and gaps between countries may widen. There are thus roles for the state to take in leading domestic firms to overcome existing international market barriers and learning costs, to create markets and correct market failures by compensating for inefficiency, and to foster supporting environments. It is not surprising that the success of the Chinese ICT industry in the early development stages is largely a story of interventionist strategies. There is no doubt that many developing countries can learn from this early development model to enter the ICT industry. While the availability of a cheap labour force has been essential for China to enter the industry, it has hardly been sufficient. China owes its success not only to the emergence of a gradualist state-led market reform and a more strategic policy towards foreign trade and investment, but also to heavy investment in R&D, technological learning, infrastructure and defence procurement so as to overcome both internal and external barriers. This, however, should not be confused with the common reactions of some developing countries to their balance of payments difficulties, such as across-the-board import substitution, or pervasive state intervention and nationalism. These are primarily the results of the failure of domestic economic adjustment in the early stage of economic liberalization. That neither of these extreme statist strategies can help with the situation is supported by the findings of this book. Yet the question is what kind of interventions really worked and how they were formed or are to be implemented in China.

Nationalist sentiment versus development orientation

China's ICT experience indicates that state intervention should be highly development-oriented rather than fulfilling nationalist sentiment. China's pre-reformed industrial development ideas were not about economics but about politics: the balance of domestic and global powers and military preparation accompanied by international political conflicts. The new reform agenda in the post-Mao era shows that the development objective is driven by a desire to raise the living standards of the masses quickly and to peacefully grow as an equitable member of international society (*heping juqi*).[1] The whole idea is to move society 'upward' by using economic and administrative means, without posing threats to global peace and stability – a fundamental and moral objective of development that was somehow missed in the 'Washington consensus' and forgotten in the Soviet and extreme statist model.

Nevertheless, the post-Mao industrial strategies strongly reflected China's leaders' political desires to regain China's pre-eminent historical status quickly, to ensure economic and technological autonomy, to attain the frontier of international competitiveness and to advance national defence. Irrational development such as repeated construction and technology imports as well as 'blind' M&A unavoidably appeared in the ICT industry. The ambition, largely influenced by ideas of political self-sufficiency, to create an independent ICT industry from upstream to downstream within China's territory certainly faced many challenges, given the international political environment and the highly dynamic nature of the industry.

All industrial strategies should therefore be used to achieve long-term growth, but not to fulfil nationalist sentiments, to keep wages constantly low, or manipulate exchange rates for mercantilist 'competitive' export expansion, breaking the fortunes of other countries. Neither are they used to control all aspects of economic activities, or to leave everything to the 'market' – particularly today, when international markets can be distorted and global innovation and production networks are controlled by MNEs in coordination and resource relocation of certain economic activities for their own interests across continents. International 'markets' can hardly be as competitive as neo-liberals have assumed, 'efficiently' allocating resources or activities for the best interests of developing nations, and this creates potential issues of maldistribution of income between developed and developing countries.

China's ICT development during the period in which it engaged in more expansive neo-liberal WTO reform shows that a massive surge of FDI has led to superficial growth of industrial output and exports. Nevertheless, the majority of domestic enterprises still suffer from a lack of technological capabilities and are locked into low-value-added and cost-reduction activities that appear 'high-tech' as finished goods, such as labour-intensive assembly production of final high-tech products for MNEs (see Chapter 6). Unfettered FDI may bring opportunities and have positive impacts on basic technological upgrading and the general economic environment in the early development stages, but it will not assist any latecomers to build up capability and to achieve sustainable competitive advantage (subsequent deepening) in the long run. The governments of developing nations thus need a clear development-oriented 'moral' objective, and to act on behalf of the benefits of their people, grasping development opportunities and realizing the potentials of their countries, rather than leaving everything to distorted market allocation and coordination. But nor should they, like China, attempt to control all aspects of industrial development to create a highly independent industry without considering international cooperation in today's globalized world.

Learning focus to combat the dynamism of the high-tech industries

This leads to the third policy lesson derived from China's experience: that the role of the state should be to target learning and be selective, as well as constantly to modify the targets according to the dynamic development of the ICT industry. As knowledge accumulation has become increasingly vital in today's economic development, China's experience shows that economic strategies should primarily serve the purpose of learning, especially in high-tech industries. Again, opening up provides opportunities such as 'learning by doing' and imitation activities, but the state may still need to provide temporary initial nutrition and protection as well as to correct distorted market signals. Providing uniform across-the-board protection for all activities makes no sense. Not only is it too costly for the state, but it is also not suitable for the development of all the different kinds of technologies.

Learning processes and externalities such as required inputs and institutional supports are technology-specific. Some technologies might be more embodied in production means while others are more complicated, contain tactical elements and are hard to absorb if no promotion measures are undertaken. China, like the East Asian latecomers, identified a few 'visionary' targeted areas (e.g. semiconductors; see Chapter 7) and embarked on coordination with factor markets, providing capital, information and institutional support as well as fostering required skills and infrastructure. Meanwhile, the government needed to demand improved performance by domestic firms in exchange for further incentives and support.

The argument here is not to exaggerate the role of the state. Governments may sometimes promote the 'wrong' visionary sectors and fail to keep upgrading and modifying measures in accordance with changes of environment, as may all types of business investment. The study of China's ICT industry shows that there is great uncertainty for the state in adjusting the strategies of the old East Asian latecomers to try to catch up with a 'moving' target led by the emergence of the global production and innovation network. Chinese enterprises tend to stay away from the core competitive areas, diversify into less specialized and related areas, and choose to take over modularized activities to complement global leaders' specialization in network-controlling and innovation activities. It is not surprising to see that both large and small businesses, and the 'walking out' and 'attracting in' strategies, have failed to enable the ICT industry to catch up with the dynamic development of the industry. While suggesting that the government leave these strategies to market forces, this book has emphasized that the state's intention to improve indigenous capabilities and to act in the interests of society is something that can hardly be provided by the 'market' alone.

In the new development era under the WTO rules, the conventional East Asian development 'ladder' has become difficult to follow, but there is still some scope for selective intervention. While accelerating liberalization, the government needs to ensure the effective use of WTO non-actionable policies to support the technological upgrading of domestic firms more directly (see Chapter 7). The agreement prevents developing countries from using policies that could discriminate against foreign firms. Together with forces promoting structural adjustment, bilateral trade agreements and pressures from rich countries, it has arguably been seen as removing necessary protection and creating obstacles for learning efforts. However, as the agreed integration conditions and speed are set, the government could look to employ those 'non-actionable' subsidies such as those for basic R&D, environment-related technological upgrading and economically disadvantaged regions. These restrictions include only 'trade-related policies', and there is still scope for developing countries to use domestic policies together with non-actionable subsidies to create learning effects. Although the NIE strategies have become difficult to pursue, China could still subsidize ICT firms investing in equipment or special skills, assist research activities conducted by firms or higher education, and support start-up firms, regardless of their size and private ownership. It could also provide assistance to set up industrial parks in the less developed northern and western regions.

Country-specific barriers

The most important lesson other developing countries should learn from China's ICT development is how to draw on the historical experiences of others to design their own strategies. China's experience shows that a successful economic policy or reform programme should not be a comprehensive and detailed duplication of the programmes of others, neither should it be based entirely on some theoretical abstraction. It must be country-specific, fitting the particular country's economic, historical and political conditions, its degree of market and institutional development, and the realities of the international market and environment. All these differences between countries imply that different interventions need to be made, depending on the conditions.

China paid little attention to these differences while attempting to replicate the East Asian latecomer strategy in its gradual transitional market reform of the command economy. It also created large international competitive firms based on unrealistic notions of what global competition is like or should be. A number of historical elements that shaped the selection of East Asian strategies were not taken into account in the promotion of the Chinese ICT industry, for example the Japanese colonial influence, the availability of local private capital, the ultimate promotion focus on private enterprises, the governing capacity of the state, as well as the differing nature of economies and international political environment (see Chapter 5). It is not surprising that China's ICT strategy did not turn out to be dynamic and sustainable, as the state failed to modify and update the NIE strategies adopted in accordance with local conditions and the constantly and rapidly changing competition in the industry. The Chinese government also faced huge social and economic adjustment costs. Intellectual, ideological and political debates and conflicts between reformists and conservatives led to an uneven, stop-and-go development of marketization, and extreme plan-style state intervention. The informal, gradualist, experimental and decentralized reform approach used to reconcile confrontation between the two parties weakened the state's ability to carry out coordinating functions between different administrative regions, which resulted in locally duplicated industrial structure and a confused development target.

This leads to a mention of the functions of SOEs in the technological learning process. While avoiding many ownership reform issues, the Chinese government attempted to convert them into profit-seeking competitive 'firms'. SOEs, as opposed to private firms, are established for purposes other than making profits in most Western economies. These mainly include reducing distributional problems in some regions, achieving particular macroeconomic goals (such as reducing inflation) and promoting private firms (Aharoni and Vernon 1981). It is therefore not justifiable to use profitability or the concept of competitiveness to measure the performance of SOEs. For example, in Taiwan's case SOEs were created as the first movers into new markets where small private firms were experiencing both financial and technological difficulties. SOEs in these selected sectors were used to stimulate initial demand and create spillover effects for private firms that entered later. Chinese SOEs could be used to address distributional concerns of economic activities among provinces. The government could assist coastal firms to shift their less productive activities to less developed regions so as to foster supporting bases. Given the country-specific barriers, these tasks remain difficult for China, as the government needs to refocus its policy on private firms and decide which SOEs it needs to privatize and how to do that legitimately.

Finally, the upgrading of industrial structures through the same NIE strategies has raised profound international political issues regarding foreign technological access, the dual-use nature of the ICT industry and related national security issues, trade surplus pressures on trading partners, foreign exchange, human rights and WTO restrictions. It is indeed very unlikely that China can reconcile the two conflicting approaches, the neo-liberal and the nationalist interventional, to promote further ICT competitiveness. Deeper integration into the global ICT production and innovation network has also proved difficult if the state cannot help firms to overcome political barriers and move away from extreme nationalism to rational development. China's nationalist ambitions have already caused the industry to integrate into the global production network in a shallow manner, and have therefore limited the possibility of pursuing specialization and network-controlling activities – the activities of the leading global enterprises. The big business strategy was used to force local vertical integration artificially and push activities into a few large firms, without considering technological connectivity. The small and medium-sized strategy was used to enhance regional supply chains so as to reduce dependence on foreign imports. The challenge China faces is finding a dynamic technological upgrading ladder. This has proved to be difficult, however. The 'breaking through' interventionist strategy that China employed to develop the semiconductor industry has faced serious political challenges and opposition based on the dual-use nature of the industry (see Chapter 7).

As real-world policy cannot be divorced from politics, political acceptance and cost should be taken into account in adopting other countries' models. In short, the rise of a particular industry is a history-dependent and country-specific process in which both exogenous and indigenous factors play important roles. Governmental involvement is not intended to replace the market and can only be beneficial if it can help the industries overcome barriers to improving competitiveness both economically and politically, and in accordance with the changes of the outside world. Perhaps both China's ICT development and those attempting to use China's model should take heed of Deng's doctrine: 'We must follow our own road in economic development as we did in revolution'.

Going forward

The rise of China's ICT sector in the global market is of course tremendous, although not as competitive as one might at first think. Its development path and the whole economic reform remain fraught with nationalism, contradictions, tensions and pitfalls in many respects. Yet some pragmatic characteristics of the 'model' and the scale of expansion China has achieved so far have already demonstrated a possible alternative approach to the disappointing neo-liberal one, although it has yet to become sustainable. Given that China is larger than any of the NIEs, its impact on the global economy and community is or will be greater than that of previous latecomers. With political and legal systems to be improved in the foreseeable future, a time might come when the Chinese ICT industry follows its own path rather than adopting those taken by others. This may not only allow a sustainable strong economy and industries to emerge, but also offer a hope for the world that a common international interest for all can be pursued in order to engender a globalization that is fair, peaceful and moral. Any mercantilist attempt, however, will not be tolerated by other countries. Because of the inseparable nature of real-world policy and politics, as well as the dual application of the ICT industry, a series of critical questions needs to be answered to ensure China's 'peaceful rise' and rapid integration into the ICT global production network. These are as follows.

- Does China still have the capacity to lead its firms to internationalization and push them up the global value chain?
- Can China become more deeply integrated into the global production network while advanced countries have political and security concerns?
- Would privatization be a more satisfactory alternative for the purpose of improving China's global competitiveness and resolving foreign political opposition?
- If so, could this be feasible within China's current 'socialist' political structure?
- How would China's industrial strategy, which aims at expansion at both ends of the value chain, ensure the industrial development of other developing countries and fulfil its 'peaceful rise' proposition?

Appendix 1
Definition of the Chinese ICT industry

The Chinese ICT industry this book discusses is set mainly within the manufacturing side of the information industry (see also Chapter 1). The characteristics of the ICT industry are difficult to define as the industry features rapid changes in technology and overlaps with many other industries. The definition of the industry also varies from country to country. The Chinese electronics industry is classified into the following sub-sectors: communication equipment, broadcast television equipment, computers, components, measuring instruments, special purpose instruments, consumer products and electronic devices (see Table A.1). In 1998, the Chinese government implemented a series of institutional reforms. The Ministry of the Information Industry (MII) was set up to replace both the former Ministry of Posts and Telecommunications and the Ministry of the Electronic Industry. The MII was established to formulate national plans, to design policies, to regulate the information industry and to promote the application of information in the national economy and social services. The MII also took up the information and network management functions of the former Ministry of Radio, Film and Television, the Space Industrial Corporation and the Aviation Industrial Corporation, and also supervises the newly established State Post Administration (MII 1999). In line with these institutional changes and the strategic development goals announced at the Sixteenth National Congress, the National Bureau of Statistics of China (NBSC) made reference to the United Nations (UN) proposal of 2002 on the classification of the information and ICT sectors. It issued a provisional prescript on the statistical division of 'the information-related industries' on 29 December 2003.[1]

In the UN proposal, it is suggested that the information industry include 'not only the electronic way of producing, storing and dissemination of information, but also the old-fashioned ways of paper and records' (Albert 2002).[2] The ICT industry is proposed to cover 'instrument[s] (product[s]) that enable the user to make use of electricity as an information vector, which means the (potential) transportation possibility to make information available for consumers of information' (Albert 2002).[3] Unlike these two UN proposed definitions, the Chinese term does not draw a distinction between the ICT and the information industries. Instead, it combines these two definitions and names them 'the information-related industries', which means a set of activities that are relevant to electronic information

Table A.1 Classification of the electronics industry by the Ministry of the Information Industry

1 Communication equipment
    Manufacture of wire transmission apparatus
    Manufacture of wireless transmission apparatus
    Manufacture of switching apparatus
    Manufacture of wire terminal units
    Manufacture of wireless terminal units
    Manufacture of other communication equipment

2 Broadcast television equipment
    Manufacture of broadcast television equipment
    Manufacture of televisions
    Manufacture of radio and sound recorders
    Manufacture of video recorders
    Repair of broadcast television equipment
    Manufacture of other broadcasting TV devices

3 Computers
    Manufacture of complete computer final products
    Manufacture of computer peripheral equipment
    Manufacture of computer associated services facilities
    Software design and manufacture
    Manufacture of calculators
    Computer repair
    Manufacture of other computer products

4 Components
    Manufacture of electrical micro-machines
    Manufacture of wires and cables
    Manufacture of electronic storage cells/accumulators
    Manufacture of electronic dry cells
    Manufacture of electronic components
    Manufacture of special materials for electronic components
    Manufacture of other component products

5 Measuring instruments
    Manufacture of electronic measuring apparatus
    Manufacture of other electronic measuring apparatus

6 Special purpose instruments
    Manufacture of electronic special devices
    Manufacture of moulds and gears
    Manufacture of other electronic instruments

7 Consumer products
    Manufacture of refrigerators
    Manufacture of electronic fans
    Manufacture of air conditioning
    Manufacture of electric heating devices
    Manufacture of electric toys
    Manufacture of other consumer products

8 Electronic devices
    Manufacture of bulbs
    Manufacture of electronic vacuum devices
    Manufacture of semiconductor discrete devices
    Manufacture of integrated circuits
    Manufacture of materials for electronic devices
    Manufacture of other devices

Source: *Yearbook of the Electronics Industry*, various years.

(see Table A.2) (NBSC 2003).[4] Table A.3 compares the OECD proposed classification and that of the NBSC.[5]

The UN classification of the information sector exists only as a proposal for the revision of the International Standard Industrial Classification (ISIC) in 2007. There is still some debate about the exact coverage of the ICT and information

Table A.2 ICT classification by China's National Bureau of Statistics

Classification	Code
I. Manufacture of electronic information equipment	
1 Manufacture of computer equipment	
Manufacture of complete computer final products	4041
Manufacture of computer network equipment	4042
Manufacture of computer peripheral equipment	4043
2 Manufacture of communication equipment	
Manufacture of transmission apparatus	4011
Manufacture of switching apparatus	4012
Manufacture of terminal units	4013
Manufacture of mobile communication and terminal units	4014
Manufacture of other communication equipment	4019
3 Manufacture of broadcast television equipment	
Broadcast television programme-producing and transmitting devices	4031
Manufacture of broadcast television receiving devices	4032
TV application equipment and other broadcasting TV devices	4039
4 Manufacture of home audio-visual equipment	
Manufacture of home movie and TV devices	4071
Manufacture of home audio equipment	4072
5 Manufacutre of electronic devices and components	
Manufacture of electronic vacuum devices	4051
Manufacture of semiconductor discrete devices	4052
Manufacture of integrated circuits	4053
Manufacture of optoelectronic and other electronic devices	4059
Electronic components and groupware	4061
Manufacture of printed circuit boards	4062
6 Manufacture of special purpose instruments and meters	
Manufacture of radar and associated facilities	4020
Manufacture of special instruments and meters for environmental monitoring	4121
Manufacture of special purpose apparatus for navigation, meteorology and oceanography	4123
Manufacture of special purpose instruments and meters for agriculture, forestry, livestock husbandry and fishing	4124
Manufacture of special purpose apparatus for geological prospecting and seismology	4125
Manufacture of nucleus and nuclear radiation measuring apparatus	4127
Manufacture of electronic measuring apparatus	4128
Manufacture of other special purpose apparatus	4129

Classification	Code
7 Manufacture of general electronic instruments and meters	
Manufacture of industrial automatic control system devices	4111
Manufacture of electronic engineering instruments and meters	4112
Manufacture of experimental analysis devices	4114
Manufacture of supply meters and other general instruments	4119
8 Manufacture of other electronic and information devices	
Manufacture of wires and cables	3931
Manufacture of light wave fibre and optical cable	3932
Calculators and special purpose devices for currency	4155
II. Sales and rental of electronics and information devices	
1 Sales of computer, software and facilities	
Wholesales of computer, software and facilities	6375
Retail of computers, software and facilities	6572
Retail of other electronics products	6579
2 Sales of communication apparatus	
Wholesales of telecommunication and broadcast television devices	6376
Retail of telecommunication devices	6573
3 Rental of computer and telecommunication devices	
Rental of computer and telecommunication devices	7314
III. Services of electronics and information transmission	
1 Telecommunications	
Fixed telecommunication services	6011
Mobile telecommunication services	6012
Other telecommunication services	6019
2 Internet communication services	
Internet communication services	6020
3 Broadcast television transmitting services	
Cable-cast television transmitting services	6031
Radio-broadcasting television transmitting services	6032
4 Satellite transmitting services	
Satellite transmitting services	6040
IV. Computer services and software	
1 Computer services	
Computer system services	6110
Data processing	6120
Computer repair	6130
Other computer services	6190
2 Software services	
Basic software services	6211
Application software services	6212
Other software services	6290

(Continued)

Table A.2 Continued

Classification	Code
V. Other information-related services	
1 Radio broadcasting, television, movies and music	
Radio broadcasting	8910
Television broadcasting	8920
Production and publishing of motion pictures	8931
Motion picture projection	8932
Audio-visual production	8940
2 News and publishing	
News	8810
Publishing of books	8821
Publishing of newspapers	8822
Publishing of journals and periodicals	8823
Publishing of music	8824
Publishing of electronic publications	8825
Other publishing	8829
3 Library and archive activities	
Library	9031
Archives	9032

Source: NBSC 2004.

Table A.3 Comparison between the ICT manufacturing industrial classifications of the OECD and China

	OECD classification	Chinese classification	Code
Manufacturing			
ISIC 3000	Office, accounting and computing machinery	Manufacture of complete computer final products	4041
		Manufacture of computer peripheral equipment	4043
		Manufacture of calculators and special purpose devices for currency	4155
ISIC 3130	Insulated wire cable	Manufacture of wires and cables	3931
		Manufacture of light wave fibre and optical cable	3932
ISIC 3210	Electronic valves and tubes and other electronic components	Manufacture of electronic vacuum devices	4051
		Manufacture of semiconductor discrete devices	4052
		Manufacture of integrated circuits	4053

(Continued)

Table A.3 Continued

	OECD classification	Chinese classification	Code
		Manufacture of optoelectronic and other electronic devices	4059
		Electronic component and groupware	4061
		Manufacture of printed circuit boards	4062
ISIC 3220	Television and radio transmitters and apparatus for line telephony and line telegraphy	Manufacture of transmission apparatus	4011
		Manufacture of switching apparatus	4012
		Manufacture of terminal units	4013
		Manufacture of mobile communication and terminal units	4014
		Manufacture of other communication equipment	4019
		Manufacture of broadcast television programme-producing and transmitting devices	4031
ISIC 3230	Television and radio receivers, sound and video recording or reproducing apparatus and associated goods	Manufacture of computer network equipment	4042
		Manufacture of mobile communication and terminal units	4014
		Manufacture of broadcast television receiving devices	4032
		Manufacture of TV application equipment and other broadcasting TV devices	4039
		Manufacture of home movie and TV devices	4071
		Manufacture of home audio equipment	4072
ISIC 3312	Instruments and appliances for measuring, checking, testing, navigating and other purposes except industrial process equipment	Manufacture of radar and associated facilities	4020
		Manufacture of electronic engineering instruments and meters	4112
		Manufacture of experimental analysis devices	4114
		Manufacture of supply meters and other general instruments	4119
		Manufacture of special instruments and meters for environmental monitoring	4121

(Continued)

	OECD classification	Chinese classification	Code
		Manufacture of special purpose apparatus for navigation, meteorology and oceanography	4123
		Manufacture of special purpose instruments and meters for agriculture, forestry, livestock husbandry and fishing	4124
		Manufacture of special purpose apparatus for geological prospecting and seismology	4125
		Manufacture of nucleus and nuclear radiation measuring apparatus	4127
		Manufacture of electronic measuring apparatus	4128
		Manufacture of other special purpose apparatus	4129
ISIC 3313	Industrial process equipment	Manufacture of industrial automatic control system devices	4111
Services			
ISIC 5150	Wholesale of machinery, equipment and supplies		
ISIC 5151	Wholesale of computers, computer peripheral equipment and software	Wholesale of computer, software and facilities	6375
ISIC 5152	Wholesale of electronic and telecommunication parts and equipment	Retail of computers, software and facilities	6572
		Retail of other electronics products	6579
		Wholesale of telecommunication and broadcast television devices	6376
		Retail of telecommunication devices	6573
ISIC 6420	Telecommunications	Fixed telecommunication services	6011
		Mobile telecommunication services	6012
		Other telecommunication services	6019
		Cable-casting television transmitting services	6031
		Radio-broadcasting television transmitting services	6032
		Satellite transmitting services	6040

(Continued)

Table A.3 Continued

	OECD classification	Chinese classification	Code
ISIC 7123	Rental of office machinery and equipment	Rental of computer and telecommunication devices	7314
ISIC 72	Computer-related activities		
ISIC 7210	Hardware consultancy	Computer system services	6110
ISIC 7221	Software publishing	Basic software services	6211
		Application software services	6212
ISIC 7229	Other software consultancy and supply	Other software services	6290
ISIC 7230	Data processing	Data processing	6120
ISIC 7240	Data activities and online distribution of electronic content	Internet communication services	6020
ISIC 7250	Maintenance and repair of office, accounting and computing machinery	Computer repair	6130
ISIC 7290	Other computer-related activities	Other computer services	6190

Source: OECD 2002, and NBSC 2004.

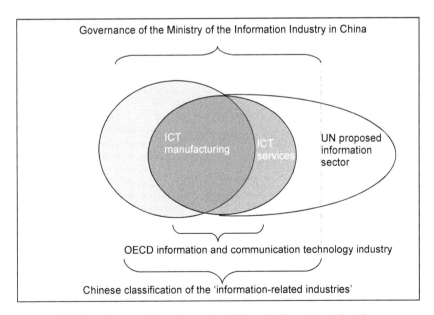

Figure A.1. Classification of the electronics, ICT and information industries.

sectors. However, a broad view of how such classifications apply in China is delineated in Figure A.1. The information industry covers both the traditional and electronic means of displaying, producing, storing and disseminating information. The electronics industry is concerned with the production of all electronic goods, including those that perform the functions listed in Table A.1. The ICT industry, then, lies at the overlap between these two sectors. Its manufacturing side forms a part of the electronics industry, which is also involved in producing information-related products, and its service side forms the electronic part of the information industry.

The governance of the MII, contrary to what is suggested by its name and the industrial classification, ranges from the electronics industry to partly cover the UN proposed information industry, but it also covers the whole ICT sector.[6] In line with the 'big business' (national champion) strategy and the ranking of the top 100 information technology enterprises (manufacturing only; see Appendix 4) carried out by the MII, this book therefore focuses on the manufacturing part of the Chinese 'information-related industry' (also known as the ICT industry) (see Table A.3). The designation 'electronics industry' is used only at points where it is necessary to show the development of the ICT industry and be consistent with the policies launched prior to 1998.

Appendix 2

Relaxation of investment restrictions

Market access in exchange for selected advanced technologies

Policies welcoming FDI, particularly in the manufacturing sectors, have contributed significantly to the expansion of trade and investment in China. A number of concessionary provisions were used to encourage the inflow of FDI.

- Limiting controls on foreign business. As is discussed in Chapter 4, China has been relaxing its restrictions on the market entry modes since 1986. In 1995, foreign investment was allowed to take the form of JVs, WFOEs and JSCs with minimum administrative interference. Additionally, foreign investors were allowed to appoint the chairman of the board and other key management members, to engage directly in foreign trade and to partner with non-state-owned enterprises in accordance with the newly modified foreign investment law of 1992. Some promotion provisions, once available only in the special economic zones and coastal open cities, were expanded to a large number of open cities along the border and inland cities. Furthermore, foreign investors were allowed to engage in equity investment via hard currencies in selected firms, which were initially listed as B shares on the Shanghai Stock Exchange in 1992. These restrictions were gradually removed in the late 1990s.
- Concessionary tax rates. Along with relaxation of market access, a series of concessionary taxation policies provided modest financial advantages to FDI and export-oriented enterprises to reduce the risk of establishment and receive incentives. Since 1991, the Chinese government has been replacing un-unified corporate income tax imposed by local authorities with a statutory standardized tax rate of 33 per cent on all FIEs across all regions; those established in SEZs and STZs (Special Technology Zones) qualified for a further reduced rate at 15 per cent; those that had been operating in China, irrespective of location, for more than ten years could receive significant tax holidays. Income tax was remitted for the first and second year of profit-making operations, and levied at 50 per cent in their third, fourth and fifth years.
- Duty-free imports of production input for export production. All investment goods and foreign-sourced material imported for self-use were exempt from tariff and import-stage value added tax.[1] Manufacturers are eligible for a tax

rebate on almost all local content that was sourced from within China for their export products. Competition among different local authorities to attract FDI also led to significant subsidies in many overt and implicit forms such as subsidized prices for land use and minimized central state tax exemption by local officials.

- Relaxing foreign exchange policies. In the mid-1990s, China also significantly liberalized its foreign exchange policy, which allowed FIEs to retain their foreign exchange revenues while domestic firms were subject to many restrictions.

All these policies provide a general framework or a model of investment and export encouragement, which, combined with a relatively cheap labour force, have made China one of the most cost-competitive production sites in the world. However, in order to obtain substantial foreign technologies and financial resources for domestic enterprises, the government realized that it had to offer foreign investors opportunities to access China's huge potential domestic market. In 1992, China opened up more areas for investment, such as commercial retailing, power generation, land, property and port development, insurance, law, accounting, airline services, hotels and restaurants, that had previously been off-limits to foreign JVs. In 1995, after the volume of FDI had grown from modest amounts of a few hundred million US dollars per year before 1991 to more than double in both 1993 and 1994, the government promulgated the Provisional Regulations for Guiding Foreign Investment.

Appendix 3

China's foreign investment guidelines on the electronics and telecommunications industry

The ICT industry (for civilian purposes) is now one of the most highly liberalized industries in China, although there are still ownership requirements that foreign investors need to fulfil. There were no prohibited or highly restricted trade and investment sectors in the industry in 1995. Once China joined the WTO/ITA agreement in 2001, many restricted areas were officially removed from the restricted guideline list. The encouraged sectors were amended according to the central development plan (see Chapters 6 and 7, the 'breaking through' strategy). The 'guidelines' for 1995 and 2004 are ddetailed below.

The guidelines for 1995

Encouraged sectors, 1995

1　Large-scale production of integrated circuits with a line width of 0.35 microns or less.
2　New-type electronic spare parts (including slice spare parts) and electric and electronic spare parts.
3　Manufacture of photoelectric components, sensitive components and sensors.
4　Manufacture of large and medium-sized computers.
5　Manufacture of compatible digital TVs, HDTVs, digital videotape recorders and players.
6　Development of semiconductors, photoelectric materials.
7　Manufacture of new-type displays (plate displays and displaying screens).
8　Development of three-dimensional computer-aided design, CAT, computer-aided manufacturing, computer-aided engineering and other computer application systems.
9　Manufacture of special electronic equipment, instruments and industrial moulds.
10　Manufacture of hydrological data collection instruments and equipment.
11　Manufacture of satellite communication equipment.
12　Manufacture of digital cross-linking equipment.
13　Manufacture of air traffic control equipment (wholly foreign-owned enterprises are not allowed).

14 Development and manufacture of high-capacity mass storage of laser disks, disks and parts.
15 Development and manufacture of new-type printing devices (laser printers, etc.).
16 Manufacture of equipment for multimedia systems of data communication.
17 Production of single-mode optical fibres.
18 Manufacture of equipment for cut-in communication systems.
19 New technical equipment supporting communication networks.
20 Manufacture of integrated services digital networks.

Restricted A, 1995

1 Satellite television receivers and key parts.
2 Exchange boards for the use of digital programmer-control bureaux and for the use of private branch exchanges.

Restricted B, 1995

1 Colour TVs (including projection television), colour kinescopes and glass shielding.
2 Video cameras (including camera-recorder in one unit).
3 Video recorders and magnetic heads, magnetic drums and movement of video recorders.
4 Analogue-type mobile communications systems (honeycomb, colony, wireless beeper call, wireless telephone).
5 Receiving equipment for satellite navigation systems and key parts (wholly foreign-owned enterprises are not allowed).
6 Manufacture of the system of very small aperture terminals.
7 Manufacturing of photo-timing digital serial communication systems of less than 2.5 GB/s and microwave communication systems of 144 MB/s and lower.

The guidelines for 2004/2006

Encouraged sectors, 2004/2006

1 Manufacture of digital televisions, digital video cameras, digital record players, digital sound-playing equipment.
2 Manufacture of new-type plate displays, medium- and high-resolution colour kinescope and glass shielding.
3 Manufacture of digital audio and visual coding or decoding equipment, digital broadcast TV studio equipment, digital cable TV systems.
4 Equipment: digital audio broadcast transmission equipment.
5 Design of integrated circuit and production of large-scale integrated circuit with a line width of 0.35 microns or smaller.

6 Manufacture of medium-sized and large computers, portable microcomputers, high-grade servers.

7 Development and manufacture of drivers of high-capacity compact disks and disks and related parts.

8 Manufacture of three-dimensional CAD, CAT, CAM, CAE and other computer application systems.

9 Development and manufacture of software.

10 Development and production of materials specific for semiconductors and components.

11 Manufacture of electronic equipment, testing equipment, tools and moulds.

12 Manufacture of new-type electronic components and parts (slice components, sensitive components, sensors, frequency monitoring and selecting components, hybrid integrated circuits, electrical and electronic components, photoelectric components, new-type components for machinery and electronics).

13 Manufacture of hi-tech green batteries: non-mercury alkali-manganese batteries, powered nickel-hydrogen batteries, lithium-ion batteries, high-capacity wholly sealed maintenance-proof lead-acid accumulators, fuel batteries, pillar-shaped zinc-air batteries.

14 Development and manufacture of key components for high-density digital compact disk drivers.

15 Manufacture of recordable compact disks (CD-R, CD-RW, DVD-R, DVD-ARM).

16 Design and manufacture of civil satellites (the Chinese partner shall hold the majority of shares).

17 Manufacture of civil satellites' effective payload (the Chinese partner shall hold the majority of shares).

18 Manufacture of spare parts for civilian satellites.

19 Design and manufacture of civilian carrier rockets (the Chinese partner shall hold the majority of shares).

20 Manufacture of telecommunication system equipment for satellites.

21 Manufacture of receiving equipment for satellite navigation systems and key components (equity joint ventures or contractual joint ventures only).

22 Manufacture of optical fibre, pre-formed.

23 Manufacture of serial transmission equipment of digital microwave synchronization of 622 MB/s.

24 Manufacture of serial transmission equipment of photo-timing synchronization of 10 GB/s.

25 Manufacture of equipment for cut-in communication networks with broadband.

26 Manufacture of optical cross-linking equipment.

27 Manufacture of ATM and IP data communication systems.

28 Manufacture of mobile communication systems (GSM, CDMA, DCS1800, PHS, DECT, IMT2000): mobile telephones, base stations, switching equipment and digital colonization system equipment.

29 Development and manufacture of high-end router, network switchboards of gigabit per second or over.
30 Manufacture of equipment for air traffic control systems (equity joint ventures or contractual joint ventures only).

Restricted B, 2004

1 Production of satellite television receivers and key parts.

Appendix 4

The top 100 large domestic ICT firms ranked by the Ministry of the Information Industry (2004)

Rank	Enterprise	Operation income (10,000 yuan)	Profit (10,000 yuan)	Tax (10,000 yuan)	Exports (10,000 yuan)	R&D (10,000 yuan)	Investment for informationalization (10,000 yuan)	Main products
1	海尔集团公司 Haier Group Company	8,064,840	145,714	176,850	490,372	385,000	8,000	Colour TVs 彩色电视机; refrigerators 电冰箱;ice boxes 电冰柜; air conditioning 空调器; washing machines 洗衣机; mobile phones 手机; computers 计算机
2	联想控股有限公司 Legend/Lenovo Holding Company	4,033,096	123,730	75,433	176,936	115,818	6,500	Computers 计算机; printers 打印机
3	TCL 集团股份有限公司 TCL Group Joint Stock Ltd Company	3,820,434	142,340	180,267	1,279,382	128,842	5,421	Colour TVs 彩色电视机; mobile phones 手机; computers 计算机; telephone sets 电话机
4	上海广电（集团）有限公司 Shanghai Guangdian SVA Group Ltd Company	3,068,636	134,906	36,402	1,239,655	104,144	1,175	Mobile phones 手机; colour TVs 彩色电视机; laser CD players 激光视盘机; set-top boxes 机顶盒; colour TV tubes 彩色显像管

	Company						Products
5	熊猫电子集团有限公司 Panda Electronics Group Ltd Company	2,632,697	56,989	46,166	768,055	31,182	1,800	Mobile phones 手机; wireless base stations 无线基站; switching apparatus 程控交换机; colour TVs 彩色电视机
6	海信集团有限公司 Hisense Group Ltd Company	2,211,327	30,749	61,428	295,171	80,184	9,524	Colour TVs 彩色电视机; air conditioning 空调器; mobile phones 手机; refrigerators 电冰箱; switching apparatus 程控交换机
7	华为技术有限公司 Huawai Technology Ltd Company	2,166,990	381,031	281,399	371,205	317,885	0	Switching apparatus 程控交换机; communication transmission apparatus 通信传输设备
8	北京北大方正集团公司 Beijing Founder Group Ltd Company	1,812,026	82,746	33,691	45,265	94,100	5,100	Electronic publishing systems 电子出版系统; computers 计算机; laser printers 激光打印机; scanners 扫描仪; displays 显示器; software 软件
9	广东美的集团股份有限公司 Guangdong Midea Joint Stock Company	1,750,000	37,200	50,000	415,000	54,000	6,000	Air conditioning 空调; compressors 压缩机; electric motors 电机; small home electronic applications 小家电

(Continued)

Rank	Enterprise	Operation income (10,000 yuan)	Profit (10,000 yuan)	Tax (10,000 yuan)	Exports (10,000 yuan)	R&D (10,000 yuan)	Investment for informationalization (10,000 yuan)	Main products
10	中兴通讯股份有限公司 ZTE Joint Stock Ltd Company	1,745,705	121,914	221,543	216,864	133,151	0	Switching apparatus 程控交换机; mobile phones 手机; mobile phone applications 小灵通
11	京东方科技集团股份有限公司 BOE Joint Stock Ltd Company	1,610,360	42,375	44,838	256,494	38,643	946	Displays 显示器; colour TV tubes 彩色显像管
12	四川长虹电子集团有限公司 Sichuan Changhong Group Ltd Company	1,581,212	28,211	38,031	543,787	79,013	2,100	ColourTVs 彩色电视机; air conditioning 空调器; laser CDs 激光视盘机; disposable batteries 次电池
13	康佳集团股份有限公司 Konka Group Ltd Company	1,280,868	13,400	81,546	70,172	48,232	2,108	ColourTVs彩色电视机; mobile phones 手机; Chinese mobile devices 小灵通; refrigerators 电冰箱
14	中国长城计算机集团公司 China Great Wall Computer Group Company	1,172,102	20,170	8,298	947,101	31,981	0	Computers 计算机; magneto-resistive heads 磁阻磁头; hard drives 硬盘

No.	Company							Main products
15	深圳创维-RGB电子有限公司 Shenzhen Skyworth RGB Electronics Ltd Company	1,028,500	8,457	25,612	165,571	42,847	234	Colour TVs 彩色电视机; laser CDs 激光视盘机; set-top boxes 机顶盒
16	深圳华强集团有限公司 Shenzhen Huaqiang Holding Ltd Company	1,024,809	12,613	10,974	817,909	30,000	980	Laser audio heads 激光拾音头; micro-motors 微型马达; colour TVs 彩色电视机; artificial intelligence entertainment products 智能娱乐仿真产品
17	上海贝尔阿尔卡特股份有限公司 Shanghai Alcatel Joint Stock Ltd Company	974,225	56,541	88,356	174,231	69,159	17,604	Digital switching apparatus 数字程控交换机; ADSL; mobile base stations 移动基站 传输设备
18	广东格兰仕集团有限公司 Guangdong Galanz group Ltd Company	969,080	48,222	11,225	389,734	54,368	253	Microwave ovens 微波炉; air conditioning 空调器; small home electronics applications 小家电
19	大连大显集团有限公司 Dalian Daxian Group Ltd Company	854,912	16,116	15,130	379,701	35,165	1,245	Black-and-white electronic guns 黑白电子枪; components for colour electronic guns 彩色枪零件; IC 线路板; precision engineering shafts 精密轴

(Continued)

Rank	Enterprise	Operation income (10,000 yuan)	Profit (10,000 yuan)	Tax (10,000 yuan)	Exports (10,000 yuan)	R&D (10,000 yuan)	Investment for informationalization (10,000 yuan)	Main products
20	浪潮集团有限公司 Langchao Ltd Company	829,351	18,763	17,869	25,496	37,843	6,365	Network servers 服务器; computers 计算机; mobile phones 手机; software and information systems 软件及系统集成
21	惠州市德赛集团有限公司 Huizhou Desay Group Ltd	785,930	34,515	31,238	465,048	24,521	2,300	Telephone sets 电话机; laser CDs 激光视盘机; automobile hi-fi 汽车组合音响; batteries 电池
22	彩虹集团公司 Rainbow Group Company	782,495	59,487	50,606	109,171	14,586	236	Colour TV kinescopes 彩色显像管
23	惠州市华阳集团有限公司 Huizou City Huayang Group Ltd	738,136	44,648	4,875	542,304	2,814	1,036	Automobile hi-fi 汽车组合音响; automobile and home hi-fi 汽车/家用组合音响机芯; laser devices 激光镭射头; precision compressors 精密冲压件; speakers 扬声器
24	侨兴集团有限公司 Cosun Group Ltd Company	695,632	35,301	16,913	16,104	2,456	897	Telephone sets 电话机; mobile phones 手机; fax machines 传真机; voice repetition recorders 复读机; walkie-talkies 对讲机

No.	Company						Products
25	夏新电子有限公司 Amoi Electronics Ltd Company	684,592	84,284	42,637	32,816	34,000	195	Mobile phones 手机; laser CDs 激光视盘机; telephone sets 电话机; AV 功放
26	厦门华侨电子企业有限公司 Xiamen overseas Chinese Electronics Ltd Company	678,962	6,905	9,523	96,063	14,050	2,400	Colour TVs 彩色电视机; colour displays 彩色显示器; fax machines 传真机
27	河南安彩集团有限责任公司 Henan Anchai Group Ltd Company	678,015	27,059	27,584	102,345	18,699	4,668	Colour TV kinescopes (shell) 彩色显像管玻壳; 通信产品; 数字 set-top boxes 机顶盒; air conditioning 空调
28	华东电子集团 Huadong Electronics Group Company	674,558	31,922	10,468	82,076	22,518	50	Colour TV kinescopes 彩色显像管; air conditioning 空调; fluorescent lights 荧光灯; getters 吸气剂
29	华立控股有限公司 Huali Holding Ltd Company	673,506	43,210	35,609	65,685	12,096	956	Electronic tariff meters 电度表; electronic multi-tariff meters 多费率表; copper-clad laminates 铜箔板; 光电存储; terminal measurements 测量终端
30	清华同方股份有限公司 Tsingha UNis Tongfang Holding Ltd Company	669,374	20,055	20,068	29,873	7,357	360	Computers 计算机; nuclear checking technology products 核技术检查系列产品; network, software and integration systems 网络软件与系统集成

(Continued)

Rank	Enterprise	Operation income (10,000 yuan)	Profit (10,000 yuan)	Tax (10,000 yuan)	Exports (10,000 yuan)	R&D (10,000 yuan)	Investment for informationalization (10,000 yuan)	Main products
31	江苏新科电子集团有限公司 Jiangsu Shinco Electronics Group Ltd Company	651,199	10,425	8,408	348,389	6,250	810	Laser CD players 激光视盘机; automobile electronics 汽车电子; air conditioning 空调器
32	广东科龙电器股份有限公司 Guangdong Kelong Holding Ltd Company	617,851	22,000	19,954	180,000	37,060	32,051	Refrigerators 电冰箱; air conditioning 空调器; freezers 冷柜; small home electronics applications
33	青岛澳柯玛集团总公司 Qingdao Aucma Hi-Tech Group Company	605,490	9,284	11,224	42,278	31,759	720	Freezers 冷柜; refrigerators 电冰箱; air conditioning 空调器; washing machines 洗衣机; Li electronics cells 锂离子电芯
34	深圳市赛格集团有限公司 Shenzhen Sage Group Ltd Company	582,756	49,339	15,002	238,812	5,188	520	Colour TV tubes 彩色显像管; TV kinescopes 彩色显像管玻壳; integrated circuits 集成电路; discrete semiconductor devices 半导体分立器件

No.	Company							Products
35	上海飞乐股份有限公司 Shanghai Feilo Joint Stock Ltd Company	533,579	88,208	11,773	178,114	26,679	5,069	Premises distribution systems 布线系统; automobile electronics 汽车电子; electronic special devices 电子专用设备
36	比亚迪股份有限公司 Byd Joint Stock Ltd Company	503,105	98,094	68,296	188,703	13,337	1,533	Ni-Cd batteries 镍镉电池; Ni-MH batteries 镍氢电池; lithium-ion batteries 锂离子电池; automobile electronics 汽车电子; LCD 液晶显示屏
37	深圳赛达电子集团有限公司 Shenzhen Sed Electronics Group Ltd. Company	454,792	13,232	2,071	213,149	1,603	1,151	Mobile phones 手机; 行输出变压器; 商业收款机; laser CDs 激光视盘机
38	许继集团有限公司 XJ Group Ltd Company	414,241	39,210	25,599	2,742	24,560	530	Electronic industrial automation systems 电力工业自动化系统; civilian automation systems 民用自动化控制系统; mobile communication systems and machines 传输收发信机
39	中国华录集团有限公司 China Hualu Group Ltd Company	393,327	17,452	1,509	288,085	14,165	73	Laser CD players 激光视盘机; laser CD components 激光视盘机机芯; DVD-ROM optics, DVD-ROM 光头

(Continued)

Rank	Enterprise	Operation income (10,000 yuan)	Profit (10,000 yuan)	Tax (10,000 yuan)	Exports (10,000 yuan)	R&D (10,000 yuan)	Investment for informationalization (10,000 yuan)	Main products
40	长白计算机集团公司 Changbai Computer Group	366,754	3,500	1,594	187,670	2,636	120	Colour TVs 彩色电视机; laser printers 打印机; IC cards 卡智能电话; CAD controlling devices 工业控制机
41	托普集团科技发展有限责任公司 Sichuan Top Group Science and Technology Development Ltd Company	355,699	20,846	8,207	513	16,953	5,972	Telecom hardware products 通讯类硬件产品; software and integrated systems 软件及系统集成
42	广州南方高科有限公司 Guangzhou Southern Technology Ltd Company	343,125	6,640	2,585	1,654	12,009	0	Mobile phones 手机
43	永鼎集团有限公司 Yongding Group Ltd Company	317,457	11,943	11,762	811	72,140	150	Optical fibre cables 通信光缆; telecom cables 通信电缆; ADSS, OPGW; 电力 optical fibre cables 光缆; optical devices 光电子器件

	Company						Products
44	广州金鹏集团有限公司 Guangdong Jinpeng Group Ltd Company	307,170	2,299	3,404	0	8,517	923	Automobile telecom station 移动通信基站; Chinese mobiles and mobile communication systems 小灵通
45	西安海星科技投资控股（集团）有限公司 Xian Seastar (Group) Holding Ltd Company	302,837	12,123	2,493	0	2,708	50	Computers 计算机; software 软件
46	中国科健股份有限公司 China Kejian Joint Stock Ltd Company	300,000	5,000	2,420	15,000	3,000	0	Mobile phones 手机
47	江苏宏图电子信息集团有限公司 Jiangsu Hongtu Electronics Information Ltd Company	298,000	3,940	5,100	72,235	0	0	Telecom devices 通信设备; electronic cables 电缆; laser CD players 激光视盘机
48	浙江浙大网新科技股份有限公司 Zhejiang Zhedawang New Tech Joint Stock Ltd Company	297,331	7,912	5,390	1,817	4,460	11,700	Network servers 服务器; network products 网络系列产品; digital monitor systems 数字监控产品; software and integrated systems 软件及系统集成
49	宇通集团有限公司 Hengtong Group Ltd Company	285,340	21,520	11,250	4,875	970	670	Optical cables 光纤; optical fibre cables 光缆; electricity cables 电缆; optical devices 光器件

(Continued)

Rank	Enterprise	Operation income (10,000 yuan)	Profit (10,000 yuan)	Tax (10,000 yuan)	Exports (10,000 yuan)	R&D (10,000 yuan)	Investment for informationalization (10,000 yuan)	Main products
50	大恒新纪元科技股份有限公司 Daheng New Epoch Technology Joint Stock Company	284,236	8,894	6,100	7,122	14,212	400	CAD and integrated systems 机械; CAD 及系统集成; electronic publications 电子出版物; laser processing devices 激光加工设备; TV network broadcasting devices 电视网络播出设备
51	横店集团东磁有限公司 Hengdian Group Dongci Ltd Company	277,086	20,668	14,145	160,280	11,763	783	Permanent magnet diodes 永磁铁氧体; 功率铁氧体; magnet direct current motors 磁电机; speakers 扬声器
52	威海北洋电气集团股份有限公司 Weihai Beiyang Group Joint Stock Ltd Company	271,747	10,694	1,888	187,288	8,942	560	Laser printers 打印机; high-speed note scanners 高速票据扫描仪; 热敏打印头接触式图像传感器; fax machines 传真机
53	富通集团有限公司 Futong Group Ltd Company	259,374	16,938	11,981	4,282	12,645	1,300	Optimal fibres 光纤; telecom optical fibre cables 通信光缆; telecom cables 通信电缆; optical devices 光器件

54	浙江富春江通信集团有限公司 Zhengjiang Fuchunjiang Telecom Group Ltd Company	256,592	8,545	7,132	3,670	3,000	300	Telecom optical cables 通信电缆; 通信光缆 optical fibre cables 光缆; optical devices 光器件; electricity cables 电力电缆
55	河南新飞电器（集团）股份有限公司 Henan Xinfei Electronics Group Joint Stock Ltd Company	251,301	11,378	13,271	24,276	2,275	3,000	Refrigerators 电冰箱; freezers 电冰柜; air conditioning 空调器; GPS 定位系统
56	上海宏盛科技发展股份有限公司 Shanghai Hongsheng Technology Development Joint Stock Ltd Company	248,620	5,852	254	247,734	267	22	Integrated circuits 集成电路; laser CD players 激光视盘机; CD-ROM; CD-RW; DVD-ROM
57	武汉邮电科学研究院 Institute of Wuhan Telecom and Post Science Research	234,460	4,237	18,609	8,138	15,258	633	Telecom transmission devices 通信传输设备; 光纤 optical fibre cables 光缆; electronic cables 电缆; optical devices 光器件; wireless receivers 无线接入产品
58	清华紫光股份有限公司 UNIS Tsinghua Ziguang Joint Stock Ltd Company	230,941	2,892	2,687	0	9,234	952	Computers 计算机; digital products 数码产品; scanners 扫描仪

(Continued)

Rank	Enterprise	Operation income (10,000 yuan)	Profit (10,000 yuan)	Tax (10,000 yuan)	Exports (10,000 yuan)	R&D (10,000 yuan)	Investment for informationalization (10,000 yuan)	Main products
59	福建实达电脑集团股份有限公司 Fujian Shida Computer Ltd Company	229,087	1,470	6,606	0	5,529	300	Printers 打印机; computers 计算机
60	上海金陵股份有限公司 Shanghai Jinling Joint Stock Ltd Company	215,791	21,881	7,214	63,303	6,470	2,150	Electronic components 电子元件; software system projects 软件系统工程; electronic tariff meters 电度表; 微电机
61	上海飞乐组合音响股份有限公司 Shanghai Feiyue Hi-Fi Joint Stock Ltd Company	209,846	16,177	3,934	42,456	3,114	170	IC cards, IC 卡, micro electronic modes 微模块; lighting 照明; software 软件; deflection cables 偏转线圈
62	航天信息股份有限公司 Aviation Telecom Joint Stock Ltd Company	209,172	43,276	10,883	0	6,275	300	Anti-counterfeit controlling systems 防伪税控系统; ICT cards, IC 卡; card readers 读卡机具
63	东软集团有限公司 Neusoft Group Ltd Company	205,321	13,770	14,897	13,307	24,430	0	Digital medical treatment devices 数字化医疗设备; software and integrated systems 软件及系统集成

	Company						Products
64	广州七喜电脑股份有限公司 Guangzhou Qixi Computer Ltd Company	204,660	6,380	3,936	450	1,200	150	Computer and peripheral equipment 计算机及外部设备
65	长飞光纤光缆有限公司 Guangfei Optical Fibre Cable Ltd Company	203,214	4,732	8,790	11,512	1,745	175	Telecommunication optical cables 通信光纤; telecommunications 通信; optical fibre cables 光缆
66	中国振华电子集团有限公司 China Zhenhua Group Ltd Company	202,297	3,952	6,909	31,076	1,332	550	Mobile phones 手机; telephone sets 电话机; electronic components 电子元器件; integrated circuits 集成电路
67	四川汇源科技产业控股集团有限公司 Sichuan Huiyuan Technology Group Holding Ltd Company	194,988	10,094	6,470	0	0	0	Optical fibre cables 光缆; optical devices 光器件; cable TVs 有线电视设备 网络及设备; software and integrated systems 软件及系统集成
68	中国四联仪器仪表集团有限公司 China Silian Instrument Group Ltd Company	181,527	6,963	11,000	10,681	0	110	CAD systems 工业自动化仪表及控制系统; 厚膜 integrated circuits 集成电路; 铜基复合材料; optical instruments 光学仪器

(Continued)

Rank	Enterprise	Operation income (10,000 yuan)	Profit (10,000 yuan)	Tax (10,000 yuan)	Exports (10,000 yuan)	R&D (10,000 yuan)	Investment for informationa-lization (10,000 yuan)	Main products
69	北京国际交换系统有限公司 Beijing International Switching Apparatus Ltd Company	178,770	21,551	14,741	179	8,598	1,467	Digital switching apparatus 数字程控交换机; routers 路由器; ADSL
70	咸阳偏转集团公司 Xianyang Deflexion Group Ltd Company	178,592	2,772	3,107	70,063	4,600	1,000	Deflection cables 偏转线圈; Li batteries 锂电池; displays 显示器; PVC-insulated power cable 漆包线
71	朝华科技（集团）股份有限公司 Chaohua Technology Group Joint Stock Ltd Company	176,245	2,130	3,024	2,272	2,356	1,215	Software and integrated systems 软件及系统集成; digital products 数码产品
72	深圳市新天下集团有限公司 Shenzhen Hasee Group Ltd Company	176,097	6,879	10,131	0	4,292	455	Computers and related devices 计算机及外部设备; computer mother boards 计算机主机板卡; digital products 数码产品

No.	Company						Main products
73	江苏赛博电子有限公司 Jiangsu Bodian Electronics Ltd Company	169,017	4,732	1,956	91,718	5,787	1,643	Colour TVs 彩色电视机; multimedia terminals 多媒体显示终端; internet TVs 网络电视; laser CD players 激光视盘机
74	石家庄宝石电子集团有限责任公司 Shijiazhuang Baoshi Electronics Group Ltd Company	161,957	6,214	12,865	2,212	1,139	110	Colour TV kinescopes 彩色显像管玻壳; lead glass tubes 铅玻璃管; colour TV electronic guns 彩色电子枪芯柱
75	广东东菱凯琴集团有限公司 Guangdong Frestech (donglingkaiqin) Group Ltd Company	155,633	7,299	0	156,283	8,000	250	Small home electronics applications 小家电
76	四川九洲电器企业集团 Sichuan Jiuzhou Electronics Ltd Company	150,592	13,584	5,683	28,419	9,869	1,153	Radar tubes 雷达产品; cable TVs 有线电视; satellite receivers 卫星接收机; optical fibre cables 光缆
77	北京益泰电子集团有限责任公司 Beijing Yitai Electronics Group Ltd Company	142,806	8,467	1,796	84,310	5,379	33	Laser CD players 激光视盘机; hi-fi 组合音响; video recorders and receivers 收录放机; syndicate systems 系统集成

(Continued)

Rank	Enterprise	Operation income (10,000 yuan)	Profit (10,000 yuan)	Tax (10,000 yuan)	Exports (10,000 yuan)	R&D (10,000 yuan)	Investment for informationalization (10,000 yuan)	Main products
78	北京 JVC 电子产业有限公司 Beijing JVC Electronics Ltd Company	142,421	2,146	1,220	124,220	0	0	Integrated video recorders and players 摄录一体机; video recorders 录像机
79	西湖电子集团有限公司 Xihua Electronics Group Ltd Company	139,666	3,236	2,292	59,141	3,050	4,767	Colour TVs 彩色电视机; mobile phones 手机; laser CDs 激光视盘机; displays 显示器
80	华伦集团 Huatuo Group	139,490	4,866	3,785	0	2,936	106	Electricity cables 电缆; optical fibre cables 光缆; optical fibres 光纤
81	江西省电子集团公司 Jiangxi Electronics Group Company	138,960	4,859	5,350	30,022	9,000	1,000	LED 芯片; LED 器件; optical fibre cables 光缆; cables 线缆
82	上海精密科学仪器有限公司 Shanghai Precision and Scientific Instrument Group Ltd Company	132,804	10,668	13,671	69,412	1,006	83	Spectrometers 分光光度计; composition analysis instruments 成份分析仪; electronic measurement instruments 电子测量仪器; electronic instruments for electricians 电工仪器仪表

No.	Company							Main products
83	宁波韵升（集团）股份有限公司 Ningbo Yunsheng Group Ltd Company	131,892	7,724	4,930	119,114	3,400	341	Permanent magnetic materials 钕铁硼永磁材料; electronic complements of music instruments 八音琴机芯; automobile electronics 汽车电子; optical telecommunications 光通信
84	上海自动化仪表股份有限公司 Shanghai Automatic Instrument Joint Stock Ltd Company	130,950	6,898	5,815	3,093	2,352	100	Automatic instruments 自动化仪表; computer controlling systems 计算机控制系统; meter instrument components 仪表元件; air pressure components 气动元件
85	江苏中天科技集团 Jiangshu ZTT Zhongtian Technology Group	128,500	11,500	7,800	800	5,800	1,000	Optical fibres 光纤; optical fibre cables 光缆; optical devices 光器件
86	哈尔滨光宇电源集团股份有限公司 Haerbin Guangyu Joint Stock Group Ltd Company	127,565	14,296	5,676	15,009	284	150	Rechargeable batteries 蓄电池; mobile phones 手机电池; electric control cabinets 电源柜
87	烟台首钢东星（集团）公司 Yantai Shougang Dongxing Group Company	126,572	9,055	14,057	0	0	0	Automobile electronics 汽车电子; permanent magnetic materials 钕铁硼永磁材料; high-pressure electronic cabinets 高低压配电柜

(Continued)

Rank	Enterprise	Operation income (10,000 yuan)	Profit (10,000 yuan)	Tax (10,000 yuan)	Exports (10,000 yuan)	R&D (10,000 yuan)	Investment for informationalization (10,000 yuan)	Main products
88	辽宁无线电二厂 (集团) Liaoning No. 2 Radio Factory (Group Company)	123,795	7,831	2,468	66,847	3,095	980	Radar 雷达; oscillographs 示波器; optical lenses 光学镜头; automobile electronics 汽车电子
89	乐山无线电股份有限公司 LRC Leshan Radio Electronics Joint Stock Ltd Company	123,416	9,494	3,833	107,261	3,700	80	Chip diode triode tubes 片式二、三极管; 塑封二极管; 玻壳二极管; bridge rectifiers 桥式整流器
90	天津市中环电子计算机公司 Tianjiang Zhonghuan Electronics Computer Company	122,006	9,983	1,923	66,369	1,092	50	Computers 计算机; ink cartridges 墨盒; POS machines POS 机; bankbook printers 存折打印机
91	宏安集团有限公司 Hongan Group Ltd Company	121,563	11,514	6,798	0	3,647	26	Telecommunication cables 通信电缆; optical fibre cables 光缆, 五号数据缆
92	广州无线电集团 Guangzhou Radio Group	120,357	23,541	5,346	9,603	8,133	595	AM/SW broadcasting stations 中、短波通信电台; telecommunications transmitter-receivers 通信发射、接收机; GPS 通信导航定向设备

93	山东中创软件工程股份有限公司 Shandong Zhongchuang Software Joint Stock Ltd Company	116,018	1,890	1,421	4,167	1,542	460	Software 软件系列产品; video recorders 录像机
94	江阴新潮科技集团有限公司 Jiangyin Xinchao TechnologyGroup Ltd Company	113,538	9,053	4,056	23,931	55,723	300	Integrated circuits 集成电路; discrete semiconductor devices 分立器件; electronics signal lights 电子信号灯; intellectual electronics instruments 智能化电力仪表
95	深圳兰光电子集团有限公司 Shenzhen Languang Electronics Ltd Company	112,642	1,020	2,741	86,433	4,200	500	Colour displays; hi-fi 组合音响系列
96	广州华南信息产业集团有限公司 Guangzhou Huanan Information Industry Group Ltd Company	109,819	8,404	2,390	98,915	1,250	557	Computers and related applications 计算机及应用系统; micro-control systems 微控制系统产品; multimedia devices 多媒体设备

(Continued)

Rank	Enterprise	Operation income (10,000 yuan)	Profit (10,000 yuan)	Tax (10,000 yuan)	Exports (10,000 yuan)	R&D (10,000 yuan)	Investment for informationa-lization (10,000 yuan)	Main products
97	江苏紫金电子集团有限公司 Jiangsu Zijin Electronics Ltd Company	109,565	5,539	4,050	500	3,835	350	Computers 计算机; printers 打印机; printed IC boards 印制电路板
98	广东生益科技股份有限公司 Guangdong Yike Technology Ltd Company	108,901	14,122	3,509	76,623	244	65	Copper-clad laminated board 覆铜板; bonding sheets 粘结片
99	广东风华高新科技股份有限公司 Guangdong Fenggao New Technology Joint Stock Company	106,000	3,500	4,300	44,900	4,750	2,850	Multilayer ceramic capacitors 片式多层陶瓷电容器; chip electronic resisters 片式电阻器; electronics materials 电子材料; electronics special devices 电子专用设备
100	成都国腾通讯（集团）有限公司 Chengdu Guoteng Telecom Group Ltd Company	103,878	7,697	5,763	0	10,160	3,540	IC telephone cards, IC 卡电话机, information devices 信息机; network controlling systems 网管系统; client machines 用户机

Source: MII, 2005, www.ittop100.gov.cn

Notes

1 Introduction

1 'High-tech products' as discussed in this book are defined as those that '[embody] relatively intensive research and development inputs, either directly at the final manufacturing stage or through the intermediate goods used in their production' (Scherer 1992: 5).

2 Economic liberalization and industrial policies: the state's role in economic development

1 For detailed discussion, see Chang (2003a: chapter 4) and Chang (2004: chapter 7).
2 The model assumes that two countries produce two goods.
3 Ricardo did not discuss the determinants of labour productivity. Later, many economists saw them as arising from differences in technology.
4 The work was refined by Paul Samuelson (1938).
5 The planned International Trade Organization was not founded, owing to its rejection by the US Congress.
6 For example, the introduction of export promotion policy to underdeveloped countries by colonial governments is believed to be in the interests of the mother country.
7 The principle was practised by Italy, Hanseatic cities (Hamburg and Lübeck in 1241), the Netherlands, England, Spain, Portugal, France, Germany, Russia and the United States.
8 For example, colonization and the Navigation Act, which required that all trade with Britain must be via British ships, allowed the British government to monopolize trade channels.
9 The rate of tariffs on imports of manufactured goods in fact was the highest (45–55 per cent) in Europe in 1820s (Bairoch 1993: 40).
10 Book IV, ch. xxxiii, the Insular Supremacy and the Continental Powers – North America and France, pp. 15–16.
11 The first Secretary of the Treasury of the United States (1789–1795), and a friend of List.
12 Chang (2002) argues that the liberal view on the direct cause–effect relationship between Smoot-Hawley tariff and the Great Depression is misleading. The tariff bill raised the degree of protection only marginally, from 37 per cent in 1925 to 48 per cent in 1931. The increase was not higher than the averaged tariff rate imposed during the US Civil War (e.g. 40–50 per cent in 1875, 44 per cent in 1913). The cause of the Great Depression needs interpreting against the background that the United States was the largest creditor nation after the First World War (1914–1918).
13 Other famous dependency theorists include, for example, Celso Furtado, Andre Gunder Frank, Hans Singer and Gunnar Myrdal.

14 One of the prominent Marxist radical critics is Andre Gunder Frank (see Frank 1967).
15 For example, the phenomenon of intra-trade among industrialized countries in the post-Second World War period, the role of the firms involved in trade, and the apparent monopolistic market conditions in the real world.
16 Market failure should be distinguished from market inadequacy which often refers to a situation in which markets cannot, because of their design, deal adequately with rapid changes such as acceleration of development, or shocks.
17 For example, Bhagwati (1958) showed that growth may lower a country's welfare under free trade conditions when distortions replace growth. Rodriguez and Rodrik's review of empirical studies argued that 'there should be no theoretical presumption in favor of finding [an] unambiguous negative relationship between trade barriers and growth rates in the types of cross-national data typically analyzed'. They concluded that 'openness (lower trade barriers) by itself is not a reliable mechanism to generate sustain economic growth'. There is 'little evidence that open trade polices in the sense of lower tariff and non-tariff barriers to trade are significantly associated with economic growth' (Rodriguez and Rodrik 1999).

3 Creation of the electronics industry: military-driven development, 1949–1978

1 Chinese democracy often refers to the ideology of a social and economic system that is established in a similar way to the capitalist revolution in the seventeenth and eighteenth centuries. Neo-democracy was to be based on an anti-imperialist, anti-feudalist and anti-crony capitalist revolution led by the proletariat, and the system it established would ultimately be a socialist one in which the means of production would be collectively owned and administered by all members of society.
2 The industry had nine domestic enterprises: one factory producing consumer radios, telegraphy devices, and broadcasting machines; two manufacturing telephones and switches; five in the field of batteries, bulbs and electrical wire production; and one radar repair plant. It also had two foreign-invested firms, Shanghai US Edison Electronics (producing light bulbs) and Shanghai Sino-US Electronics Joint Venture (producing radio devices).
3 The 'ten relationships' refer to Mao's views on how to solve ten different economic and political problems that China faced in the 1950s.
4 Mao believes that steel and grain were crucial for economic development. When Khrushchev announced that the USSR would surpass the United States within 15 years, Mao predicted that China could catch up with the United Kingdom within 15 years. At the 1958 Politburo meeting, he decided to follow his agricultural–industrial parallel development strategy to double China's steel production within two years. Large numbers of peasants were withdrawn from agricultural production to 'backyard factories' established in every commune. It was hoped that steel could be made out of scrap metal. This left an insufficient number of people in the agricultural sector and caused a reduction in agricultural production. However, local officials, under huge pressure from the central government, had no choice but to announce exaggerated results. As a result, economic disasters soon emerged and spread all over the country during the 'Three Years of Natural Disasters' period from 1959 to 1962.
5 For example, uprisings in East Germany, Poland and Hungary.
6 The total number of electronics factories is different from the total of number of centrally and locally owned enterprises because of duplicated ownerships among these enterprises.

4 The 'opening up' reform and state-led growth, 1978–1993

1 The 'Four Modernizations' were in the fields of agriculture, industry, science and technology, and the military. The modernization ideas were initially introduced by Prime Minister Zhou Enlai in 1964.

2 On 4 June 1985, at an enlarged meeting of the military commission of the CCP's central committee, Deng said: 'It is possible that there will be no large-scale war for a fairly long time to come and that there is hope of maintaining world peace'.

3 'Cluster economies' include the availability of a market and a range of physical inputs, human resources, supporting services and technological spillovers.

4 In 1985, Deng Xiaoping declared a reduction in the number of military personnel from 4 million to 3 million. The process continued until 1987.

5 For example, Li Xiannian, vice-prime minister, concluded that one of the main pitfalls of Mao's economic reforms was that enterprises did not have an 'independent status' (autonomy). In order to improve their efficiency and productivity, they should be given rights of self-management and operation. His proposition rests on Mao's early decentralization policies (see 'ten relations'; Li 1989: 330).

6 From 1978 to 1981, household income had increased from 55 per cent to 66 per cent of national disposable income.

7 *see also* the 'Technology leverage' section in this chapter (p. 67).

8 The abortive reform was characterized by a 'big bang' rather than a gradualist approach. Material incentives rather than 'spiritual' incentives and political appeals were used to motivate the labour force.

9 A 'tax for profit' system was introduced in a similar fashion to encourage enterprises to improve efficiency and to establish a clear income and investment distribution rule among enterprises, local governments and the central government.

10 The real unemployment rate may have been much higher.

11 The number of employees was determined based on the definition of 'exploitation' in Marx's *Capital* (1867).

12 This was mostly for small-scale 'individual firms' (*siying qiye*) with more than eight employees, and foreign-invested firms.

13 For example, the Shanxi Number 4400 Colour TV Tube and Wuxi Jiangnan Number 170 Radio Device factories.

14 For example, in 1973, a group of Chinese officials from the MEI went to RCA to discuss the possible purchase of television-tube production lines in the United States. They also visited Corning, a specialist manufacturer of glass for high-tech components, in order to compare its technologies with Chinese technology. On their departure, Corning's staff gave Chinese officials glass snails as souvenirs. Jiang Qing (Mao's wife) believed that the souvenirs represented the United States' political criticisms of China's slow technological progress. This is known as the 'snail event', which delayed China's first attempt to import electronics technologies from the United States. The 'Gang of Four' was a leftist faction of four Chinese Communist Party officials: Jiang Qing, Zhang Chunqiao, Yao Wenyuan and Wang Hongwen.

15 Notable events in strategic cooperation between China and the United States were the visit of the heads of US technical agencies, led by Frank Press (science adviser to President Carter), in July 1978, the visit of Energy Secretary James Schlesinger in the autumn of 1978, and defence-technical meetings with William Perry, Undersecretary of Defense.

16 Wang Dahang (nuclear scientist), Chen Yufang (nuclear scientist), Yang Jiaxu (aviation scientist) and Wang Ganchang (nuclear physicist).

17 The digits represent the date of the programme's promotion: '86' is the year 1986, and '3' is the month of March.

Introduction to Part III

1 For further reading, Naughton (1995) and Wang (1998).

2 The 'industrial policy' adopted by the conservatives covers energy and heavy industries as well as material, transportation and agriculture. Its priorities were the same as under the command economy.

5 The big business strategy and the small and medium-sized enterprise strategy

1 Except for the semiconductor sector, where the government lacked a clear vision regarding the promotion of domestic production (Sung 1997).
2 For example, the first was the Korean Institute of Electronics and Technology.
3 Except for the video cassatte recorder (VCR) and semiconductor industries, where the government intervened intensively (Dahlman *et al.* 1993).
4 For example, the Industrial Technology Research Institute (ITRI).
5 For example, the Hsinchu Science and Industrial Park.
6 Refer to the ministerial statement on the MII's website, www.mii.gov.cn.
7 Marx (1867: part IV, ch. 15 in paragraph IV.XV.167; part VII, ch. 25 in paragraph VII.XXV.15).
8 Decision of China's Central Communist Party Regarding State Owned Enterprise Reform and Related Crucial Issues (22 September) (Beijing: Xinhua News Agency, 1999).
9 State-controlled enterprises (SCEs) are those in which the state has the largest ownership share.
10 *see also* Chapter 6 for data concerning industrial output, export and domestic sales of private enterprises.

6 The 'attracting in' and 'walking out' trade and investment strategy

1 All the strategies are related and were launched at the same time. The 'walking out' strategy and the big business strategy complemented each other in achieving scale economies on a world scale.
2 For example, outward investment in Third World countries was used in exchange for support of China's UN permanent membership, isolation of Taiwan and enhanced rights with other socialist countries (excluding the USSR).
3 Also see Hu Qili's 'stimulating internal through external resources'.
4 Tariffs for ICT products as agreed in the Information Technology Agreement have been reduced to zero. China also committed itself to abolishing all quotas, licensing or other quantitative restrictions in 2005.
5 The strategy also refers to the national champion/big business strategy (see Chapter 5).
6 For example, John Dunning's eclectic ownership, location and internalization (OLI) paradigm of international production. See Cai (1999) for an application of the OLI model to China's outward investment. Also see Ning (2007) for the case study of Korea.
7 The World Bank studies argued that a significant part of the increase in China's FDI flows was due to recycled capital of Chinese origin. Chinese firms often moved money offshore (e.g. to Hong Kong) and then recycled it back into China disguised as FDI in order to take advantage of the special tax and preferential policies only available to FDI. The World Bank estimates that about 25 per cent of FDI inflows in 1992 were recycled (Harrold and Lall 1993; Lardy 2001).
8 Sources: WTO statistics and OECD ITS database, 1999–2004.
9 Foreign-owned R&D units were mainly from Western Europe, the United States and Taiwan, and increased in the field of the computer, communications, electronics, chemical and automobile industries. According to Chinese official statistics, there were 629 FDI-related R&D, technology services and geological prospecting technology projects. Contracted value and value actually achieved were US$1.006 billion and US$0.294 billion in 2004 (MOC 2006).
10 For example, Huawei, China's largest telecommunication and networking equipment manufacturer, ranked sixth in terms of turnover (US$3.8 billion, 27 per cent of which was made up of exports) out of the top 100 firms in 2005, had already established branch offices in more than 40 nations, with nine regional headquarters, and a number of R&D institutes in the United States, Sweden, India and Russia. The total number of

employees reached 56,333, of whom 48 per cent are researchers, and 3,000 are overseas nationals. Huaiwei also established two JV production facilities worth US$80 million, in Russia and Brazil, and won production contracts in Ecuador, Egypt, Germany and Kenya. The company is engaging in research collaborations with Texas Instruments, Motorola, IBM, Intel, Agere Systems, Sun Microsystems, Altera, Qualcomm, Infineon and Microsoft.

11 This refers to objects in 'China's Fifth Five-Year Plan of the ICT Industry and 2020 Mid- and Long-Term Plan' announced by the MII in 2006.

12 Even if the World Bank estimate that 25 per cent of FIEs were disguised Chinese-funded enterprises were true, the shares of FIEs in industrial output and exports were still significantly larger than for all domestic firms.

13 Although China Mobile was ranked 43rd in 2004, it primarily served the domestic market and has not yet expanded internationally.

14 Data gathered from MOFCOM 2006: http://www.mofcom.gov.cn/.

15 Supplier-oriented industrial upgrading refers to the development steps from being MNEs' outsourcing suppliers, accumulating learning effects, mastering manufacturing and designing capabilities, to gradually becoming original brand manufacturers in the world market. See Sturgeon and Lester (2004: 35–88).

16 For example, the percentage of production of developed countries' manufacturing firms that takes places abroad increased significantly from 1986 to 1995: for the United States, from 20 per cent to 25 per cent; for Germany, from 15 per cent to 20 per cent; and for Japan, from 4 per cent to 10 per cent (Nolan 2001: 31).

17 The theory of the global flagship model; see Ernst (2003).

18 Sturgeon and Lester (2004) have discussed five possible upgrading routes for East Asian firms. (1) They could acquire or create a global brand and sell production under this brand name to markets that the global leaders are not so interested in. (2) They could follow the classic ODM route by developing internal design and capability to handle production for multiple clients, allowing them to introduce a new design model to global leaders, and thus reducing competition through raising the market entry threshold. (3) They could follow the OEM route with a strong focus on continuous improvement in process-specific technologies to provide low-cost, high-quality manufacturing and related services in order to meet the specifications of global leaders. (4) They could become a higher-tier supplier, serving as an intermediate between global leaders, local suppliers and suppliers from the country's own mini-GPNs, as in Tawian. (5) They could adopt the 'global flagship' model, shedding manufacturing activities and engaging in global network management.

19 For example, China's largest computer producer, Lenovo/Legend, was created within the Computer Institute of the Chinese Academy of Sciences in 1984. The firm was converted into a 'modern market-oriented firm' during the reform of SOEs. The ownership shares were initially bought by its employees, and further ownership diversification came through listing of its shares in Hong Kong in 1994. The actual state ownership has become very vague, but still exists (CCID News 2006). Hu Qilin, minister for the electronics industry from 1993 to 1998, regarded Legend as 'the son of the ministry'. It was included in China's big business strategy and frequently received special attention from the ministry. In 2006, Yang Yuanqing, the CEO of Lenovo, gave a talk in San Francisco after the US government cancelled a purchase order from IBM Lenovo in consideration of national security issues raised by uncertainty resulting from the Chinese government's involvement in Lenovo; see http://it.sohu.com/20060511/n243187031.shtml. Yang denied majority ownership by the state and state intervention in the firm's operation and decision-making process. The logics of China's 'opening up' strategy, however, clearly imply that the state influence still remains strong in the industry as a whole. Most Chinese MNEs do not provide data on their ownership structures. Exceptionally, the TCL Group Co. did offer such information in 2004: 12.8 per cent, state ownership (the largest proportion); 13.4 per cent,

individual shareholders; 6.3 per cent, Philips; 1.0 per cent, Toshiba; 0.2 per cent, Sumitomo; 10 per cent, other foreign investors; 7.7 per cent, trade unions; 48.1 per cent, others. See the financial information available from http://www.tcl.com/main/others/investor/.

7 The 'breaking through' strategy of China's ICT industry: dynamic technological catching up and challenges in developing the semiconductor sector

1 The best-known successful projects include large-scale and very large-scale integrated circuits (1976–1979), and played a crucial role in assisting Japanese firms in upgrading their technologies.
2 Fairchild was the third largest US firm in the 1960s.
3 By 1974, there were nine US-owned and seven Japanese-owned firms located in Korea engaging in labour-intensive semiconductor assembly and testing operations.
4 After the Chinese Civil War, the Kuomintang government in Taiwan established an independent state–firm relationship in order to prevent corruption by separating politicians from business communities. Accordingly, policies were designed to broaden its support base to include the general public and small businesses, as opposed to just a few large corporations.
5 For example, Winbond with HP and Toshiba, MXIC/Powerchip with Matsushita and Sun, New PC Consortium with IBM and Motorola.
6 It refers to what Chinese officials called 'strategic adjustment of the industrial structure'.
7 A US producers' petition was filed with the assistance of the Department of Commerce against Japanese manufacturers in the field of erasable programmable read-only memory and dynamic random access memory under Title VII of the Tariff Act of 1930. An investigation was soon launched by the US International Trade Commission. Japanese imports were determined to be dumping memory devices in the US market and to have materially injured the US semiconductor industry.
8 Although the European Community complained to the GATT that this unilateral action was illegal, particularly the price floor set by the United States, Japan had to accept unconditionally the United States' terms as it was threatened by further protectionist measures and political actions. As the GATT panel was unable to respond to its complaint, the European Community used all means possible to conclude an agreement with Japan for 5 per cent market access in 1988.
9 Antidumping Duty Order and Amended Final Determination: Dynamic Random Access Memory Semiconductors of One Megabit and Above from the Republic of Korea, 58 Fed. Reg. 27,520 (1993). Since 1994, LG and Hyundai had begun to request the Department of Commerce to review the anti-dumping order, but no decision was given. After three years, Korea brought this case to the WTO Dispute Settlement Body. The Department of Commerce finally revoked the order in 2000.
10 In both cases, very minor import duties were placed on Samsung products. The charges have been amended and are currently activated.
11 Notice of Final Determination of Sales at Less than Fair Value: Static Random Access Memory Semiconductors from Taiwan, *Federal Register*: 23 February 1998 (vol. 63, no. 35); Static Random Access Memory Semiconductors from Taiwan: Notice of Revocation of Antidumping Duty Order and Termination of Antidumping Duty Administrative Reviews and New Shipper Review, *Federal Register*: 14 January 2002 (vol. 67, no. 9); Notice of Final Determination of Sales at Less than Fair Value: Dynamic Random Access Memory Semiconductors of One Megabit and Above ('DRAMs') from Taiwan, *Federal Register*: 19 October 1999 (vol. 64, no. 201).
12 China's world market shares as reported by the Chinese Ministry of Information Industry were arguably 3.64 per cent in 2001, 3.64 per cent in 2001, 4.81 per cent in 2002, 4.98 per cent in 2003 and 5.64 per cent in 2004.

13 The technological level of the semiconductors is indicated by the diameter in inches of the silicon wafer and the thickness in microns of the ICs. The greater the diameter and the thinner the ICs, the more advanced the technology.

14 For more details on these conditions, please refer to Ning (2007).

15 According to the CCID 2005 report, China's semiconductor imports accounted for 23.1 per cent of world semiconductor sales, worth US$62.04 billion in 2004, and with an average growth rate of 46.5 per cent from 2001 to 2004.

16 Although the Wassenaar Arrangement identifies the equipment of sophisticated semi-conductor manufacturing for export control, licensing decisions were left for each member to make its own judgements on. Unlike the United States, neither the European Union nor Japan believed that China's importation of semiconductor manu-facturing equipment would cause international and regional instability. However, because of the strong US objections, they might not license export of state-of-the-art equipment to China. The effectiveness of the Wassenaar Arrangement in seeking to deny China access to 0.25-micron semiconductor manufacturing technology is ques-tionable, as a number of the Chinese chip producers announced plans for 0.18-micron (and below) wafer processes in 2004.

9 Theory and policy lessons: rethinking China's ICT development experience

1 A phrase frequently used by Hu Jintao and Wen Jiabao during their foreign visits in 2004 to mean that China will never seek hegemony, even while growing at a rapid pace. It will continuously seek to bring its people out of poverty through embracing economic globalization and improving relations with the rest of the world.

Appendix 1 Definition of the Chinese ICT industry

1 This proposal revises the criterion established for the ISIC Revision in 2007. For fur-ther details, refer to Albert (2002).

2 Propositions made by the North American Industry Classification System (NAICS).

3 This definition is a modified version of the OECD definition.

4 These activities mainly include (1) manufacturing, sales and rental activities concern-ing telecommunication equipment; (2) manufacturing, sales and rental activities concerning computers; (3) manufacturing of electronic equipment and components for observing, measuring and recording; (4) services of electronic information transmis-sion; (5) services involving processing, disposal and management of electronic information; (6) services involving processing, production, dissemination and man-agement of cultural information products through electronic technology (source: NBSC 2003).

5 This comparison does not include the sub-sector of contents and infrastructure. It only refers to the dissemination sector.

6 For example, the General Administration of Press and Publication of the People's Republic of China is in charge of the press and publication sectors.

Appendix 2 Relaxation of investment restrictions: market access in exchange for selected advanced technologies

1 The tax exemption policies were suspended in 1996 to ensure equal competition between domestic and foreign-funded firms, but continued to be implemented to attract more FDI into China when other East Asian countries were in financial crisis around 1997.

References

Aghion, P. and Blanchard, O. J. (1993). 'On the Speed of Transition in Central Europe'. Working Paper 93, Massachusetts Institute of Technology (MIT), Department of Economics.

Aharoni, Y. and Vernon, R. (1981). *State-Owned Enterprises in Western Economies*. New York: St. Martin's Press.

Albert, J. (2002). *A New Industry Structure for Information*. Online. Available at http://unstats.un.org/unsd/class/intercop/techsubgroup/02-01/tsg0201-8.htm (accessed 4 May 2005).

Amsden, A.-H. (1989). *Asia's Next: South Korea and Late Industrialization*. New York: Oxford University Press.

Amsden, A.-H. (2001). *The Rise of 'the Rest': Challenges to the West from Late-Industrializing Economies*. Oxford: Oxford University Press.

Amsden, A.-H. and Chu, W.-W. (2003). *Beyond Late Development: Taiwan's Upgrading Policies*. Cambridge, MA: MIT Press.

Armbrecht, F. (2003). 'Sitting Industrial R&D in China: Notes for Pioneers', slide presentation, Arlington, VA: Industrial Research Institute (12 March).

Arndt, S. W. and Kierzkowski, H. (eds) (2001). *Fragmentation: New Production Patterns in the World Economy*. Oxford: Oxford University Press.

Arrow, K. (1962). 'The Economic Implications of Learning by Doing'. *Review of Economic Studies*, 29: 155–173.

Atiyas, I., Dutz, M. and Frischtak, C. (1992). 'Fundamental Issues and Policy Approaches in Industrial Restructuring', Industry and Energy Department Working Paper, World Bank Industry Series Paper.

Bairoch, P. (1982). 'International Industrialization Levels from 1750–1980', *Journal of European Economic History*, 11: 269–333.

Bairoch, P. (1993). *Economics and World History: Myths and Paradoxes*. Brighton: Wheatsheaf.

Bairoch, P. (1996). 'Globalization Myths: Some Historical Reflections on Integration, Industrialization and Growth in the World Economy', UNCTAD Discussion Papers, UNCTAD/OSG/DP/113.

Balassa, B. (1967). *Trade Liberalization among Industrial Countries*. New York: McGraw-Hill.

Balassa, B. A. (1988). 'Interest of Developing Countries in the Uruguay Round', *World Economy*, 11: 39–54.

Baldwin, R. E. (1971). 'Determinants of Trade and Foreign Investment: Further Evidence', *Review of Economics and Statistics*, 61: 40–48.

Bauer, P. T. (1984). *Reality and Rhetoric: Studies in Economics of Development*. London: Weidenfeld and Nicolson.

Bell, M. and Pavitt, K. (1993). 'Technological Accumulation and Industrial Growth: Contrasts between Developed and Developing Countries', *Industrial and Corporate Change*, 2: 185–203.

Bell, M. and Pavitt, K. (1995). 'The Development of Technological Capabilities'. In Hague, I. (ed.), *Trade, Technology, and International Competitiveness*, Washington, DC: World Bank.

Bergsten, C. F. (1998). 'Fifty Years of the GATT/WTO: Lessons from the Past for Strategies for the Future', paper presented at the symposium on the world trading system 'Fifty Years: Looking Back, Looking Forward'. Geneva: World Trade Organization and Graduate Institute of International Studies.

Bhagwati, J. (1958). 'Immiserizing Growth: A Geometric Note', *Review of Economic Studies*, 25: 201–205.

Bhagwati, J. (1998). 'Free Trade: What Now?', paper presented at the International Management Symposium, Switzerland: University of St Gallen.

Bhagwati, J. (2002). *Free Trade Today*. Princeton, NJ: Princeton University Press.

Bhagwati, J. N. (1982). 'Directly Unproductive, Profit Seeking (DUP) Activities', *Journal of Economic Studies*, 35: 481–485.

Bharadwaj, R. (1962). 'Factor Proportion and the Structure of Indo-US Trade', *Indian Economic Journal*, 10: 105–116.

BIS (2004). 'Lattice Semiconductor Settles Charges of Illegal Exports to China', Bureau of Industry and Security. Online. Available at www.bis.doc.gov/News/2004/ Lattice_Sep14.htm (accessed 2 January 2005).

Brander, J. A. and Krugman, P. R. (1983). 'A "Reciprocal Dumping" Model of International Trade', *Journal of International Economics*, 15: 313–321.

Breznitz, D. (2005). 'Development, Flexibility and R&D Performance in the Taiwanese IT Industry: Capability Creation and the Effects of State–Industry Co-evolution', *Industrial and Corporate Change*, 14: 153–187.

Brown, C. and Linden, G. (2005). 'Offshoring in the Semiconductor Industry: A Historical Perspective', *Brookings Trade Forum*, 2005: 279–322.

Burenstam-Linder, S. (1961). *An Essay on Trade and Transformation*. New York: Praeger.

Burton, J. (1983). *Picking Losers? Political Economy of Industrial Policy* (Hobart Papers). London: Institute of Economic Affairs.

Business Korea. (1999). 'Corporate Korea Takes a Whipping', *Business Korea*, October: 30–32.

Cai, K. (1999). 'Outward Foreign Direct Investment: A Novel Dimension of China's Integration into the Regional and Global Economy', *China Quarterly*, 160: 856–880.

Cai, Y. (1998). *A Study on China's Strategy of Industrial Technology Development*. Beijing: China Labour Publisher.

Cao, S. (1994). *China's Shift of Military Production Towards a Civilian Orientation*. Beijing: China Economics Publisher.

Caprio, G. J., Hunter, W. C., Kaufman, G. G. and Leipziger, D. M. (1998). *Preventing Bank Crises: Lessons from Recent Global Bank Failures*. Washington, DC: World Bank.

CASS (1986). *Zhong Guo Dang Dai Dian Zi Gong Ye* (China's Contemporary Electronics Industry). Beijing: Chinese Academy of Social Sciences (CASS).

CASS (1987). *The Contemporary Chinese Electronics Industry*. Beijing: Chinese Academy of Social Sciences.

CCID (2005). *A Report on the Development of the Semiconductor Industry in China.* Beijing: CCID.

CCID News (2006). 'CEO Yang Yuanqing Reiterated Lenovo Is Not a SOE'. Online. Available at http://it.sohu.com/20060511/n243187031.shtml (accessed 5 January 2007).

Chandler, A. (1990). *Scale and Scope: The Dynamics of Industrial Capitalism.* Cambridge, MA: Harvard University Press.

Chandler, A., and Hikino, T. (1997). *Big Business and the Wealth of Nations.* New York: Cambridge University Press.

Chandra, V. and Kolavalli, S. (2006). 'Technology, Adaptation, and Exports: How Some Developing Countries Got It Right'. In Chandra, V. (ed.), *Technology, Adaptation, and Exports: How Some Developing Countries Got It Right.* Washington, DC: World Bank.

Chang, H.-J. (1994a). *The Political Economy of Industrial Policy.* New York: St Martin's Press; London: Macmillan.

Chang, H.-J. (1994b). 'State, Institutions and Structural Change', *Structural Change and Economic Dynamics*, 5: 293–313.

Chang, H.-J. (2002). *Kicking Away the Ladder: Development Strategy in Historical Perspective.* London: Anthem Press.

Chang, H.-J. (2003). *Rethinking Development Economics.* London: Anthem.

Chang, H.-J. (2003c). *Globalization, Economic Development and the Role of the State.* London and Penang: Zed Books.

Chang, H.-J. (2004b). 'Institutional Foundations for Effective Design and Implementation of Selective Trade and Industrial Policies in the Least Developed Countries: Theory and Evidence'. In Chang, H.-J., *Globalization, Economic Development and the Role of the State.* London and Penang: Zed Books.

Chang, H.-J. and Grabel, I. (2004). *Reclaiming Development: An Alternative Economic Policy Manual.* London: Zed Books.

Chang, P.-L. and Tsai, C.-T. (2000). 'Evolution of Technology Development Strategies for Taiwan's Semiconductor Industry: Formation of Research Consortia', *Industry and Innovation*, 7: 185–197.

Chen, N., Xu, H. and Wang, Y. (1994). *Zhongguo Xiangzhen Fazhan De Zhengce Daoxiang Yanjiu.* (Development and Policy Studies of China's Rural Industries). Beijing: Economics and Management Publisher.

Chen, Y. (1953). *To Implement Central Control Policy on Grain Supply and Sale: A Collection of Chen Yuan's Articles (1949–1956).* Vol. 2. Beijing: People's Publisher.

Cherry, J. (2003). 'The "Big Deals" and Hynix Semiconductor: State–Business Relations in Post-crisis Korea', *Asia Pacific Business Review*, 10: 178–198.

China Statistical Yearbook. (1986–2006). *China Statistical Yearbook.* Beijing: China Statistics Press.

Chow, G. (2002). *China's Economic Transformation.* Oxford: Blackwell.

Coase, R. (1960). 'The Problem of Social Cost', *Journal of Law and Economics*, 3: 1–44.

Coe, D. T. and Helpman, E. (1995). 'International R&D Spillovers', *European Economic Review*, 39: 859–887.

Corden, W. M. (1974). *Trade Policy and Economic Welfare.* Oxford: Clarendon Press.

Corden, W. M. (1997). *Trade Policy and Economic Welfare*, 2nd edn. Oxford: Oxford University Press.

Dahlman, C.-J. (1990). 'Electronics Development Strategy: The Role of Government', Industry and Energy Department Working Paper, 37, World Bank Industry Series.

Dahlman, C. J. (1979). 'The Problem of Externality', *Journal of Law and Economics*, 22: 141–162.

Dahlman, C. J., Miller, A. and Wellenius, B. (1993). *Developing the Electronics Industry.* Washington, DC: World Bank.

Dahlman, C. J., Ross-Larson, B. and Westphal, L. E. (1987). 'Managing Technological Development: Lessons from the Newly Industrializing Countries', *World Development*, 15: 759–775.

Dasgupta, P. and Stiglitz, J. E. (1974). 'Benefit–Cost Analysis and Trade Policies', *Journal of Political Economy*, 82: 1–33.

Deng, X. (1978a). 'Emancipate the Mind, Seek Truth from Facts and Unite as One in Looking to the Future. *Selected Works of Deng Xiaoping*, Online. Available at http://english.peopledaily.com.cn/dengxp/vol2/text/b1260.html (accessed 4 March 2005).

Deng, X. (1978b). 'Hold High the Banner of Mao Zedong Thought and Adhere to the Principle of Seeking Truth from Facts'. *Selected Works of Deng Xiaoping*. Beijing: People's Publisher. Online. Available at http://english.peopledaily.com.cn/dengxp/vol2/text/b1260.html (accessed 4 March 2005).

Deng, X. (1978c). Speech at the Opening Ceremony of the National Conference on Science, 18 March 1978. *Selected Works of Deng Xiaoping*. Beijing: People's Publisher. Online. Available at http://english.peopledaily.com.cn/dengxp/vol2/text/b1260.html (accessed 4 March 2005).

Deng, X. (1982). 'China's Historical Experience in Economic Construction', *Selected Works of Deng Xiaoping*, 6 May (electronic text).

Deng, X. (1984a). 'Defense and Military Construction'. *Selected Works of Deng Xiaoping*: 99. Beijing: People's Publisher. Online. Available at http://english.peopledaily.com.cn/dengxp/vol2/text/b1260.html (accessed 4 February 2005).

Deng, X. (1984b). 'Make a Success of Special Economic Zones and Open More Cities to the Outside World'. *Selected Works of Deng Xiaoping*. Beijing: People's Publisher. Online. Available at http://english.peopledaily.com.cn/dengxp/vol2/text/b1260.html (accessed 4 March 2005).

Deng, X. (1988). 'China Must Take Its Place in the Field of High Technology', 24 October. *Selected Works of Deng Xiaoping*, vol. 3. Beijing: People's Press. Online. Available at http://web.peopledaily.com.cn/english/dengxp/vol3/text/c1920.html (accessed 4 March 2005).

Deng, X. (1993). 'Hold High the Banner of Mao Zedong Thought and Adhere to the Principle of Seeking Truth from Facts', 16 September 1978. *Selected Works of Deng Xiaoping*. Beijing: People's Publisher. Online. Available at http://english.peopledaily.com.cn/dengxp/vol2/text/b1260.html (accessed 4 February 2005).

Dicken, P. (2003). *Global Shift: Reshaping the Global Economic Map in the 21st Century*, 4th edn. London: Sage.

Dosi, G., Freeman, C., Nelson, R. and Soete, L. (1988). *Technical Change and Economic Theory*. London: Pinter Publishers.

Duncombe, R. and Heeks, R. (1999). 'Information, ICTs and Small Enterprise: *Findings from Botswana*', Development Information Working Paper 7. Manchester: Institute for Development Policy and Management, University of Manchester.

Ellman, M. (1989). *Socialist Planning*, 2nd edn. Cambridge: Cambridge University Press.

Ernst, D. (2003). 'The New Mobility of Knowledge: Digital Information Systems and Global Flagship Networks', Economics Study Area Working Papers 56, East–West Center, Economics Study Area.

Ernst, D. (2004). 'Global Production Networks in East Asia's Electronics Industry and Upgrading in Malaysia.' In Yusuf, S., Altaf, M. A. and Nabeshima, K. (eds), *Global Production Networking and Technological Change in East Asia*. Washington, DC: World Bank and Oxford University Press.

Ernst, D., Mytelka, L. and Ganiatsos, T. (1998). 'Technological capabilities in the context of export-led growth a conceptual framework'. In D. Ernst, T. Ganiatsos and L. Mytelka (eds), *Technological Capabilities and Export Success in Asia.* London: Routledge, pp. 5–35.

Evans, P. (1995). *Embedded Autonomy: States and Industrial Transformation.* Princeton, NJ: Princeton University Press.

Feigenbaum, E. A. (1999). 'Who's Behind China's High-Technology "Revolution"? How Bomb Makers Remade Beijing's Priorities, Policies, and Institutions'. *International Security*, 24: 95–126.

Five Year Plan (1986–2004). *Yearbook of the Chinese Electronics Industry.* Beijing: China Electronics Industry Press.

Frank, A. G. (1967). *Capitalism and Underdevelopment in Latin America: Historical Studies of Chile and Brazil.* New York: Monthly Press Review.

Flamm, K. (1996). *Mismanaged Trade? Strategic Policy and the Semiconductor Industry.* Washington, DC: Brookings Institution Press.

Fong, G. R. (1998). 'Follower at the Frontier: International Competition and Japanese Industrial Policy', *International Studies Quarterly*, 42: 339–366.

Forbes (2004). 'Toshiba to Move All Asian PC Output to China-Paper'. Online. Available at http://www.forbes.com/reuters/newswire/2004/04/08/rtr1328209.html (accessed 9 April 2004).

Fransman, M. (1986). 'International Competitiveness, Technical Change and the State: The Machine Tool Industry in Taiwan and Japan', *World Development*, 14: 1375–1396.

Furman, J. L. and Stern, S. (1999). 'Understanding the Drivers of National Innovative Capacity: Implications for the Central European Economies', NBER Working Paper.

Gangnes, B. and Assche, A. V. (2004). 'Modular Production Networks in Electronics: The Nexus between Management and Economics Research', SMU Economics & Statistics Working Papers 21–2004.

GAO (1987). 'International Trade Observations on the US–Japan Semiconductor Arrangement', Briefing Report to the Honorable Lloyd M. Bentsen, United States Senate.

GAO (2002). 'Export Controls Rapid Advances in China's Semiconductor Industry Underscore Need for Fundamental US Policy Review', Report to the Ranking Minority Member Committee on Governmental Affairs, US Senate.

Gao, Y. (1993). *Fazhan, Keji, Zhengfu* (Development, Technology and the Government). Beijing: National Defence Publisher.

Gartner (2005). Gartner Dataquest Announces Final 2004 Semiconductor Market Share, Gartner Teleconference, Online. Available at http://www.gartner.com/ (accessed 7 April 2006).

GATT (1947). Preamble of the General Agreement of Tariffs and Trade. Online. Available at http://unstats.un.org/unsd/class/intercop/techsubgroup/02-01/tsg0201-8.htm (accessed 1 May 2006).

Gerschenkron, A. (1962). *Economic Backwardness in Historical Perspective.* Cambridge, MA: Harvard University Press.

Gertz, B. (2007) 'US–China company merger deemed "threat"' , *The Washington Times*, November 29. Online. Available at http://washingtontimes.com/apps/pbcs.dll/article?AID=/20071129/NATION/111290108/1001 (accessed 29 November 2007)

Gilboy, G. (2003). Nodes without Roads: Pockets of Success, Networks of Failure in Chinese Industrial Technology Development, Department of Political Science, MIT.

Gordon, R. J. (2002). 'Technology and Economic Performance in the American Economy', Working Papers 8771, National Bureau of Economic Research.

Grossman, G. M. and Helpman, E. (1991). *Innovation and Growth in the Global Economy*. Cambridge, MA: MIT Press.

Grubel, H. G. and Lloyd, P. J. (1975). *Intra-industry Trade: The Theory and Measurement of International Trade in Differentiated Products*. London: Macmillan.

Guo, G. and Cao, R. (1994). *Woguo Dianzi Guoye Jiegou Yanjiu* (Study on the Industrial Structure of Chinese Industry). Shanxi: Taiyuan Publisher.

Haberler, G. (1950). 'Some Problems in the Pure Theory of International Trade', *Economic Journal*, 60: 223–406.

Harrold, P. and Lall, R. (1993). 'China: Reform and Development in 1992–1993', World Bank Discussion Paper 215, 24 August.

Hausmann, R. and Rodrik, D. (2003). 'Economic Development as Self-Discovery', *Journal of Development Economics*, 72: 603–633.

Helpman, E. and Krugman, P. R. (1985). *Market Structure and Foreign Trade: Increasing Returns, Imperfect Competition and the International Economy*. Brighton: Wheatsheaf Books.

Hirst, P. and Thompson, G. (1995). 'Globalization and the Future of the Nation State', *Economy and Society*, 24 (3): 408–442.

Hobday, M. (1995a). 'East Asian Latecomer Firms: Learning the Technology of Electronics', *World Development*, 23: 1171–1193.

Hobday, M. (1995b). *Innovation in East Asia: The Challenge to Japan*. Aldershot, UK, and Brookfield, VT: Elgar.

Hobday, M., Cawson, A. and Kim, S. R. (2001). 'Governance of Technology in the Electronics Industries of East and South-East Asia', *Technovation*, 21: 209–226.

Hobday, M., Davies, A. and Prencipe, A. (2005). 'Systems Integration: A Core Capability of the Modern Corporation', *Industrial and Corporate Change*, 14 (6): 1109–1143.

Howell, R. T., Bartlett, L. B., Noellert, W. A. and Howe, R. (2003). China's Emerging Semiconductor Market: The Impact of China's Preferential Value-Added Tax on Current Investment Trends. Online. Available at http://www.sia-online.org/pre_stat.cfm?ID=225 (accessed 11 February 2004).

Hu, Q. (1993). 'Making the Electronics Industry the Pillar Industry for the National Economy'. In Hu, Q. (ed.), *Exploration and Practice of China's Informationalisation*. Beijing: Publishing House of Electronics Industry.

Hu, Q. (2001). *China's Informationalisation: Exploration and Practice (a Collection of the Minister's Speeches)*. Beijing: Publishing House of Electronics Industry.

Hu, Q. (2006). *Xinlu Licheng* (The Path to the Development of the Chinese Semiconductor Industry). Beijing: Publishing House of Electronics Industry.

Hu, Z. (1996). *Zhongguo Zhizhu Chanye Fazhan Zhanlue* (The Development Strategy of China's Pillar Industries). Beijing: Beijing Jing Ji Guan Li Chu Ban She.

Hughes, H. (1993). 'Is There an East Asian Model?', Economic Division Working Paper 4, Research School of Pacific Studies, Australian National University, Canberra.

IMF (1997). 'Korean Memorandum on the Economic Program, Letter of Intent of the Government of Korea', 3 December. Online. Available at http://www.imf.org/external/np/loi/120397.HTM (accessed 15 December 2004).

Information Technology Yearbook. (2004). *Yearbook of China's Information Technology*. Beijing: China City Press.

Information Technology Yearbook (2005). *Yearbook of China's Information Technology*. Beijing: Publishing House of Electronics Industry.

Irwin, D. A. (1994). 'Trade Politics and the Semiconductor Industry', NBER Working Paper Series, 4745.

Jiang, Z. (1989) 'Opinions on the Characteristics of Global Information Industry Development and China's Strategic Development Issues'.

Jiang, Z. (1992). 'Speeding up the Pace of Reform, Opening Up and Modernization, Capturing the Great Success of China's Socialist Pursuit', Report at the Fourteenth Congress of the CCP, 12 October 1992.

Jiang, Z. (1993). 'Discussion on the New Features of the Development of the World Electronics Industry and the Development Strategy of Our Country's Information Industry', *Academic Journal of Shanghai Transportation University*, issue 6, 1986. Reprinted in China Electronics News Agency (ed.), *Reviving the Electronics Industry and Rapid Informationisation*. Beijing: Beijing Electronics Publishing House.

Jiang, Z. (1997). 'Implementing "Attracting-In" and "Walking-Out" Combined Opening Up Strategies'. In *Selected Works of Jiang Zemin*. Beijing: People's Publisher.

Jiang, Z. (2002). 'Build a Well-Off Society in an All-Round Way and Create a New Situation in Building Socialism with Chinese Characteristics', full text of Jiang Zemin's report at the Sixteenth Party Congress, 8 November, 2002. Online. Available at http://english.peopledaily.com.cn/200211/18/eng20021118_106983.shtml (accessed 15 May 2006).

Johnson, H. G. (1970). 'The Efficiency and Welfare Implications of International Corporations'. In Kindleberger, C. P. (ed.), *The International Corporation*. Cambridge, MA: MIT Press.

Johnson, H. G. (1975). 'Technological Change and Comparative Advantage: An Advanced Country Viewpoint'. In Kojima, K. and Wionczek, M. S. (eds), *Technology Transfer in Pacific Economic Development*. Tokyo: Economic Research Centre.

Juster, K. I. (2003). 'Keynote Address of Under-Secretary of Commerce for Industry and Security at the U.S.–Taiwan Business Council and the Fabless Semiconductor Association', Keynote speech presented at Conference on Taiwan and China Semiconductor Industry Outlook, 2003.

Katz, J. (2000). 'Structural Change and Productivity in Latin American Industry, 1970–1996', *CEPAL Review*, 71: 63–81.

Keller, W. W. and Pauly, L. W. (2000). 'Crisis and Adaptation in East Asian Innovation Systems: The Case of the Semiconductor Industry in Taiwan and South Korea', *Business and Politics*, 2: 327–352.

Keynes, J. M. (1926). *Official Papers of Alfred Marshall*. London: Macmillan.

Kim, S. R. (1996). 'The Korean System of Innovation and the Semiconductor Industry: A Governance Perspective', SPRU/SEI-Working Paper, University of Sussex.

Knowles, L. C. A. (1921). *The Industrial and Commercial Revolutions in Great Britain during the Nineteenth Century*. London: Routledge.

Kong, X. and Xing, C. (2005). '*Zhongguo Dianzi Gongye De Chengzhang: Tizhi Bianqian Jidui Zhenzhangde Gongxian*', (The Growth of China's Electronics Industry: Institutional Transformation and Contribution to the Economic Growth), *Zhongguo keji luntan*, (China Technology Forum) 5: 90–93.

Krueger, A. O. (1974). 'The Political Economy of the Rent-Seeking Society', *American Economic Review*, 64: 291–303.

Krueger, A. O. (1978). *Foreign Trade Regimes and Economic Development: Liberalization Attempts and Consequences.* Cambridge, MA: Ballinger for the National Bureau of Economic Research.

Krueger, A. O. (1997). 'Trade Policy and Economic Development: How We Learn'. NBER Working Paper.

Krugman, P. R. (1987). 'Is Free Trade Passé?' *Journal of Economic Perspectives*, 1: 131–144.

Krugman, P. R. (1990). *Rethinking International Trade.* Cambridge, MA: MIT Press.

Krugman, P. R. (1991a). *Geography and Trade.* Cambridge, MA: MIT Press.

Krugman, P. R. (1991b). 'Myths and Realities of US Competitiveness'. *Science*, 254 (5033): 811–815.

Krugman, P. R. (1998). 'The Confidence Game', manuscript. Cambridge, MA: Economics Department, MIT.

Kuznet, P. W. (1977). *Economic Growth and Structure in the Republic of Korea.* London: Yale University Press.

Lakenan, B., Boyd, D. and Frey, E. (2001). 'Why Cisco Fell: Outsourcing and Its Perils', *Strategy+Business*, 24 (3rd quarter): 54–65.

Lall, S. (2001). 'The Technological Structure and Performance of Developing Country Manufactured Exports, 1985–98', QEH Working Paper Series, Oxford University.

Lall, S. (2004). *Reinventing Industrial Strategy: The Role of Government Policy in Building Industrial Competitiveness.* United Nations Conference on Trade Development Group of Twenty-four: 9. New York and Geneva: United Nations.

Lall, S. and Kraemer-Mbula, E. (2005). '*Industrial Competitiveness in Africa: Lessons from East Asia*'. Rugby, UK: ITDG Publishing.

Lall, S. and Teubal, M. (1998). '"Market-Stimulating" Technology Policies in Developing Countries: A Framework with Examples from East Asia', *World Development*, 26: 1369–1385.

Lall, S. and Urata, S. (2003). *Competitiveness, FDI and Technological Activity in East Asia.* Cheltenham, UK: Edward Elgar.

Langlois, R. and Steinmueller, W. E. (1999). 'The Evolution of Competitive Advantage in the Worldwide Semiconductor Industry, 1947–1996.' In Mowery, D. C. and Nelson, R. R. (eds), *The Sources of Industrial Leadership.* New York: Cambridge University Press.

Lardy, N. (2001). 'The Role of Foreign Trade and Investment in China's Economic Transformation.' In Garnaut, R. and Huang, Y. (eds), *Growth without Miracles: Readings on the Chinese Economy in the Era of Reform.* Oxford: Oxford University Press.

Leamer, E. E. (1980). 'The Leontief Paradox, Reconsidered', *Journal of Political Economy*, 88: 495–503.

Leamer, E. E. (1993). 'Factor-Supply Differences as a Source of Comparative Advantage', *American Economic Review*, 83: 436–439.

Lemon, S. (2003). 'Intel Plans Second Assembly Plant in China'. Online. Available at http://www.pcworldmalta.com/news/2003/Aug/281.htm (accessed 28 Aug 2003).

Leontief, W. (1953). 'Domestic Production and Foreign Trade: The American Capital Position Re-examined', *Proceedings of the American Philosophical Society*, 97: 331–349.

Leontief, W. (1956). 'Factor Proportions and Structure of American Trade: Further Theoretical and Empirical Analysis', *Review of Economics and Statistics*, 38: 386–407.

Levi-Faur, D. (1997). 'Friedrich List and the Political Economy of the Nation-State', *Review of International Political Economy*, 4: 154–178.

Li, M. (1997). *China's 863*. Jiangsu: Jiangsu Literature Publisher.

Li, T. (1981). 'The Minister's Report on the Electronics Industry', speech on the Electronics Industry Official Meetings. Beijing: Xinhua News.

Li, T. (1986a). 'The Minister's Report on the Electronics Industry', speech on the Electronics Industry Official Meetings. Beijing: Ministry of the Electronics Industry.

Li, T. (1986b). 'A Study of the Development of the Electronics Industry and Reform'. In China Electronics News Agency (ed.), *Reviving the Electronics Industry and Rapidly Informationalising*. Beijing: Beijing Electronics Publishing House.

Li, T. (1993). 'A Study of the Development of the Electronics Industry and Reform 1986'. In China Electronics News Agency (ed.), *Reviving the Electronics Industry and Rapidly Informationalising*. Beijing: Beijing Electronics Publishing House.

Li, X. (1989). Report at the 1978 Third Plenum of the 11th CCP Congress, *Selected Works of Li, Xiannian*. Beijing: People's Publisher.

Li, Y. (1986). *The Basic Principles of China's Economic Reform*. Beijing: China Perspective Publisher.

Li, Z. (1997). *Dagongye Yu Zhongguo* (Large Industries and China). Nanchang: Jiangxi People's Publisher.

Lin, J.-Y., Cai, F. and Li, Z. (1996). *The China Miracle: Development Strategy and Economic Reform*. Friedman Lecture Fund Monograph series. Hong Kong: Chinese University Press for the Hong Kong Centre for Economic Research and the International Center for Economic Growth.

Linden, G. (2004). 'China Standard Time: A Study in Strategic Industrial Policy', *Business and Politics*, 6 (3) Online. Available at http://www.bepress.com/bap/vol6/iss3/art4 (accessed 5 October 2007).

List, F. (ed.) (1841). *The National System of Political Economy*. London Longmans, Green.

List, F. (1938). *The Natural System of Political Economy* (Henderson's translation, 1983). London: Frank Cass.

Little, I., Scitovsky, T. and Scott, M. (1970) *Industry in Trade in Some Developing Countries – A Comparative Study*, London, Oxford University Press.

Liu, S. (1993). *Sannian Zhunbei Shinian Jianshe* (Three-Year Preparation, Ten-Year Construction). Beijing: Central Documentary Publisher.

Liu, X. (2005), China's Development Model: An Alternative Strategy for Technological Catch-up. Hitotsubashi University, Institute of Innovation Research Working Paper, March 22.

Liu, Y. (2004). *Chunsong: Dengxiaoping Yu Zhonguguo Keji Shiye* (Spring Eulogy: Deng Xiaoping and China's Technology). Beijing: Publisher of Science and Technology Literature.

Lou, Q. (2003). *Zhongguo Dianzi Xinxi Chanye Fanzhan Yanjiu* (A Study on the Development Model of China's Information Industry). Beijing: Chinese Economics Publishing House.

Lu, X. (2002). '20 Year Splendid "Reform and Opening Up" Canto of the Electronics Industry', Internal Report by Vice Minister of the Information Industry. Beijing: Minister of the Information Industry.

McKinsey (1998). *Productivity-Led Growth for Korea*. Seoul and Washington, DC: McKinsey Global Institute.

Mao, Z. (1950). 'Buyao Simian Chuji' (Don't Attack from All Directions). *A Collection of Mao's Works*. Beijing: Beijing People's Publisher.

Mao, Z. (1955). 'Guanyu Nongye Hezuohua Wenti' (Regarding Agricultural Cooperation on 31 July). *A Collection of Mao's Works*. Beijing: People's Publisher.

Mau, Z. (1977a) 'China Will Take a Great Stride Forward', 13 December 1963, quoted in *Peking Review*, no. 52, December 1977.

Mao, Z. (1977b). 'Discussion on Ten Relationships 1956', *A Collection of Mao's Works*, Beijing: People's Publisher.

Marshall, A. (1920). *Principles of Economics*. London: Macmillan.

Marx, K. (1867). *Capital (Das Kapital): A Critique of Political Economy*, vol. I: *The Process of Capitalist Production*. Trans. Moore, S. and Aveling, E., ed. Engels, F. Chicago: Charles H. Kerr (1906).

Mathews, J.-A. and Cho, D.-S. (2000). *Tiger Technology: The Creation of a Semiconductor Industry in East Asia*. Cambridge Asia-Pacific Studies. Cambridge: Cambridge University Press.

Mehdi, S. (2000). 'What Did Frederick List Actually Say? Some Clarifications on the Infant Industry Argument', UNCTAD Discussion Papers, UNCTAD/OSG/DP/149.

Mehdi, S. (2005). *Trade Policy at the Crossroads: The Recent Experience of Developing Countries*. Basingstoke, UK: Palgrave Macmillan.

MII (1998). *Report of the Working Plan of the Ministry of the Information Industry*. Beijing: Ministry of Information Industry.

MII (1999). *Zhongguo Dianzi Guoye Wushi Nian* (Fifty-Year History of the Chinese Electronics Industry). Beijing: Publishing House of Electronics Industry.

Mill, J. (1821). *Elements of Political Economy*. London: Baldwin, Cradock & Joy.

MOC (2006). *Statistical Bulletin of China's Outward Foreign Direct Investment 2005*. Beijing: Ministry of Commerce.

Myint, H. (1958). 'The "Classical Theory" of International Trade and the Underdeveloped Countries', *Economic Journal*, June: 317–337.

Myrdal, G. (1968). *Asian Drama: An Inquiry into the Poverty of Nations*. Harmondsworth, UK: Penguin.

Naughton, B. (1988). 'The Third Front: Defence Industrialization in the Chinese Interior', *China Quarterly*, 115: 351–386.

Naughton, B. (1995). *Growing out of the Plan*. Cambridge: Cambridge University Press.

Naughton, B. and Ernst, D. (2005). 'China's Emerging Industrial Economy: Insights from the IT Industry', paper prepared for the East-West Center Conference on China's Emerging Capitalist System, Honolulu, Hawaii.

Naughton, B. and Segal, A. (2003). 'China in search of a workable model: technology development in the new millennium'. In Keller, W. W. and Samuels, R. J. (eds), *Crisis and Innovation in Asian Technology*. Cambridge: Cambridge University Press, pp.160–86.

NBSC (2003). 'The Provisional Prescript on the Statistical Division of the Information Related Industries, 29 December 2003'. Online. Available at http://www.stats.gov.cn (accessed 10 October 2004).

NBSC (2004). 'Temporary Provision of Statistical Classification of the Information Related Industry, 10 February 2004'. Online. Available at http://www.stats.gov.cn (accessed 10 February 2004).

NDRC (1949–2005). *Five Year Economic Plan*. Online. Available at http://www.ndrc.gov.cn/ (accessed 20 June 2005).

Nelson, D. (1987). 'The Domestic Political Preconditions of US Trade Policy: Liberal Structure and Protectionist Dynamics', paper presented at Conference on Political Economy of Trade: Theory and Policy. Washington, DC: World Bank.

Nelson, R. R. (1987). 'Innovation and Economic Development: Theoretical Retrospect and Prospect.' In Katz, J. M. (ed), *Technology Generation in Latin American Manufacturing Industries*. New York: St Martin's Press.

Nelson, R. R., and Pack, H. (1997). 'The Asian Miracle and Modern Growth Theory'. World Bank Policy Research Working Paper 1881.

Ning, L. (2007). 'Economic Liberalization for High-Tech Industry Development? Lessons from China's Response in Developing the ICT Manufacturing Sector Compared with the Strategies of Korea and Taiwan', *Journal of Development Studies*, 43: 562–587.

Nolan, P. (2001). *China and the Global Business Revolution*. Basingstoke, UK: Palgrave Macmillan.

Nolan, P. (2002). 'China and the Global Business Revolution', *Cambridge Journal of Economics*, 26: 119–137.

Nolan, P. (2004). 'Politics, Planning, and the Transition from Stalinism: The Case of China.' In Nolan, P. (ed.), *Transforming China: Globalization, Transition and Development*. London: Anthem Press.

Nolan, P. and Wang, X. (1998). 'Beyond Privatization: Institutional Innovation and Growth in China's Large State-Owned Enterprises', *World Development*, 27: 169–200.

Nolan, P., Zhang, J. and Liu, C. (2007a). *The Global Business Revolution and the Cascade Effect: Systems Integration in the Aerospace, Beverages and Retail Industries*. Basingstoke, UK: Palgrave Macmillan.

Nolan, P., Zhang, J. and Liu, C. (2007b). 'The Global Business Revolution, the Cascade Effect, and the Challenge for Firms from Developing Countries', *Cambridge Journal of Economics*, Advance Access published online on 13 August 2007, 1–19.

OECD (2000). 'Policy Brief: Science, Technology and Innovation in the New Economy'. Online. Available at www.oecd.org/publications/Pol_brief/ (accessed 23 June 2004).

OECD (2002). 'Measuring the Information Economy 2002'. Online. Available at http://www.oecd.org/dataoecd/16/14/1835738.pdf (accessed 23 June 2004).

OECD (2003a). *The Economic Impact of ICT Measurement: Evidence and Implications*. Paris: OECD Publishing.

OECD (2003b). *OECD Science, Technology and Industry Scoreboard 2003: Towards a Knowledge-Based Economy*. Online. Available at http://www1.oecd.org/publications/e-book/92-2003-04-1-7294/ (accessed 15 August 2004).

OECD (2004a). *OECD Information Technology Outlook*. Paris: OECD Publishing.

OECD. (2004b). *Science and Innovation Policy: Key Challenges and Opportunities*. Online. Available at www.oecd.org/publications/Pol_brief/ (accessed 23 June 2004).

OECD (2005). *OECD Economic Survey: China*. Paris: OECD Publishing.

OECD (2006a). 'OECD Finds That China Is Biggest Exporter of Information Technology Goods in 2004, Surpassing US and EU'. Online. Available at http://www.oecd.org/document/8/0,2340,en_2825_293564_35833096_1_1_1_1,00.html (accessed 1 November 2006).

OECD (2006b). *OECD Information Technology Outlook*. Paris: OECD Publishing.

Ohlin, B. G. (1933). *Interregional and International Trade*. Cambridge, MA: Harvard University Press.

O'Riain, S. (2000). 'The Flexible Developmental State: Globalization, Information Technology and the "Celtic Tiger"'. *Politics and Society*, 28: 157–193.

O'Riain, S. (2004). *The Politics of High Tech Growth: Developmental Network States in the Global Economy*. Cambridge: Cambridge University Press.

Ozawa, T. (1974). *Japan's Technological Challenge to the West, 1950–1974: Motivation and Accomplishment*, Cambridge, MA: MIT Press.

Pack, H. (1987). *Productivity, Technology, and Industrial Development*. New York: Oxford University Press.

Pavitt, K. (2005). 'Specialization and Systems Integration: Where Manufacture and Services Still Meet'. In Prencipe, A. Davies, A. and Hobday, M. (eds), *The Business of Systems Integration*. Oxford: Oxford University Press.

People's Daily (2001). 'Japan's Toshiba to Shift Television Output to China'. Online. Available at http://english.people.com.cn/english/200103/19/eng20010319_65362. html (accessed 11 November 2004).

Perdikis, N. and Kerr, W. A. (1998). *Trade Theories and Empirical Evidence*. Manchester: Manchester University Press.

Perez, C. (2000). 'Technological Change and Opportunities for Development as a Moving Target', paper presented at High-Level Round Table on Trade and Development: Directions for the Twenty-first Century, 12 February, Bangkok.

Pinder, J. (1982). 'Causes and Kinds of Industrial Policy'. In J. Pinder (ed.), *National Industrial Strategies and the World Economy*. London: Croom Helm.

Posner, R. A. (1987). 'The Constitution as an Economic Document', *George Washington Law Review*, 56: 4–38.

Prebisch, R. (1950). *The Economic Development of Latin America and Its Principal Problems*. Lake Success, NY: United Nations.

Prebisch, R. (1958). *The Economic Development of Latin America and Its Principal Problems*. New York: United Nations.

Prebisch, R. (1984) 'Five Stages in My Thinking on Development'. In Meier, G. M. and Seers, D. (eds), *Pioneers in Development*. Oxford: Oxford University Press.

Preeg, E. H. (2005). *The Emerging Chinese Advanced Technology Superstate*, Washington, DC: Manufacturers Alliance and Hudson Institute.

Przeworski, A. (1998). 'The State in a Market Economy'. In Nelson, J., Tilly, C. and Walker, L. (eds), *Transforming Post-communist Political Economies*. Washington, DC: National Academy of Science.

PWC (2004). *China's Impact on the Semiconductor Industry*. London: Pricewaterhouse Coopers.

Qian, Y. (1999). 'The Process of China's Market Transition (1978–98): The Evolutionary, Historical, and Comparative Perspectives', paper presented at the Journal of Institutional and Theoretical Economics symposium on 'Big-Bang Transformation of Economic Systems as a Challenge to New Institutional Economics', June 1999, Wallerfangen/Saar, Germany.

Qian, Y. and Xu, C. (1993). 'Why China's Economic Reforms Differ: The M-Form Hierarchy and Entry/Expansion of the Non-State Sector', *Economics of Transition*, 1: 135–170.

Reinert, E. S. (1994). 'Competitiveness and Its Predecessors: A 500-Year Cross-national Perspective', paper prepared for the Business History Conference, Williamsburg, Virginia: Step Groups.

Ricardo, D. (1817) On the Principles of Political Economy and Taxation, 3rd edn, 1821. London: John Murray.

Rodriguez, F. and Rodrik, D. (1999). 'Trade Policy and Economic Growth: A Skeptic's Guide to Cross-national Evidence', NBER Working Paper W7081: 5, 13–14.

Rodrik, D. (1996). 'Coordination Failures and Government Policy: A Model with Applications to East Asia and Eastern Europe', *Journal of International Economics*, 40: 1–22.

Rodrik, D. (2004). 'Industrial Policy for the Twenty-first Century', Working Papers for UNIDO.

Romer, P.-M. (1990). 'Endogenous Technological Change', *Journal of Political Economy*, 98: 71–102.

Sachs, J. D., Warner, A., Aslund, A. and Fischer, S. (1995). 'Economic Reform and the Process of Global Integration, 25th Anniversary Issue', *Brookings Papers on Economic Activity*, 1995: 1–118.

Sala-i-Martin, X. and Barro Robert, J. (1995). *Economic Growth*. New York: McGraw-Hill.

Samuelson, P. A. (1938). 'Welfare Economics and International Trade', *American Economic Review*, 28: 261–266.

Samuelson, P. A. (1939). 'The Gains from International Trade', *Canadian Journal of Economics and Political Science*, 5: 195–205.

Samuelson, P. A. (1962). 'The Gains from International Trade Once Again', *Economic Journal*, 72: 820–829.

Scherer, F. M. (1992). *International High-Technology Competition*. Cambridge, MA: Harvard University Press.

Schotter, A. (1985). *Free Market Economics: A Critical Appraisal*. New York: St Martin's Press.

Schumpeter, J. (1942). *Capitalism, Socialism, and Democracy*. New York: Harper.

Segal, A. (2002). *Digital Dragon: High Technology Enterprises in China*. Ithaca, NY: Cornell University Press.

Shafaeddin, S. M. (2005). 'Trade Liberalization and Economic Reform in Developing Countries: Structural Change or De-industrialization?', paper presented at United Nations Conference on Trade and Development, Discussion Papers 179.

SIA (2004). *Comments of the Semiconductor Industry Association for the 2005 National Trade Estimate Report on Foreign Trade Barriers: China December 21, 2004*. San José, CA: Semiconductor Industry Association.

Singer, H. W. (1950). 'The Distribution of Gains between Borrowing and Investing Countries', *American Economic Review*, 40: 473–485.

Smith, A. (1776). *An Inquiry into the Nature and Causes of the Wealth of Nations* (1976 reprint). Chicago: University of Chicago Press.

Smith, H. (2000). *Industry Policy in Taiwan and Korea in the 1980s: Winning with the Market*. Cheltenham: Edward Elgar.

Smyth, R. (2000). 'Should China Be Promoting Large-Scale Enterprises and Enterprise Groups?', *World Development*, 28: 721–737.

Steinfeld, E. (2004). 'China's Shallow Integration: Networked Production and the New Challenges for Late Industrialization', *World Development*, 32: 1971–1987.

Stern, R. M. and Maskus, K. E. (1981). 'Determinations of the Structure of US Foreign Trade 1958–1976', *Journal of International Economics*, 11: 207–224.

Stigler, G. (1975). *The Citizen and the State: Essays on Regulation*. Chicago: University of Chicago Press.

Stiglitz, J. E. (1994). *Whither Socialism?* Cambridge, MA: MIT Press.

Stiglitz, J. E. (2002). *Globalization and Its Discontents*. London: Penguin Books.

Stiglitz, J. E. and Charlton, A. (2005). *Fair Trade for All: How Trade Can Promote Development*. Oxford: Oxford University Press.

Stiglitz, J. E. and Newbery, D. (1984). 'Pareto-Inferior Trade', *Review of Economic Studies*, 51: 1–12.

Stolper, W. and Samuelson, P. A. (1941). 'Protection and Real Wages', *Review of Economic Studies*, 9: 58–73.

Sturgeon, T. J. (2004). 'Modular Production Networks: A New American Model of Industrial Organization', *Industrial and Corporate Change*, 11: 451–496.

Sturgeon, T. and Lester, R. (2004). 'The New Global Supply-Base: New Challenges for Local Suppliers in East Asia'. In Yusuf, S., Altaf, M. A. and Nabeshima, K. (eds), *Global Production Networking and Technological Change in East Asia*. Washington, DC: World Bank and Oxford University Press.

Subramanian, A. and Wei, S.-J. (2003). 'The WTO Promotes Trade, Strongly but Unevenly', NBER Working Paper.

Sung, G. H. (1997). *The Political Economy of Industrial Policy in East Asia: The Semiconductor Industry in Taiwan and South Korea*. Cheltenham: Edward Elgar.

Suttmeier, R. P. and Yao, X. (2004). 'China's Post-WTO Technology Policy: Standards, Software, and the Changing Nature of Techno-nationalism', National Bureau of Asian Research Special Report 7.

Swerling, B. C. (1954). 'Capital Shortage and Labor Surplus in the United States', *Review of Economics and Statistics*, 36: 275–296.

Tatemoto, M. and Ichimura, S. (1959). 'Factor Proportions and Foreign Trade: The Case of Japan', *Review of Economics and Statistics*, 41: 442–226.

Teubal, M., Foray, D., Justman, M. and Zuscovitch, E. (1996). *Technological Infrastructure Policy: An International Perspective*, vol. 7: *Economics of Science, Technology and Innovation*. Dordrecht: Kluwer Academic.

Thomas, V., Matin, K. and Nash, S. (1990). *Lessons in Trade Policy Reform*. Washington, DC: World Bank.

Torrens, R. (1815). *Essay on the External Corn Trade*. London: J. Hatchard.

Tung, A.-C. (2001). 'Taiwan's Semiconductor Industry: What the State Did and Did Not', *Review of Development Economics*, 5: 266–288.

UNCTAD (1999). *African Development in a Comparative Perspective*. New York and Geneva: UNCTAD published for and on behalf of the United Nations.

UNCTAD. (2001). *World Investment Report 2001: Promoting Linkages*. New York and Geneva: United Nations.

UNDP (2001). *Human Development Report*. Oxford: Oxford University Press.

UNDP (2004). *Human Development Report*. Oxford: Oxford University Press.

USTR (2004). *US Files WTO Case against China over Discriminatory Taxes That Hurt US Exports*. Online. Available at http://www.ustr.gov/Document_Library/Press_Releases/2004/March/U.S_Files_WTO_Case_Against_China_Over_Discriminatory_Taxes_That_Hurt_U.S._Exports.html (accessed 20 June 2004).

Vaggi, G. and Groenewegen, P. (2003). *A Concise History of Economic Thought: From Mercantilism to Monetarism*. New York: Palgrave Macmillan.

Vernon, R. (1966). 'International Investment and International Trade in the Product Cycle', *Quarterly Journal of Economics*, 80: 190–207.

Wade, R. (1990). *Governing the Market: Economic Theory and the Role of Government in East Asian Industrialization*. Princeton, NJ: Princeton University Press.

Wade, R. (1998). 'The Asian Debt and Development Crisis of 1997? Causes and Consequences', *World Development*, 26: 1535–1553.

Wade, R. (2004). *Governing the Market: Economic Theory and the Role of Government in East Asian Industrialization*. Princeton, NJ: Princeton University Press.

Walsh, K. (2005). Testimony before the US–China Economic and Security Review Commission, Hearing on China's High-Technology Development, April 2005, Washington, DC.

Wang, H. (1998). *The Industrial History of People's Republic of China*. Shanxi: Shanxi Economic Publisher.

Wang, H. (2001). *Xinzhongguo De Jingjishi* (The Industrial History of the New China, 1979–2000). Beijing: Economic Management Publisher.

Wang, R. (1990). 'Against Capitalist Liberalization', *Qiushi*, 4.

Wang, Y. (1996). *WaiShang Zhi JieTou Zi Ying Xiang ZhongGuo GuoJi ShouZhi De RuoGan Yinsu* (The Effects of FDI on China's Direct Trade Balance and Its Causes). Beijing: Zhong Guo Jing Ji Chu Ban She.

Wang, Y. C. (1966). *Chinese Intellectuals and the West, 1872–1949*. Chapel Hill: University of North Carolina Press.

Weber, M. (1946). *From Max Weber: Essays in Sociology*. New York: Oxford University Press.

Wei, H. (2001). *Congchongfujianshe Zouxiang Youzhi Jingzheng* (From Repeated Construction to Competitive Orders). Beijing: People's Publisher.

Westphal, L. E. (1990). 'Industrial Policy in an Export-Propelled Economy: Lessons from South Korea's Experience', *Journal of Economic Perspectives*, 4: 41–59.

White House. (1999). 'Briefing on the Clinton Administration Agenda for the World Trade Organization. Material Summary of the US–China Bilateral WTO Agreement, November 17', The White House Office of Public Liaison, Washington, DC.

Williamson, J. (2000). 'What Should the World Bank Think About the Washington Consensus?' World Bank Research Observer, 15(2): 251–264

Winters, L. A. (2003). 'Trade Policy as Development Policy'. In Toye, J. (ed.), *Trade and Development: Directions for the Twenty-first Century*. Cheltenham, UK: Edward Elgar.

Wolf, C., Jr (1979). 'A Theory of Non-market Failure: Framework for Implementation Analysis', *Journal of Law and Economics*, 22: 107–139.

Woo, J.-E. (1991). *Race to the Swift: State and Finance in Korean Industrialization*. New York: Columbia University Press.

World Bank. (1993). *The East Asian Miracle: Economic Growth and Public Policy*. World Bank Policy Research Report Series. Oxford: Oxford University Press.

WTO (2004). 'Subsidies Request from the United States to China Pursuant to Article 25.8 of the Agreement on Subsidies and Countervailing Measures', Committee on Subsidies and Countervailing Measures, G/SCM/Q2/CHN/9 (6 October 2004).

WTO (2005). 'International Trade Statistics 2005'. Online. Available at http://www.wto.org/english/res_e/statis_e/its2005_e/its05_bysector_e.htm (accessed 10 Jan 2007).

Wu, J. C. (2003). *The Minister's Working Report at the National Information Industry Conference*. Beijing: Ministry of Information Industry.

Wu, J. L. (1985). 'Economic Reform Mechanism and Complementary Reforms'. In Wu, J. L. (ed.), *Selected Works of Wu Jinlian*. Taiyuan: Shanxi Publisher.

Wu, J. L. (2003a). *Dangdai Zhongguo Jingji Gaige* (Economic Reform in Contemporary China). Shanghai: Shanghai Yuandong Publisher.

Wu, J. L. (2003b). *Suggestions for the Reform of the State Economy after the Establishment of the State Ownership Committee*. Beijing: China Economic Daily.

Xinhua News Agency (2005). 'Ministry of Commerce: China's FDI Accumulated to 44.8 Billion USD'. Online. Available at http://news.xinhuanet.com/fortune/2005–10/30/content_3701957.htm (accessed 4 June 2006).

Xue, M. (1982). 'Several Theoretical Questions of the Reform of the Economic Management System.' In Magazine, H. (ed.), *Collected Essays on the Planned Economy and Market Adjustment*. Beijing: Hongqi.

Yearbook of China's High Tech Industries (2005), *Yearbook of China's High Tech Industries*. Beijing: China Statistics Press

Yearbook of the Electronics Industry (1986–2001). *Yearbook of the Electronics Industry*, Beijing: Publishing House of Electronics Industry.

Yearbook of World Electronics Data (2004). *Yearbook of World Electronics Data 2004/2005: Emerging Countries and World Summary*. Wantage, UK: Reed Electronics Research.

Yoshitaka, O. (2000). *Competitive-cum-Cooperative Interfirm Relations and Dynamics in the Japanese Semiconductor Industry*. Tokyo: Springer.

Yu, Z. (1989). *The Development of China's Electronics Industry. China's Medium and Large Enterprises*, Economic Technology and Social Development Research Centre, State Department and Bureau of Statistics: 9. Beijing: Urban Economy and Society.

Yu, Z. (1990). *Zhongguo Dianzhi Gongye Sishinian Jubian* (The Huge Changes of the Chinese Electronics Industry in the Past 40 Years), *China's Economic Structure Reform*, 1: 11–12.

Yusuf, S. (2004). 'Competitiveness through Technological Advances under Global Production Networking'. In Yusuf, S., Altaf, M. A. and Nabeshima, K. (eds), *Global Production Networking and Technological Change in East Asia*. Washington, DC: World Bank and Oxford University Press.

Yusuf, S., Altaf, M. A. and Nabeshima, K. (2004). *Global Production Networking and Technological Change in East Asia*. Washington, DC: World Bank and Oxford University Press.

Zedtwitz, M. V. (2005). 'China Goes Abroad'. In Passow, S. and Runnbeck, M. (eds), *What's Next? Strategic Views on Foreign Direct Investment*. Geneva: UNCTAD and Invest in Sweden Agency.

Zedtwitz, M. V. (2007). *Connecting Science to Innovation: Managing R&D on a Global Scale*. London: Edward Elgar.

Zhao, X. (1995). *Zhongguo Gongyehua Sixiang Ji Fazhan Zhanlue Yanjiu* (A Study on China's Industrialization Thought and Development Strategies). Shanghai: Shanghai Academy of Social Science.

Zhu, R. (1999). 'Significant Progress Seen in China–US Talks on China's WTO Bid', *People's Daily*, 10 April.

Zhu, R. (2000). 'Explanation of Propositions for the Tenth Five-Year Plan for National Economic and Social Development', 20 October.

Index

For Product Safety Concerns and Information please contact our EU
representative GPSR@taylorandfrancis.com
Taylor & Francis Verlag GmbH, Kaufingerstraße 24, 80331 München, Germany

www.ingramcontent.com/pod-product-compliance
Ingram Content Group UK Ltd.
Pitfield, Milton Keynes, MK11 3LW, UK
UKHW021118180425
457613UK00005B/141